Joni Eareckson Tada

Secret STRENGTH

...for those who search

MULTNOMAH

Portland, Oregon 97266

Edited by Larry R. Libby
Design by Brenda Jose and Bruce DeRoos
Cover painting and interior paintings by Joni Eareckson Tada
Author photos by Steven Harvey

SECRET STRENGTH
© 1988 by Joni, Inc.
Published by Multnomah Press
Portland, Oregon 97266

Multnomah Press is a ministry of Multnomah School of the Bible, 8435 Northeast Glisan Street, Portland, Oregon 97220

Printed in the United States of America

Library of Congress Cataloging-in-Publication Data

Tada, Joni Eareckson.
   Secret strength/Joni Eareckson Tada.
     p. cm.
   Includes index.
   ISBN 0-88070-238-9
   1. Meditations, I.Title.
BV4832.2T3 1988
248.4—dc19   88-12053
                                       CIP
88 89 90 91 92 93 94 95 — 8 7 6 5 4 3 2

For Mom and Dad Tada

Contents

PART 1

Secrets of His Strength

PART 2

Secrets of His Character

PART 3

Secrets of His Grace

PART 4

Secrets of Praise

Acknowledgments

I wish I could remember all the times and the places where I've learned those . . . unforgettable things. A lingering phrase from someone's long ago sermon that has stuck with me. A poem, a catch phrase, a memorized paragraph that hasn't shaken itself from my mind.

Like you, I read a little here, gather some ideas there, and somehow the Lord weaves these flashes of thoughts into the fabric of my own study of God and His Word. I wish I could exactly recall each author or speaker, pastor or friend from whom I've gleaned so much. I would want, here and now, to give them full acknowledgment and my special thanks.

A few names come immediately to mind—Steve Estes, Elisabeth Elliott, C. S. Lewis, Dr. Martin Lloyd-Jones, Phil Yancey, John MacArthur, Kay Arthur, Bill Gothard, to name a few. I beg the indulgence of others whom I'm regrettably unable to list here. My hope is that if they see the fleeting imprint of their original ideas in my book, they will be pleased that those ideas are having an impact for the Lord Jesus on new and different readers.

I especially want to thank Bev Singleton, our Media Coordinator here at *Joni and Friends* for the years of tirelessly helping me research, write, compile and organize my radio programs. Also a word of thanks to our friends at Ambassador Advertising Agency who keep giving me deadlines so I can research and write more. For this book I have chosen those radio messages that have touched my heart the most.

Also, I have occasionally drawn from some of my favorite parts of *A Step Further*.

And my lasting thanks remain with Larry Libby, my friend and editor at Multnomah Press. From him I am learning to slow down, enjoy words, and write with my heart.

An Opening Thought

What's so secret about God?

Nothing. And yet everything.

It is God's nature to hide things. I discovered that early on in my life with Christ. Somehow I knew if I desired a deeper, more intimate knowledge of the Lord, I would be sent on a search. There were treasures to dig. Precious gems to mine.

I was surprised—and a little nettled—when I stumbled across a Scripture verse which told me that "the secret things belong to the Lord our God." God had secrets? It seems that He did—some to keep and some to tell. That fact unquieted me, made me restless. It was as though the Father had cupped His hand to my ear and whispered something I couldn't quite catch.

What was that Lord? What did You say??

I didn't realize it then, but I was responding to an age-old yearning of the spirit . . . an incurable urge to solve secrets, to delve into mysteries, to walk the higher and hidden roads.

And it is our God. our wonderfully mysterious God wrapped in glorious enigma, who has placed that yearning within us. As Solomon wrote, "It is the glory of God to conceal a matter . . . He has also set eternity in the hearts of men; yet they cannot fathom what God has done from beginning to end" (Proverbs 25:2, Ecclesiastes 3:11b, NIV).

He is the treasure we seek . . . the precious gem to be mined. Have you heard His whispers? I think you have—or else you would not have been drawn to a book written "for those who search."

If you are a believer, you already have everything you need for the journey. You have been initiated into the fellowship of the skies. You have His Word, the key to heaven's hieroglyphics. You have the mind of Christ. Now you must find His heart! He waits, tenderly and compassionately, to reveal Himself to you.

Would you like a little help in your search? Then I invite you, my fellow seeker, to enjoy this book as a companion on your venture.

You will seek me and find me, when you search for me with all your heart (Jeremiah 29:13).

May you find that secret strength that is His to give and yours to receive.

No, we speak of God's secret wisdom, a wisdom that has been hidden and that God destined for our glory before time began. None of the rulers of this age understood it, for if they had, they would not have crucified the Lord of glory. However, as it is written:

> *"No eye has seen,*
> *no ear has heard,*
> *no mind has conceived*
> *what God has prepared*
> *for those who love him"*—

but God has revealed it to us by his Spirit (1 Corinthians 2:7-10, NIV).

Secrets of His Strength

PART 1

Secrets of His Strength

CHAPTER 1

In Weakness Made Strong

Just who does God delight in using to accomplish His plans?

Consider Gideon. Israel had been under virtual siege by the Midianites for seven weary years. Gideon was threshing wheat— crouching in a winepress to avoid detection by the enemy—when the Lord Himself appeared with a message.

The LORD is with you, mighty warrior (Judges 6:12, NIV).

You can almost visualize Gideon's head popping up out of the winepress. "Er, excuse me? Were you talking to me?" He'd probably been called a lot of things by his friends and family, but never *that*.

Scripture tells us "the LORD turned to him and said, 'Go in the strength you have and save Israel out of Midian's hand. Am I not sending you?'" (6:14).

Gideon, apparently, wasn't aware of *any* strength. He sputtered and stuttered and reminded this Stranger that he was the weakest member of the weakest clan of the weakest tribe in the weak nation of Israel. Definitely no West Point graduate. If God was looking for warrior material, He must have been peering into the wrong winepress.

But no, God wanted Gideon. When that fact finally sunk in, the reluctant general began to gather a large army around him— only to find out God wanted to complete the assignment with a mere three hundred men.

The task was ridiculously large. The biblical account affirms the enemy soldiers filled a great valley, "thick as locusts. Their camels could no more be counted than the sand on the seashore" (7:12).

Yet God accomplished His plans through Gideon's little band, "in order that Israel may not boast against me that her own strength has saved her" (7:2).

Within a few pages of the Gideon account, we read about Deborah. The men of Israel had lost all heart for battle, intimidated by a Canaanite commander named Sisera with his nine hundred iron chariots. Scripture says he "had cruelly oppressed the Israelites for twenty years" so "they cried to the LORD for help" (Judges 4:3, NIV). Deborah, who led the nation at that time, sent her commander-in-chief to lead Israel's beleaguered army into battle against Sisera. General Barak's response was less than manly. Barak said to her, "If you go with me, I will go; but if you don't go with me, I won't go."

"Very well," Deborah said, "I will go with you. But because of the way you are going about this, the honor will not be yours, for the LORD will hand Sisera over to a woman" (4:8-9).

Israel's troops won the fight with the Canaanites, but Barak wouldn't dare include the battle in his memoirs. Deborah, "a mother in Israel" had rallied the troops on the front line and a housewife named Jael dispatched the mighty Sisera with a hammer and a tent peg.

"On that day," Scripture tells us, "God subdued Jabin, the Canaanite king, before the Israelites. And the hand of the Israelites grew stronger and stronger . . ." (Judges 4:23-24).

God used a woman—in all her weakness—to overthrow a dictator and his roughneck army. Deborah probably couldn't even find a size twelve suit of armor to wear, yet the Lord used her as an object lesson to all the following generations. God will show Himself mighty through weak men and women who lean hard on His strength and grace.

Perhaps you feel a bit like Deborah or Gideon today. Your gifts aren't many. Your talents are few. You'll never make the cover of *Gentleman's Quarterly* or *Vogue*. You're not sure you could make the church softball team, you're a poor hand at balancing the checkbook, and you frankly wonder where people get the energy to accomplish all they do. Like Gideon, you have to admit you're not the brightest or strongest member of your own family.

Take a look, my weak friends, at 1 Corinthians 1:26-29:

Brothers, think of what you were when you were called. Not many of you were wise by human standards; not many were influential; not many were of noble birth. But God chose the foolish things of the world to shame the wise; God chose the weak things of the world to shame the strong. He chose the lowly things of this world and the despised things . . . so that no one may boast before him (NIV).

Start chasing this theme through the pages of your Bible and you'll be at it for months! God picked David, a teenaged shepherd, to slay one of the greatest fighting men the world had ever seen. He plucked elderly Sarah from the social security rolls to birth a new nation. Her gynecologist would have laughed. So did everyone else. But after nine months, they were laughing with joy over a chubby baby boy.

When I feel weak, I ponder these examples. It pleased God to pick the unlikely, unlovely, and unheralded to get His job done. He picked weak and ordinary me. He's even picked you . . . with all your weakness and inadequacy, in spite of your mistakes and fumbled opportunities, regardless of your questionable track record, poor health, and lackluster résumé.

Then, when the task is completed and God's work has been accomplished through your life, guess who gets the glory?

Sometime beyond all time, we'll stand together before His throne and acknowledge that He did it all . . . through His strength, in keeping with His character, by His incredible grace, and to the praise of His glory.

And to think He included you and me!

STRONGHOLD

Read 1 Corinthians 2:1-5. Can you imagine the apostle Paul weak and fearful—even trembling? Why do you think he thought of himself that way? How does his example speak to you? Take heart knowing that if God did such great things through a man who often trembled in weakness and fear, He can surely use you!

e Warning

slammed into the Carolina networks were there with fort of our living rooms, we -per-hour winds overturned ..., and drove pleasure craft into beach house bedrooms. A wind so fierce that it even bent streetlights in half.

But out of all of those televised scenes of Diana's wrath, one image lingers in my mind. On a dark back street, one lone man in a yellow slicker clung to a telephone pole as torrents of rain and a screaming wind sought to hurl him backwards into the darkness.

I've returned to that mental snapshot a number of times in the intervening years. I think of it as I come across verses in the Bible that speak of how absolutely weak we really are—mentally, physically, and spiritually. God keeps bringing home the fact that we *dare not* trust ourselves to find or follow the right road.

For that very reason, God also spends a great deal of time in His Word reminding us how strong, secure, and dependable He really is.

Who has said it better than David?

From the end of the earth I will cry to You,
When my heart is overwhelmed;
Lead me to the rock that is higher than I.

For You have been a shelter for me,
And a strong tower from the enemy.
I will abide in Your tabernacle forever;
I will trust in the shelter of Your wings
(Psalm 61:2-4, NKJV).

Some have suggested this psalm was composed when David was driven from his throne and from Jerusalem during the rebellion of his son, Absalom. It may have been the darkest day in the king's tumultuous life. He was faced with the humiliation of a successful coup that overthrew his leadership, as well as with the defection of some of his closest friends and most trusted aides. But not only that. He also had to endure the knowledge that this rebellion and rejection came at the hands of his own dearly-loved son. The Bible tells us that as David fled, he "continued up the Mount of Olives, weeping as he went; his head was covered and he was barefoot" (2 Samuel 15:30, NIV).

How did David feel? Psalm 61:2 says that his heart was *overwhelmed*. He felt weak and faint. Possibly sick. Hardly able to stand. The dark winds of adversity and sorrow had never blown so hard.

What did he pray? "Lead me to the rock that is higher than I." God, this is over my head! I'm absolutely drowning. I need a Rock that I can hang onto before I go under, a Tower of Refuge where I can hide and find rest.

My mind goes back to that man in the yellow slicker. Exposed to the raw force of the real world and all its destructive power, he clutched tightly to the only thing that wasn't moving—a telephone pole. In the same way, God at times exposes us to the raw forces of the real world, the real flesh, and the real devil. Assaulted by a barrage of heartaches and hardships, it is as though He overwhelms us with a sense of our own inadequacy—our moral and mental weakness.

When that happens, we are driven to cling to Him all the more closely, aren't we? We learn the same lesson as that man in the middle of the hurricane. Find the best refuge, the strongest rock, the firmest and most unshakable defense and *hold on with all your heart.* As though your very life depended on it.

Hurricane Diana is now little more than a memory. A parade of subsequent tropical storms has paid calls on the gulf and eastern seaboard, with names that blur in the passing of time. When the weather is fine it's hard to remember the terror of the storm.

Maybe today there are no great storms in your life. The sun is shining, the clouds small and puffy, the swells gentle. But life is unpredictable. Winds of change gust suddenly, catching us unawares. Testing can fall out of the clear blue. And though the network cameras may not catch all the action, the world watches when God's children get caught up in the storm.

In a world like this, it makes sense to stay close to the Shelter.

STRONGHOLD

"He's really _____ to that pole in the storm!" If you were a news reporter describing the man in the yellow slicker, what verbs would come to mind? Clinging? Grabbing? Clutching?

Now, what verbs would you use to describe how *you* have held on to God when you were hit hard with storms?

The next time you see a storm brewing in your life, hang on to this "telephone pole"—Deuteronomy 4:29-31.

Flexibility

A good friend of mine, injured only a short while ago, is still going through all the painful adjustments of life in a wheelchair. She's a beautiful girl who was a top student on her feet. For that matter, she's still making top grades in her graduate work.

But even though she's loaded with beauty and brains, that doesn't make coping with the problems of her disability any easier.

She let down with me a little the other day and spilled out some of the frustration. I understood completely.

I'll admit, right along with her, that it's tough finding slacks which hang just right when you're sitting down. It's hard finding clothes that fit well when you're always having to be reaching and pulling and pushing in your wheelchair. It's a difficult thing to have other people do your make-up or comb your hair just right.

I told my friend that I knew exactly how she felt. For instance, there are five different women who on various mornings help me go through my getting-up routine. Now, some of those girls do some things one way, and others do things a little differently. On Monday, my hairstyle is an original creation by Irene. On Tuesday it has the Judy touch to it. On Wednesday it features the Beverly bouffant and on Thursday Francie gives it a special flair. On Friday I come to work with a Lynda look.

Now, to be sure, I wear my hair basically the same way every day. But you can't expect five different women to artfully handle a brush and comb in exactly the same way you might want to do it yourself. Obviously, some things are just going to be done a little differently.

Ditto for make-up. I wear the same color lipstick and blush every day. But everybody has her own special way with make-up. So my mascara may be a little clumpy one day and hardly even there the next.

But one thing I've been able to tell my friend in her adjustments is that a disability can really teach you how to be *flexible*. We know, for instance, that Paul had a disability. Yet he was a man who didn't always insist on having things exactly his own way. He wasn't picky.

In a letter to friends at Philippi, the battered apostle wrote these remarkable words:

I have learned to to be content in whatever circumstances I am. I know how to get along with humble means, and I also know how to live in prosperity; in any and every circumstance I have learned the secret of being filled and going hungry, both of having abundance and suffering need (Philippians 4:11-12).

And what was that "secret" Paul had learned? He gives it away in the very next breath.

I can do all things through Him who strengthens me (4:13).

There's something commendable in that kind of approach to life. There are simply some things—whatever our disability or life situation might be—about which we need to be flexible.

Leaning on the strength of his Lord, Paul learned to be satisfied. With an empty stomach or a full one. In days of health or when he had to depend on others in his disability. In the comfortable homes of dear Christian friends or deep in the bowels of a Roman dungeon. In Christ, he was flexible. And because of that flexibility, God blessed him with great contentment.

Well, my young friend who is new to a wheelchair has a lot to learn. But God will fashion her into a beautiful woman, I'm sure. Her hair may not look just perfect, her clothes may not always lay the way she would like, and her make-up may be a little uneven on some days.

But *she* will be beautiful—because she will be flexible.

And she'll be content.

STRONGHOLD

Complaints, murmurings, and grumbling. That's how the Israelites are remembered for their lack of contentment. For a closer look, start at Exodus 16:3-5. Manna from heaven wasn't enough, was it?

Now flip to Numbers 11:4-10. Would you like to know how the Lord finally satisfied their desires? Read aloud—and laugh aloud—through verses 18-20.

Project: Compile your wants and God's wants. How many of them match?

Prayer: Help me, Father, to subtract my desires . . . to not be picky, to not always insist on having things exactly my own way. Forgive me if I keep adding more and more wants, for You know just what I need. And in that I am content.

No Different Story

The writer of Hebrews describes Scripture as a sharp sword. From my perspective, it often feels more like a needle.

One verse that has needled me for years is 1 Corinthians 10:13:

> *No temptation has seized you except what is common to man. And God is faithful; he will not let you be tempted beyond what you can bear. But when you are tempted, he will also provide a way out so that you can stand up under it* (NIV).

Why does that verse prick me so? Because every now and then I'm tempted to think that God *couldn't* expect from me what He does from others. Obviously it's a "different story" in my case, right?

I remember lying on my hospital bed years ago thinking that God was putting me through more than I could take. *Paralysis. Total and permanent.* But then there was good ol' 1 Corinthians 10:13 reminding me that God is faithful . . . He will not let me be tempted beyond what I can bear.

The verse came back to pierce me again when I was in my late twenties, single, and with every prospect of remaining so. Sometimes lust or a bit of fantasizing would seem so inviting— and so easy to justify. After all, hadn't I already given up more than most Christians just by being disabled? Didn't my wheelchair entitle me to a little slack now and then? Yet the words stared up at me from the pages of my Bible . . . *God is faithful . . . He will not let you be tempted beyond what you can bear . . . He will provide a way out . . . you can stand up under it.*

When God allows you to suffer, do you have the tendency to use your very trials as an excuse for sinning? Or do you feel that since you've given God a little extra lately by taking such abuse, He owes you a "day off"?

I have a hunch we've all experienced this inner battle. But when we sit down and examine our lame protests in the strong light of a verse like 1 Corinthians 10:13, the excuses just fade away, one by one.

The truth of the matter is, when we sin during our sufferings, it's not because ours is a "different story" and we're forced to disobey.

We don't sin because we have to. We sin because we *want* to.

God gives me grace to live in a wheelchair which He doesn't give you if you can walk. But He gives you grace to endure an unwanted divorce or the death of a spouse or the loss of your job or the rebellion of a child, which He doesn't give me. God provides the way of escape, the means by which we may bear up under our individual trials.

The question is never, "Can you obey?"

It's more like, "*Will* you obey?"

STRONGHOLD

"Will you obey?" That's a good question. The verse in our reading, 1 Corinthians 10:13, is good. But go a step further and start reading from the very first verse in chapter 10. How are the examples of Moses and his followers a warning to you?

If you have ever said, "Oh, I would never behave like that," type out verse 12 on a card, stick it on your bathroom mirror, and memorize it for your own good.

CHAPTER 5

Lines of Communication

Explaining spinal cord injury is confusing, but never more so than when you try to explain it to a child.

A little boy stood by my wheelchair, poked my knee and insisted, "You can make your leg move, just try!"

"But I *am* trying," I chuckled.

"No, you're just not thinking hard enough."

There was no way I could convince this boy. I attempted to explain that although I had great ideas in my head, it was of no use. I could give all the commands I wanted, but if the lines of communication were down, there was no way my legs and arms were going to respond.

Bodies are amazing, aren't they? Most of us like to take good care of our bodies. We try to eat reasonably well, and exercise whenever we can. It's fortunate that our bodies hardly ever go on strike. They ordinarily do an adequate job of taking directions from the head.

Paul used the analogy of head and body to illustrate our relationship with Christ, describing the Lord as our "Head, from whom the whole body, supported and held together by its ligaments and sinews, grows as God causes it to grow" (Colossians 2:19, NIV).

A healthy spiritual body of believers takes its direction from Christ, the Head. Jesus gives us instruction through His Word. We, His body, trust and obey, responding in prayer.

But what happens when those communication lines break down?

The person who refuses to trust and obey damages the lines of communication between himself and God. Actually, the Bible underscores that almost verbatim. "Such a person goes into great detail about what he has seen, and his unspiritual mind puffs him up with idle notions. He has lost connection with the Head . . ." (Colossians 2:18-19, NIV).

I think my own body is the best visual aid. My head, you see, has a whole lot of great plans and dreams for my hands and my legs. Unfortunately, my body refuses to listen. My spinal cord injury severed the communication lines between my head, and my hands and feet. As a result, all of those fine plans and ideas simply remain in my mind. Personally, I think my body's really missing out. But the lines have been damaged, rendering my limbs useless.

Is it all that different a situation from the spiritual condition of many believers today? Our Head, Christ, has some grand things in store for us—good ideas that He would love us to carry out, using you and me, His hands and legs down here on earth. But sad to say, our communication lines are often damaged and God's Word isn't getting through. We don't trust or obey. We don't respond in prayer.

The result? Well, a body like mine.

Numb and useless. Or weak and frail, at best.

Listen, none of us have suffered a fatal spiritual injury. Nor is there some grand cosmic spinal cord injury in the body of Christ today. The lines *are* open—we just need to use them! We need to allow God to communicate with us through His Word and then, like any good, healthy body, respond in prayer, praise, and thanksgiving . . . trusting and obeying as we carry out the plans and commands of Christ our Head.

Are your lines of communication open today? Listen to God's Word. Pray in return. Keep spiritually healthy. To paraphrase that little boy, you *can* make the right moves . . . if you try.

STRONGHOLD

Let's keep the lines of communication open today between us, Christ's body, and Jesus, our Head. To test those open lines, begin with Matthew 6:6-13. What inspires—or convicts—you most about this Scripture? Is your communication with God two-way?

The lines *are* open, so make sure you use them this week.

CHAPTER 6

Clay and Wax

"The same sun that hardens clay, melts wax."

As an artist I enjoy watching other artists at work—not just painters, but anyone with an an artistic bent.

I recall visiting a sculptor's studio. She was working on several designs, large lumps of clay in various stages of completion. Each piece sat on a turnstile, covered with damp cheesecloth, in a shaded section of her studio. The sculptor moved from one design to another, assured that each piece would remain soft, pliable, and supple until she returned.

The clay could readily harden if the humidity or temperatures in her studio changed even slightly. But not so with the wax my sculptor friend used in designing pieces for reproduction. It remained soft and pliable, easy to work with. Whenever she wanted to create a work of art, she would warm the wax with a hair dryer and it was immediately ready for work.

Hardened clay is brittle, easily damaged. If dropped, it can fracture into a thousand pieces. Dropped wax, however, only bends from the pressure of the fall. Impressionable and pliable, it can be quickly remolded.

People are like that. People who are hardened in their resolve against God are brittle, their emotions are easily damaged. But those who bend to the will of God find perfect expression in however God molds them.

I thought of these things some time back when I was in bed, depressed, as a result of a pressure sore. For three months I struggled to remain pliable and open to God's will—even though having to spend twelve long weeks away from my work, my desk, and my art easel seemed pointless.

God, it seems, was less interested in my work and most interested in my response.

"The same sun that hardens clay, melts wax." That's true. There is no change or variation in the sun itself. It's just the way the clay or wax responds. Trials and suffering will harden some just like breakable clay, baking in bitterness and resentment. The same circumstances can melt others, teaching them patience and endurance. The trials have no value or intrinsic meaning in themselves. It's the way we *respond* to those trials that makes all the difference.

I know a number of people who, like me, are confined to wheelchairs. But their paralysis has only driven them deeper into resentment and bitter despair. They even see their disability as "proof" of the nonexistence of a loving God. Many others of us see our wheelchairs as the very hallmark of a loving God who desires to purify and perfect His children.

In one of those mad, midnight moments during my long convalescence, teetering between a hardened clay or a melted wax response, I came up with a song. Since I couldn't jump out of bed and get a pad of paper and pen, I carefully pondered and memorized each phrase as it came. When the whole poem was complete in my head, I didn't feel so brittle, so depressed about the will of God.

I have a piece of china, a pretty porcelain vase
It holds such lovely flowers, captures everyone's
  gaze
But fragile things do slip and fall as everybody
  knows

And when my days came crashing down, my tears
began to flow.

But don't we all cry when pretty things get broken,
Don't we all cry at such an awful loss?
But Jesus will dry your tears as He has spoken
Cause He was the one broken on the cross.

My life was just like china, a lovely thing to me
Full of porcelain promises of all that I might be.
But fragile things do slip and fall as everybody
knows
And when my life came crashing down, my tears
began to flow.

But Jesus is no porcelain prince, His promises
won't break
His holy Word holds fast and sure, His love no one
can shake.
So if your life is shattered by sorrow, pain, or sin
His healing love will reach right down and make
you whole again.

STRONGHOLD

What makes the difference between the wax and the
clay? If the Holy Spirit has got your heart even slightly
ready, then you can be the wax that melts, too. I hope
you will see yourself as that wax today, ready to be
molded and melted into Jesus' image. Don't bother
that you've been responding to the small irritations as
some chunk of old, dry, hardened clay. As you go about
the rest of *this* day, facing those everyday pressures, let
the Son do His work. The wax will melt, and you'll be all
the better for it. Read 1 Peter 4:12-19, 5:6-11.

Dirty Laundry

None of us would like to hang out our dirty laundry for public view. Those ugly stains, embarrassing blotches, smears, and smudges are for our eyes only.

We sometimes feel the same way as believers. We catch ourselves hanging out a "laundered" version of the Christian life to attract unbelievers into our fold. We play down the problems, gloss over the hardships, throw a cover over the trials and tragedies, hide the handicaps, and push all our weak or wounded brothers and sisters to the rear.

By all means, keep the dirty laundry in the basket! Keep it off the line where everyone can ogle it! We don't want anyone thinking, "Look how this so-called loving God treats His devoted followers." And we certainly don't want the handicaps, heartaches, divorces, and dissensions in our church to be ugly smears against God's good name.

It's strange when you consider that our Lord Jesus did not seek to avoid the embarrassing blotches of His society. He actually sought out the company of prostitutes, outcasts, and indigents, apparently fearing no harm to God's reputation. He claimed responsibility for a man's blindness, put His arm around the leper, and gave special honor to the weak and heavy-laden. While studiously avoiding the crisply-laundered Pharisees, Jesus didn't seem embarrassed to hang around, or for that matter, hang out, the dirty laundry.

There was this difference, however. The most obvious way God used suffering to glorify Himself back then was to miraculously *remove* it. Jesus went about restoring sight to the blind, healing the lepers, raising the dead—doing all sorts of awesome things to ease human misery.

And sure enough, even when unbelievers and scoffers saw the miracles, they marveled and glorified God.

But what about all the dirty laundry today? Jesus is no longer with us in bodily form, walking the hills of Judea, doing all the things He once did. Today, God has another way of using suffering to glorify Himself—a less obvious, but certainly not less powerful way.

Strange as it may seem, God often not only allows but actually insures that you and I, His children, undergo and endure long periods of difficulty, pain, and struggle.

And He lets all this take place within plain view of unbelievers!

But look what happens when these Christians on whom God has sent trial after trial refuse to complain. Look what happens when instead of cursing, complaining, and shaking rebellious fists at heaven, they respond with praise to their Creator.

Unbelievers take notice. They see something that, according to all logical methods of accounting, simply doesn't add up. They are drawn to this God who inspires such loving loyalty from real people with real problems.

If you and I enjoyed nothing but ease and comfort, our world would never learn anything very impressive about God. It would never learn that our God is *worth* serving—even when the going gets tough.

So let unbelievers see what God is doing in your life. Let them identify with your dirty laundry. Don't hide your heartaches and struggle areas, hypocritically pretending they don't exist. Instead, concentrate on staying loyal to your God in the midst of them.

It may be the most convincing argument your neighbors ever see or hear about the God you love.

STRONGHOLD

Sometimes we feel more secure if we can present a clean, starched impression of our Christian walk. But look at what Paul says in 1 Corinthians 1:26-29. The fellowship of Christ includes even the people whom some consider "embarrassing blotches." How can you see yourself in this portion of Scripture? Think of how you might reach out to those believers you know are in pain or are embarrassed by failure. Find some practical ways to encourage them. Help them see that their example could be a convincing and convicting testimony to unbelievers.

Coming Glory

At some point in his dramatic rise to prominence, he took a fork in the road. And never looked back.

Up until then, his followers had rallied around him. He had stood up to the city councils and federal bureaucrats. He had revealed the self-serving hypocrisy of prominent men of the cloth. Yet he could talk to anybody, from common workers to elite civic leaders. From the hookers on skid row to fishermen on the wharf. He gave stirring speeches about better days ahead. Like any good politician, he backed up his promises with solid performance. He could plunge into a crowd with the best of them, pressing the flesh, shaking hands, kissing babies.

Then, abruptly, unexplainably, his style changed.

He started spending more time alone. Withdrawing with just a few of his inner circle. Telling strange, at times incomprehensible, stories. Avoiding the very crowds that were longing to thrust him to the top.

And though he was a young man, hardly into his prime, he began to talk more and more about death . . . his death.

Jesus' disciples must have been blown away. Bewildered. Even Peter, one of the privileged inner circle, tried to stop all the illogical talk about betrayal, humiliation, and death. He was stunned when the Teacher turned on him with a harsh reprimand.

"Get behind me, Satan! You are a stumbling block to me; you do not have in mind the things of God, but the things of men" (Matthew 16:23, NIV).

Jesus would have no more political agendas pushed on Him. From then on, He would clarify the agenda of His Father. At the same time, however, the Lord was aware that His men were bruised and shaken over the turn of events. They needed encouragement. So after six more days of talk about "denying yourself" and "taking up your cross" and "losing your life to find it," the Lord did something amazing for them.

After six days Jesus took with him Peter, James and John the brother of James, and led them up a high mountain by themselves. There he was transfigured before them. His face shown like the sun, and his clothes became as white as the light . . . A bright cloud enveloped them, and a voice from the cloud said, "This is my Son, whom I love; with him I am well pleased. Listen to him!"

When the disciples heard this, they fell facedown to the ground, terrified. But Jesus came and touched them. "Get up," he said. "Don't be afraid." When they looked up, they saw no one except Jesus (Matthew 17:1-3, 5-8, NIV).

What an uplift that must have been to those men, so down at heart over all the talk of death. Up on that hilltop, Christ helped them to see *beyond* the cross . . . into the splendor of the resurrection.

For that matter, the encounter must have been encouraging to Jesus Himself as He heard the voice of His Father from heaven, "This is my Son, whom I love; with Him I am well pleased." Perhaps the long shadow of the cross didn't seem quite so foreboding after hearing those comforting words. God the Father was setting a seal of approval on His sinless Son—the One who so soon would be nailed to the cross to bear our sins.

Yes, there would be suffering—unspeakable agony—ahead.

But after that . . . glory.

Can you and I hold onto that thought in the middle of our deepest heartaches . . . when we are most bewildered and perplexed . . . when life seems heavy, almost unendurable? Can we remember that glory is coming? That we, too, are being transfigured?

There are times when our Lord must long for us to look beyond the heaviness of our circumstances and catch a glimpse of the splendor and glory to come. Eternity lies ahead—really just a few steps down the path. What's more, the transforming might of the resurrected Christ is at work in your life *today*, this very moment, shaping you into a mature man or godly woman. Changing you to resemble Him.

There's something glorious coming. It's already breaking across the horizon . . . I can see it in your face.

STRONGHOLD

If you're hurting right now, hold on to the thoughts expressed in 2 Corinthians 4:11-18. What reasons does Paul offer for not losing heart in our daily struggles? Look closer at verses 16-18. What is Paul's counsel? As you close this book, take a few moments to "fix your eyes" on the Lord Jesus.

CHAPTER 9

Partakers in Christ

I remember her name, her face, and where she went for first-period class, but little else.

Donna Rutley was a senior when I was a lowly freshman, but she took time to invite me to a high school Young Life meeting. Donna was a Christian and everybody knew it and admired her for it. She was involved in high school clubs, student government, sports, and to me she seemed to move through the halls with her feet inches above the floor. The classic blonde-haired, blue-eyed beauty, she seemed oblivious to her good looks, choosing not to spend her break times primping in front of the girls' room mirror, but instead reaching out to new kids in the hall like me.

I studied her. Admired her. Mimicked her mannerisms and copied her style. I tried hard to be a miniature Donna Rutley. *I was going to do my best to be like her.* That smile, that hairstyle, those sorority sweaters and circle pins, her cute expressions—everything to be like Donna.

Long after she graduated, when I was a senior, I realized something. I never got to know Donna Rutley. I knew *about* her . . . but didn't know her. We'd rarely talked. I knew nothing of her home and family, goals and dreams. I've no idea where she is now. She might have gone on to be a homemaker. Or beauty queen. Or TV announcer. She might already be in heaven. Though I "worshiped her from afar" she stepped out of my life, completely and permanently. Yet thinking back on that memory, Donna Rutley has taught me a spiritual lesson I'll never forget.

It's not enough to do our best to be like Christ.

To "be like Christ" does not mean we copy His lifestyle or mimic his mannerisms, trying our best to be patient and tolerant, loving and kind. To "be like Christ" is to partake of His very nature.

The writer of Hebrews tells us that we "have become partakers of Christ," and should be "partakers of His holiness" (Hebrews 3:14, 12:10, KJV). Peter tells us that through God's promises we can be partakers of His divine nature (2 Peter 1:4).

Those thoughts sparked my curiosity. I looked up the word *partakers* in Webster's, and found that partakers are people who "take part of, have a share within, or a portion of something."

As we see from Scripture, you and I as Christians have a share, or a portion, in the life of Jesus Christ.

The sufferings we encounter in life—even garden-variety sorts of trials—are meant to *help* us partake of Christ. For when we enter the fellowship of His sufferings, God strips us of our "self-help" mindset. We are forced to our knees and driven to lean on His grace. Then—and it seems only then—can God impart His Son's character to us. In so doing, we are "made like Him."

When I struggle with this wheelchair, for instance, I can become more like Christ if I respond rightly. But I don't become more like Christ through some positive thinking, self-help approach. I don't become more sensitive or patient through a hang-in-there, stick-to-it-and-pull-yourself-up-by-your-bootstraps way of looking at hardships.

No, *we* don't build up Christ's character in our own lives. He takes responsibility for building us when we become partakers of Him. All of my flesh efforts—my teeth-gritting determination—have nothing to do with becoming more like

Jesus. It's only when I partake of Him, when I share in His life, read His Word, abide in His presence, converse with Him in prayer, seek His counsel, and delight in His fellowship that I become more like Christ in my sufferings.

Now, we've all been caught "trying our best" to be more patient or sweet-spirited in some given trial. But maybe we ought to concentrate all that effort on simply being partakers of Jesus. Then we can leave to *Him* the whole process of being made more like Christ. For as we partake of Him, sharing in His nature, it's inevitable that we'll become more like Him.

Wherever you are, Donna Rutley, thanks for the lesson.

STRONGHOLD

Ask yourself—do you long to know Christ? Or do you only know *about* Him. Take a look at Philippians 3:7-11. When Paul says he wants to know Christ in verse 10, what does his desire also include? How about it . . . would you like to join the fellowship of sharing Christ's suffering? How can you be "like Him in His death"?

Beating the Waves

Good morning! A California summer morning beckons outside my window.

It's a day to head for the beach . . . or a lake . . . or a swimming pool. Yes, me too. Even though I'm in a wheelchair, I'm by no means immune to the summer siren song. Ken and I are going beach camping in a couple of hours—one of my favorite things to do.

I've always loved the ocean. I treasure special memories of camping at Bethany Beach in Delaware when I was a girl. The waves would come in over a long sandbar, breaking up to seven feet high, spilling creamy surf over acres of sand.

Now, when you're a child—and I couldn't have been more than six or seven—those waves can look pretty high. When I saw them coming, my first inclination was to swim the other way. But that was a mistake, because the rolling, foaming, surf would toss you every which way, sometimes holding you underneath the water for what seemed to be forever.

No, I learned young the best thing to do when those waves swelled was to swim fast *toward* them and dive *under* the wave before it had a chance to break on top of you. You really had to hold your breath as you dove through the wave. But, oh, the relief you felt as you broke the surface and could hear that huge great wave breaking behind you. *You had beat the wave*, and it was exhilarating.

Funny how the lessons you learn at a young age stick with you through the years. Because even though I don't dive or swim anymore, I still feel like I can "beat the waves."

Waves of crisis or difficulty roll in from the horizon and threaten to break over my life. Looking up at them, they seem so high, so insurmountable. My first inclination is to run the other way, fleeing from those frightening problems. But I've learned that there is no fast escape. Running from problems only tosses me in a foaming fury of entanglements and frustrations and emotions later on.

Jonah learned that lesson in a tough college course called Obedience 101. When he tried to run from the clear challenge God had laid before him, life became exceedingly complicated. In the inhospitable confines of a fish's belly, the reluctant prophet reflected on his attempted escape.

> LORD . . . *You hurled me into the deep,*
> *into the very heart of the seas,*
> *and the currents swirled about me;*
> *all your waves and breakers swept over me.*
>
> *The engulfing waters threatened me,*
> *the deep surrounded me;*
> *seaweed was wrapped around my head*
> (Jonah 2:3, 5, NIV).

Jonah would agree with me that the best way to beat those waves of trials and tough challenges is to *face* them. Head on. Almost anticipating them. Sometimes I find myself literally diving into the middle of a problem before it has a chance to crash on top of me.

And when by God's grace I come through it all? Oh, the relief when I know that problem is behind me. With God's help, I've beaten it. What an invigorating feeling!

Well, I'm on my way to a camping trip, so I have to close. I'll sit by the shoreline tonight and watch the waves roll in. I'll hear the thunder of the breakers, the restless roar of that big ocean.

And if only I could swim . . . I think I could still beat those waves!

STRONGHOLD

When it seems problems are about to break on top of you, don't bury your head in the sand . . . face them with courage and confidence. What will help you stand your ground? Look at the first three sentences in James 4:7-8. Underline the verb of action in each sentence and make a commitment today to face your problems with that advice in mind.

The Exchange

I'm intrigued by the crosses people wear around their necks.

My niece has a delicate little cross of pearls and gold. An Episcopalian friend of mine has one of those big chunky crosses made of brass. (To me it looks rather heavy to be hanging from someone's neck.) My brother-in-law has a silver cross with turquoise bits on it on a necklace of leather.

What intrigues me most is the idea of wearing a cross at all. After all, a cross is an instrument of torture. An execution machine. Some might say it would be the same as wearing a little silver guillotine, a gilded hangman's noose, or an electric chair made of tiny pearls.

Sounds strange, doesn't it? What makes a cross different from other devices of torture? Simply this: Christians have exchanged its meaning for something entirely new and wonderful. To us, the very contrivance which killed our Lord Jesus has become the trademark of our hope and salvation. What was once a symbol of horrible death miraculously becomes a symbol of eternal life.

Perhaps that's what has happened with this wheelchair of mine. To many, it's something which symbolizes confinement, alienation, illness, and suffering. But because of the grace of God in my life, it's meaning has been exchanged for something new and yes, wonderful. This paralysis of mine has drawn me so much closer to Christ. It has given me such a richer experience of His grace, encouragement, and sustaining power.

Perhaps something similar has happened in your experience with Christ as well. Your symbol may be a back brace instead of a wheelchair. Or a cane, a hearing aid, or a pair of thick eyeglasses. Or perhaps a birthmark or a disfigurement of some sort. Maybe an event or a series of circumstances. Perhaps even a handicapped child.

Suffering in itself, of course, is a distressing, negative experience. But when Christ exchanged the meaning of the cross for something new, He was then able to open up whole new possibilities in the realm of suffering for all. Through the victory of His cross, He enables us to gain victory in our suffering. So much so that we, too, can ascribe radiant new meaning to otherwise distressing and sorrowful circumstances.

I don't need to go so far as to wear a little turquoise wheelchair around my neck. But the principle is still the same. My handicap . . . your heartaches . . . can take on new meaning through Christ.

STRONGHOLD

Dig into a jewelry box, find a cross which hasn't been worn in a while and hang it where you'll be able to see it often. Let it be a reminder, for a while, of the high price Christ paid on His cross for you.

The horrible realities of the crucifixion tend to become obscured with the passage of time. Perhaps now would be an appropriate time to refresh your memory about the sacrifice your Lord offered on your behalf.

Carve out some time today so that you can spend several quiet and secluded moments with Matthew 27:27-50.

Competent to Comfort

When you think of comforting someone . . . what comes to your mind?

An arm around a friend's shoulder? A hug for a child with a scraped knee? An encouraging note in the mail? Perhaps you picture yourself at a neighbor's kitchen table with a cup of coffee, a listening ear, and a handy tissue.

It's almost a pleasant picture, isn't it? Giving out parcels of comfort along life's path doesn't sound all that threatening—especially when the problems fall within the circle of our own experience.

But can you picture yourself comforting a belligerent alcoholic who's trying to kick the habit?

Or a cousin who's raging because she's just learned she has multiple sclerosis?

Or a teen who's deeply depressed over a poor self-image?

Or a forty-year-old executive who's just gone through bankruptcy?

Or a young woman who has just been sentenced to prison?

Or a grieving parent with a homosexual son?

For most of us, at least some of those situations seem outside of our understanding, outside of our experience—and certainly outside of our "comfort" zone.

Perhaps we'd like to help, but feel that "somebody else" would be, well, better qualified. There must be others, we tell ourselves, who will move into that situation and know what to say or do. We reason that our experience has only prepared us for comforting another in a similar situation, certainly not in struggles beyond our understanding.

Be careful about letting yourself off the hook with those thoughts. God's Word seems to indicate something else. In his second letter to the Corinthians, Paul writes:

Praise be to the God and the Father of our Lord Jesus Christ, the Father of compassion and the God of all comfort, who comforts us in all our troubles, so that we can comfort those in any trouble *with the comfort we ourselves have received from God* (2 Corinthians 1:3-4, NIV).

It doesn't say we can only comfort those with whom we can identify . . . the common dilemmas, the everyday obstacles, the minor bumps and bruises. It says *any* trouble. *Any* heartache, disease, or injury.

All too often we feel reluctant, insecure, or anxious when called upon to comfort someone in troubles greater than our own. But God says it's possible. And our rich resource of enabling is the Father of compassion and the God of all comfort. He'll give you the right words to say. Or the wisdom to say none at all. His love will speak through you and His grace will flow out of you.

You don't have to have a degree in sociology. You don't have to be a drug-rehabilitation specialist, family counselor, psychologist, or seminary graduate. And no, you don't have to have survived a divorce to comfort someone else through a divorce. You needn't have lost a child in order to comfort a mother through her miscarriage.

Love doesn't require technical training. It isn't qualified by a degree or limited by a job description. Anyone can demonstrate love to anyone else, and since God comforts us in *all* our troubles, is it asking too much to comfort others in *any* trouble?

I wonder if within this past week you've heard of an acquaintance, business colleague, or family member devastated by something deeply painful. Did you politely, reservedly stay at arms' length? Did you think to send a card and then change your mind? Were you going to offer a hand but then naively assumed that others were probably in there helping and consoling? Or did you wrongly decide that your words would be inadequate because the problem seemed outside of your understanding or experience?

It's not too late to do something about it. The comfort we've been blessed with is adequate to cover anyone, with any kind of trouble. In Christ, so are we.

STRONGHOLD

The question bears repeating: Were you going to help someone this past week but then politely, reservedly stayed at arm's length? How about that card of encouragement . . . did you ever send it? Stop right now and put your letter-writing paper and telephone book in clear view as a reminder to carry through before the day is done. Memorize 2 Corinthians 1:3-4.

Higher Service

My husband is the strong, silent type—the picture of a robust, athletic man. As such, he can be an intimidating force on the racquetball court.

Perhaps that's why a few of his racquetball buddies express surprise when they learn Ken is married to a quadriplegic in a wheelchair.

"It's really amazing," they say, "that you've given up your life to serve a handicapped woman."

Those sorts of comments aren't uncommon. You hear people talking about the burden of caring for an elderly mother, the sacrifice of serving a sick child, or of devoting years to a handicapped youngster. Sometimes people will say a woman has "given her husband the best years of her life," or a missionary couple has given themselves to "tireless service" in a foreign country.

Pondering statements like these has led me to a question: *Just whom do we think these people are serving?*

Listen to Paul's words:

Whatever you do, do your work heartily, as for the Lord rather than for men; knowing that from the Lord you will receive the reward of the inheritance. It is the Lord Christ whom you serve (Colossians 3:23-24).

Ken has not given his life to serve a handicapped woman. He's given his life to serve Christ. He just happens to be married to someone with a disability.

It's the same with anyone who serves in the Lord's name. How can service to the Lord Christ be a tedious, boring effort—or even a sacrifice? Certainly we tire of our service to men, "causes," organizations, companies, or academic institutions. No doubt Ken gets very tired of helping me through my nightly routine. I get tired, too. Yet, however tiring our work may be, how could it ever be *tiresome*? How could it be anything less than a joy to serve the One who has given us all things for life and enrichment and enjoyment—Jesus, who suffered so much to secure our salvation.

Have you ever sensed a lack of purpose in your work? Have you struggled to see the reward for all your effort? Is it all getting a little wearisome?

Why go the extra mile for this company? They'll never reward me for it.

Why put fabric softener on his shirt? He'll never notice anyway.

He never says anything about my new recipes. Why do I keep trying?

Why should I put myself out on this English assignment? It'll be graded by some graduate assistant, anyway. The prof will never see it.

Maybe—just maybe—you've been doing your work for the notice and praise of men. Maybe you've been laboring for your own personal gratification. Talk about tiresome! That kind of service can get very old and stale. Fast.

It's the motive that counts. Doing your work wholeheartedly "as for the Lord" can transform virtually any task you're called on to perform . . . whether it's counting widgets in a widget factory, writing a term paper in economics, cleaning the kitchen for the umpteenth time, or giving loving care to someone who fails to acknowledge or appreciate you.

The Lord Jesus will neither overlook nor forget the tasks you perform in His name. Nor will He fail to reward you.

Therefore, my dear brothers, stand firm. Let nothing move you. Always give yourselves fully to the work of the Lord, because you know that your labor in the Lord is not in vain (1 Corinthians 15:58, NIV).

STRONGHOLD

Make time this week to read the book of Ruth (don't worry, it's only four chapters long!). Get an inside look at the way friends and relatives should care for one another. Notice the way Ruth, Naomi, and Boaz supported each other in a godly way.

Is there someone in your family you've been caring for? For whose notice and praise have you been laboring? Do you want to impress your relative and those who notice? Or do you perform your tasks as a service of praise to God? Learn from Ruth those principles of higher service.

Shadows

The shadow of a mighty Rock within a weary land . . .

One of my favorite times of the day is late afternoon when shadows steal across our backyard. Ken and I like to pour a cool drink and sit out back, quietly watching the shadows shift and change. We position our chairs in the shade of our neighbor's big pine to escape the heat of the California sun. Trouble is, we have to keep inching our chairs to the left to keep up with that shadow.

Shadows. Always moving, changing with the seasons, shifting with the sun, never constant, never the same. The comfort we seek from them is temporary at best. Like Jonah crouching under the gourd vine, we find shadows fickle friends.

Ah, but there is Someone who casts an unchanging shadow.

James 1:17 tells us that, "Every good thing bestowed and every perfect gift is from above, coming down from the Father of lights, with whom there is no variation, or shifting shadow."

That shadow never shifts, because our Father never changes. He's not evolving, as some theologians would have us believe. He's not transmutable, as other religions profess. No, He is constant and changeless. Always compassionate. Always merciful. Always just. Always holy. Always full of love.

The relief we find in His presence does not change with the passing of the hours, days, or years.

The encouragement we find in His promises will not fail us when the heat of adversity bears down upon us.

The security we find in His character will never vary though our lives turn upside down and the world changes around us.

How wonderful to have His shadow fall across us. Psalm 91 begins by saying, "He who dwells in the shelter of the Most High will abide in the shadow of the Almighty." The psalmist goes on to detail the many ways God protects His own, making them feel secure. In verse 11 we're told, "For He will give His angels charge concerning you, to guard you in all your ways. They will bear you up in their hands, lest you strike your foot against a stone."

Psalm 121 assures us that:

He who watches over you will not slumber;
indeed, he who watches over Israel
    will neither slumber nor sleep.

The LORD watches over you—
    the LORD is your shade at your right hand;
the sun will not harm you by day,
    nor the moon by night.

The LORD will keep you from all harm—
    he will watch over your life (vv. 3-7, NIV).

If we are willing to put our lives in His hands and our faith in His Word, He will richly reward us by making the passing of each day's shadows a sign of His blessings to come.

You may fail Him, but He will never fail you. Place your chair in the shadow of the cross and you will never have to move it.

STRONGHOLD

Read Isaiah 25:4-5. Think of the last time you enjoyed
a picnic at the park or a party in your back yard on a
summer day. Describe the relief you felt sitting in the
shade, thinking of at least three ways you were comforted. Have you felt the same kind of comfort resting
in the shadow of God's presence?

CHAPTER 15

Strength . . . While You Wait

Years ago my family and I took a camping trip up into the wilderness reserve of Jasper Provincial Park in Alberta, Canada. I remember boarding a chairlift that cabled us to the top of a huge, glacier-scarred mountain overlooking a broad expanse of pine forest below. There our eyes met the spectacle of wild, rugged terrain and turquoise lakes shimmering in the sun. We shivered inside our down jackets, half from the icy cold and half from the awesome view. We yelled our delight to one another over the violent roaring of the wind at the mountaintop.

I marveled at the sight of a soaring eagle moving far across the wooded valley. Just a tiny speck against the distant mountain range. I watched as the eagle circled and dove, admiring his grace and ease.

Eagles seem to go with big things—mountains, canyons, great depths, immense heights. It's always at the most stupendous and alluring spectacles of nature that we find them.

God talks about eagles. In one of the most well-loved passages of the Old Testament, He uses their flight to describe the adventure that will unfold to the suffering Christian who waits for Him.

Though youths grow weary and tired,
And vigorous young men stumble badly,
Yet those who wait for the LORD
Will gain new strength;

They will mount up with wings like eagles,
They will run and not get tired,
They will walk and not become weary
(Isaiah 40:30-31).

Most of us think of "waiting on God" as passive, something we have to do before the "real action" begins. Tiresome—at best boring—waiting is viewed only as a wearisome means to a better end. We wait in line at a grocery check-out counter, watch the clock on the wall at the dentist's office, glance at our watch while in a bank teller's line.

But waiting on God is far different. It's not passive, it's active. And it's not as though we *first* wait and *then* finally get the chance to mount up with wings, run without tiring, and walk without weariness. No, those good things actually happen *while* we are waiting! Waiting on God is an active, confident trusting . . . an instant obedience.

Isaiah promises a new and exciting perspective when we wait on the Lord. Waiting on God gives us the kind of perspective that an eagle must have who mounts up above the trees, lakes, and mountains. Our surroundings come into focus. Our horizons are broadened. We see our place in the scheme of things.

When the Bible talks about waiting on God in my suffering, it means confidently trusting that God knows how much I need and can take. It means looking expectantly toward the time when He will free me from my burdens.

But not get weary? Not get tired or stumble?

How can that be when these are the very trademarks of those who suffer? Yet God's promise is clear. Those who wait for Him in their distress will receive strength and endurance which others know nothing about.

Because I know that one day I'll receive a new body, I am now "able to mount up with wings like an eagle." My expectancy and hope give me endurance and strength.

My body is now held by the limits of this wheelchair. But the waiting hope I have in God's future for me gives me the freedom to soar to heights of joy and explore the canyon depths of God's tender mercies.

All in all, it's worth the wait.

STRONGHOLD

How would you describe the difference between "passive" and "active" waiting. Read Hosea 12:6. What does this verse advise us to do while we wait? How long must we wait on God? Get into the habit of actively waiting, and before you know it you'll feel those eagle wings underneath you!

God Chooses the Weak

Have you ever thought of the Bible as an adventure story?

The King's most trusted officer turns renegade, gathers a powerful army around him, and leads a rebellion. Through treachery and deceit, the rebel leader usurps the authority of the rightful King, sets up his own rival government, and enslaves the citizens of the kingdom. In order to free the captives and retake the Kingdom, the King sends His own Son into the heart of enemy territory . . . with a battle plan more shocking than anyone could imagine.

It sounds like epic fiction, or the plot for an action-adventure movie. But it's not. The story is as current as this morning's headlines. The battle blazes white-hot even as you read these words.

Yes, those are real bullets zinging past your head. If anything on this beleaguered planet is real, it is the ceaseless warfare being waged for the hearts and minds of men and women, boys and girls. The stakes in the battle are high, the consequences eternal.

Now, if I were God, seeking to gather a winning team around Jesus Christ, how would I get the job done?

Well, let's see. I'd need a strong economic base. So I guess I'd go after the best brain trust I could pull together. All the Wall Street wizards, Harvard economists, and Fortune 500 guys.

For my strategy team, I'd go after Nobel Prize laureates, MIT computer analysts, and all the brightest young men and women from the professional world.

Umm . . . for public relations I'd need to hire some big Madison Avenue firm. I'd need to find a front man, of course . . . probably a rugged looking actor with a deep, smooth voice and a recognizable face.

I'd need a tough-minded manager. Maybe the President's chief of staff, a career miltary man, or the CEO of a multinational conglomerate.

With so many educated, blue-chip people, the job would surely get done.

But *I'm* not running the world, God is. And He has already written the most magnificent script imaginable for invading Satan's territory and retaking the Kingdom of Earth under the banner of His Son. But He has peopled the script with the weak and the poor and the unlikely. He casts the roles employing the sick, the lonely, the ungifted, and the unlovely.

Paul said it well in his first letter to the Corinthians:

Notice among yourselves, dear brothers, that few of you who follow Christ have big names or power or wealth. Instead, God has deliberately chosen to use ideas the world considers foolish and of little worth in order to shame those people considered by the world as wise and great. He has chosen a plan despised by the world, counted as nothing at all, and used it to bring down to nothing those the world considers great, so that no one anywhere can ever brag in the presence of God (1:26-29, TLB).

He's chosen such people on His team for a special reason. You see, Satan scoffs at the people God decides on. He jeers at the insignificant, average, everyday sort of folks the Lord crowds onto His team. But this is the catch. If God, by sheer grace, overcomes in spite of the odds, winning the world by using weak and inferior people, guess Who receives even greater glory?

Just like it says in 2 Corinthians 12:9. God's power shows up best in weak people. And if God's power resides in the weakest of us, if we, through suffering and disappointment, are being groomed for active duty on God's Team, why should we complain?

Instead, let's say with Paul, "I will boast all the more gladly about my weaknesses, so that Christ's power may rest on me. That is why, for Christ's sake, I delight in weaknesses . . . for when I am weak, then I am strong" (2 Corinthians 12:9b-10, NIV).

Now that's a story worth telling.

STRONGHOLD

If you were to lead an army against the Midianites, Amalekites, and a host of hostile foreigners, how many people would you want on your team? Would thirty-two thousand trained soldiers be enough? Gideon thought so, but the Lord had other ideas. For a good story on how God delights to use weak people (and weakened armies!) read Judges chapter 7.

CHAPTER 17

Thoughts in the Corner

There you are. In the corner again. Facing an agonizing choice—a do-or-die challenge. Yes, you've been there before. But now God is asking you to come through for Him once again.

Do I hear a murmur in your heart of hearts? A faint note of protest?

Now, come on God, what do You expect from me? Blood? None of my friends seem to be faced with such faith-challenging, heart-wrenching tests. What do you think I am? Some kind of martyr? Joan of Arc?

Back in the corner. We've all stood where you're standing, at one time or another. We've all toyed with the thought that just maybe, God might be asking too much of us.

To set the record straight, what does the Bible say about all this? The writer of Deuteronomy has an answer—and what an answer it is!

What does the LORD your God ask of you but to fear the LORD your God, to walk in all His ways, to love Him, to serve the LORD your God with all your heart and all your soul, and to observe the LORD's commands and decrees that I am giving you today for your own good? (Deuteronomy 10:12, NIV).

That sums it up neatly, doesn't it? What does God ask of us? Only to fear Him . . . to love Him . . . to serve Him . . . to obey Him—*and to do so with all our heart and with all our soul.*

All God is asking for is everything.

Early on in my disability there were times when I felt He was asking too much of me: to trust and obey Him in spite of severe paralysis and a life sentence in a wheelchair. I felt like a martyr. That martyr complex, I've come to realize, was fostered by concentrating too much on what God asked of me—and not enough on what God had *given* me.

If you're tempted, like I was, to think that "everything" sounds like too much, stop a moment and think about what God has given you.

How much did *He* hold back? Anything? Of course not. In fact, He gave more than everything. He gave His own life, His own Son.

> *He who did not spare his own Son, but gave him up for us all—how will he not also, along with him, graciously give us all things?* (Romans 8:32, NIV)

That's the beauty behind it all, isn't it? For if we're tempted to get a little fainthearted in not only fearing God with all our hearts and souls but loving and serving and obeying Him, too, let's remember that God has promised us even more than His own Son. He's promised us power through the Spirit—power that will help us do all that He asks of us . . . power that will strengthen our weak knees and faint hearts.

As Paul put it, "I can do all things through Him who strengthens me" (Philippians 4:13).

So what does God expect of you today? Does it seem like a bit too much? Do you feel backed into a corner?

Remember, all He asks from you is everything. And all He offers you is the power to do just that.

STRONGHOLD

When you look at today's responsibilities, do you feel God expects too much of you? If so, read Ephesians 3:16-19 for strength and encouragement.

CHAPTER 18

The Refuge

Kids and hiding places go together.

Whether they live in the country or the city, give a couple of kids an hour or two and they will be nested away in some secret shelter.

It could be as simple as a bedspread tent draped between two chairs in the living room or as elaborate as a hollowed-out cave in the blackberry vines or a homemade raft hidden in the backwater willows.

I treasure some happy memories of my sister Kathy and me constructing a special treehouse back when we lived on the farm. It was some distance from the farmhouse, so it was private—far away from the intruding eyes of grownups. We lugged wood and confiscated nails and borrowed hammers and put together a very fine and well-constructed house (or at least we thought so) up in the inviting arms of an old tree.

A shelter? A place to hide? Oh yes, but it was more than that to me. In my childish thinking it was a *fortress*—a high tower soaring above the wild frontiers! The storms would swirl and howl outside of that little house, the rain would beat on the tin roof and the wind would make the house sway in the branches of the tree.

But we were safe. Protected. Dry and cozy.

Don't you ever find yourself wishing it were that easy again? Because the storms don't stop as we grow up, do they? The clouds can become darker than we ever imagined and the wind can shake us with a fury that seems more than we can endure. Sometimes, we long for a hiding place.

We're not alone in that desire. Even some of the greatest men in the Bible expressed such a longing. In one of his deepest moments of pain and sorrow over the sin of his people, Jeremiah cried out to God:

"O that I had in the desert
A wayfarers' lodging place;
That I might leave my people,
And go from them!
For all of them are adulterers,
An assembly of treacherous men"
(Jeremiah 9:2).

There were times when David, too, wished with all his heart for a shelter from the storms of life.

"Oh, that I had wings like a dove!
I would fly away and be at rest.
Behold, I would wander far away,
I would lodge in the wilderness.
I would hasten to my place of refuge
From the stormy wind and tempest"
(Psalm 55:6-8).

The wonderful thing about the Bible is that it doesn't leave us in our despair. Scripture tells us that there *is* a hiding place. A shelter much stronger than a fragile refuge of our own making. Mightier than earth's most powerful citadel.

"The Lord is my rock and my fortress and my deliverer," wrote David, "My God, my rock, in whom I take refuge. My shield and the horn of my salvation, my stronghold . . . my God, in whom I trust! Under His wings you may seek refuge; His faithfulness is a shield and bulwark. . . . The

Lord is with me; I will not be afraid. What can man do to me?" (Psalms 18:2, 91:2, 4; 118:6, NAS, NIV).

What better hiding place could there be? What better shelter for anxious hearts and weary minds?

My little tree house taught me a lot about the meaning behind a "refuge" or "high tower." But like most adults, I put childish things behind me. When I need a refuge now, I no longer go to a place . . . I come to a *Person*. In Jesus Christ I have an Everlasting Rock, a High Fortress, a Tower of Refuge, a Shield . . . a Savior.

The storms? Oh yes, they're still there. Sometimes only inches away. Maybe you, too, hear the wind today. Maybe your branches are shaking so hard you feel you'll never be able to hang on. Climb up with me into His love, under His sheltering grace.

Together, let's say, "The Lord is with us, we will not fear."

STRONGHOLD

The writer of the book of Hebrews also thought of God as a shelter. Take a look at Hebrews 13:4-6. Notice that he even quotes Psalm 118:6, adding this wonderful thought: "He Himself has said, 'I will never desert you, nor will I ever forsake you.'"

Our friend in Hebrews is describing exactly what we have been thinking about for the last couple of pages: Our Lord is a *shelter* for His much-loved sons and daughters. But He makes these statements in the context of a discussion on (1) Sex and marriage, and (2) money (verses 4-5). Take some time to read through these few verses, considering how the Lord's beautiful offer of refuge, help, and security apply to these two crucial areas of our lives.

Pruning

It never fails. Each spring I'm amazed by those first, tentative signs . . . little green shoots poking out of the soil . . . little green buds bursting off the vine.

I'm amazed because I'm so *ruthless* with my clippers in the fall. I prune my plants and shrubbery unmercifully. Blossoms are severed as soon as they fade. Sturdy young branches are consigned to the dumpster. Nothing escapes the bite of those shears. Through the winter the Tada foliage looks stark, chastened—even lifeless.

But spring always changes things. As I pen these words on this first day of spring, life is beginning all over again in my garden.

So it's been since the beginning. Back in ancient Uz, the thoughts of a godly man named Job turned to spring—a spring he believed he would never see.

> *There is hope for a tree:*
> *If it is cut down, it will sprout again,*
> *and its new shoots will not fail.*
> *Its roots may grow old in the ground*
> *and its stump die in the soil,*
> *yet at the scent of water it will bud*
> *and put forth shoots like a plant*
> (Job 14:7-9, NIV).

Job could not imagine a future renewal in his own life. The Lord's sharp shears had clipped his life so close to the roots he didn't see how it could ever grow back. Everything dear to him had been slashed away in cruel, successive strokes. "Only a few years will pass before I go on the journey of no return," he told his friends. "My spirit is broken, my days are cut short . . ." (16:22-17:1, NIV).

Some of you reading these words can well understand Job's anguish. A family, shattered by divorce . . . a teenager, crushed by rejection or loneliness . . . a single parent, struggling to keep food on the table . . . a father, learning how to make those first adjustments to a handicapped son—a boy who will never throw a football or cast a fly rod.

Like Job, we feel at those times that there's more hope for a fallen tree than for us. Like Job, we voice our questions and wrestle with our pain.

God's pruning shears seem merciless. Nothing escapes the cutting edge of His will. Not the blossom of youth, not the bloom of good health, not the fruit of prosperity, not the sturdy, growing family. None of these fall outside the pruning effects of God's purposes.

But spring comes, doesn't it?

Much to his amazement, it even came to Job. A spring of such fragrance and beauty that his long, bitter winter must have seemed like a bad dream. (Read Job 42:10-16.)

Hope returns. New life pokes up from the dead stump. Joy reappears . . . ever so slowly, almost shyly, and not all at once. But it comes. Fresh new grace enables us to endure. Bright, hopeful promises offer a strong trellis to which we can cling. The sweet, heady fragrance of the Holy Spirit blows across our lives, waters us with His Word, and encourages us to reach for all the good things God has in store for us.

In God's order, winter always gives way to spring. The iron grip of January yields to the sunshine of His love. If not now, then soon.

Spring will not tarry. New life is on the way.

STRONGHOLD

If you're going through a winter time in your soul, read Romans chapter 6 today. To gain extra insight, read it once in your regular Bible, and again in a paraphrase of the Scriptures such as *The Living Bible*. Let the promise of "newness of life" in verse 4 remind you that spring can begin *today* in your heart.

The Noble Spork

I was having lunch at a friend's home recently, a wise Christian woman with discerning eyes. Before we ate, I had to borrow one of her spoons and have her bend and twist it in a contorted angle.

She then inserted the spoon in my hand splint and I was able to feed myself. But as we ate and casually talked, I noticed her eyes. She kept looking at the bent spoon. When lunch was over, she pulled the spoon out of my arm splint and set it by my plate. I was a little embarrassed that I had to bend one of her nicest pieces of flatware. With that ugly twist of the metal, it looked as though I had ruined the spoon.

I offered to have my husband straighten out the spoon—to return it to its original shape.

"Oh, no," she said. "I want to keep this spoon just the way it is."

"But it looks ugly like that," I protested, "and besides, you won't be able to use it."

By this time she had the spoon in her hand, gently fingering the twist in the handle, admiring it as though it were a thing of beauty rather than something bent and misshapen. To her, the spoon had a special meaning.

"You see, Joni," she explained, "you can only use a spoon that's been bent to meet your needs. A straight one just won't do. A twisted tool in your hand can better accomplish a task."

I've nicknamed my special utensil a "spork." I can't tell you how many times I've gone into a restaurant and had busboys or a waitress spy it and try to take it away.

"Ugh! Where did this come from? It must have gotten mangled in the dishwasher," they'll say.

Or a busboy may pick it up and without saying a word, bend it back to its original shape, thinking he's doing me a favor.

"Oh no," I tell them. "It's *supposed* to look like that. It's bent perfectly so I can use it."

Isn't that the way God works in our lives? He knows He can better accomplish His unique plan when He bends us to suit His will. He can best use us when we're molded and shaped for His special design. Now, certainly, this spork of mine isn't very attractive. It's obviously unlike the rest of the utensils in the kitchen drawer. And we might come to think that we, in our weakness, are unlike all the rest.

But in the hand of God we serve an express purpose. The metal of our souls may be hard and difficult to bend, but when we allow God the privilege of shaping our lives, we discover new depths of purpose and meaning. What a joyful thought to realize you are a chosen vessel for God—perfectly suited for His use.

> *In a large house there are articles not only of gold and silver, but also of wood and clay; some are for noble purposes and some for ignoble. If a man cleanses himself from the latter, he will be an instrument for noble purposes, made holy, useful to the Master and prepared to do any good work* (2 Timothy 2:20-21, NIV).

Even a spork can be noble . . . if it's placed in the Master's hand.

STRONGHOLD

The dictionary says that *noble* means, "Grand, splendid, magnificent; having greatness of character and excellent qualities." Wouldn't you like to be one of God's chosen vessels for *noble* use? You can be, you know. Read again 2 Timothy 2:21, paying special attention to the last part of the verse. What kind of work could be considered noble? How can you prepare yourself to be used for noble purposes?

CHAPTER 21

A Tool in the Master's Hand

He's been my art coach for many years now and has taught me wonderful things about the world of painting.

James Sewell is a fine gentleman who has studied extensively and traveled all over the world. More than just an artist, he's a concert pianist, an accomplished writer, and a mathematician. He's a master—a kind of Renaissance man. I feel privileged to call him a friend.

When we're able to get together for an art session, he always brings in big old books from his library, new kinds of paint, or different and unusual brushes.

Once Jim brought in some of his own brushes from his studio. I was startled by the condition they were in. These brushes, he told me, were over thirty years old. Frankly, they looked it. The paint on the handles was worn and chipped. The brushes themselves were discolored and bristly, and had obviously seen incredible wear and tear.

If I hadn't known better, I would have said they were useless . . . not fit for painting anything of real beauty or value. But then I had the chance to watch Jim at work in front of his easel with those very brushes.

Suddenly, in his hands, the brushes became not only useful, but *priceless*. I watched him swirl and sweep the paint on the canvas. I marveled how each brush had its own purpose. One brush for a certain kind of line, another for a special kind of stroke.

Jim knew just how to use each one of his brushes. He knew what each could do and not do in his hands. Even the ugliest brush—an ancient thing with stiff and ragged bristles—was reserved for special duty as Jim continued to paint. He knew his tools well.

It was no surprise that he never even picked up one of my nice, new, soft sable brushes. No, he preferred to work with his well-worn, well-proven tools.

Someone once said that a tool unto itself is of little importance. But placed in the proper hands it can create a masterpiece.

That day as I watched Jim at work with his old brushes, he created a beautiful painting right before my eyes. I was smart enough to know that if I had placed those same brushes in my mouth, there's no way I could have created such a masterpiece. I'm simply not a master. But Jim had proven to me that any tool in his hand—even the most unlovely and unlikely—could be used with mighty purpose.

In a similar way, perhaps, you may find yourself thinking you're unfit for service in the kingdom of God. Your potential, you tell yourself, is small—maybe non-existent. You may feel you've gone through too much, wandered too far, or seen too much wear and tear to accomplish anything wonderful for the Lord.

Ah, that's the problem with concentrating on the *tool*. No tool, in and of itself, has great importance. But placed in the proper hands it can create a masterpiece.

What an encouragement to realize that God has reserved you and me for a special task in His great work.

In His hands we're not only useful . . . but priceless.

Those parts of the body that seem to be weaker are indispensable, and the parts we think are less honorable we treat with special honor . . . but God has combined the members of the body and has given greater honor to the parts that lacked it, so that there should be no division in the body, but that its parts should have equal concern for each other (1 Corinthians 12:22, 24-25, NIV).

STRONGHOLD

Do you use a favorite toothbrush that's worn and thin? Or an old comb with missing teeth? Or a dog-eared address book filled with marks and scribbles? Or a spatula that's been flipping pancakes for twenty years? Or an antiquated Underwood manual typewriter? Or an ancient Boy Scout jackknife with a stiff blade? In your hands, these trusted items perform best. You prefer them. You choose them.

Let one of these simple, everyday items be a reminder to you of how God wants to use you and your strengths and weaknesses. Why do you think God has chosen you for the special tasks He's given you? Why do you think He prefers to use you for the ministry He has in mind for your family? Your co-workers? Your neighbors?

Resources for the Journey

"Lo, I am with you always . . ." (Matthew 28:20).

In her book, *A Slow and Certain Light*, Elisabeth Elliot tells of two young adventurers who came to see her in Ecuador. The two men were on their way to the rain forests east of the Andes. Both were weighted down with huge packs of equipment— most of it more cumbersome than helpful. Yet they didn't want her evaluation of their supplies. Nor did they ask for counsel or advice about their trip. All they wanted were a few phrases of the Indian language. They were certain this was all they lacked to be fully prepared for their journey. She writes:

> Sometimes we come to God as the two adventurers came to me—confident and, we think, well-informed and well-equipped. But it has occurred to us that with all our accumulation of stuff something is missing. There is just one thing we will have to ask God for, and we hope He will not find it necessary to sort through the other things. There's nothing there that we're willing to do without. We know what we need—a yes or no answer, please, to a simple question. Or perhaps a road sign. Something quick and easy to point the way.
>
> What we really ought to have is the Guide Himself.
>
> Maps, road signs, and a few useful phrases are good things, but infinitely better is Someone who has been there before and knows the way.[1]

You and I want all the maps, guides, and compasses we can get our hands on as we plan our journey into marriage, a career, or a family. We want the blueprint spread out before us if we're going through a crisis. We need to make sense out of our suffering. But through it all, Jesus says that He is with us always. It is His presence that makes the real difference between acceptance or anger, hope or despair.

Jesus Christ has been there ahead of us. He knows the way. He understands the journey and, what's more, He offers to walk with us through it all.

Maps and guidebooks are fine. But when the sky grows dark and the path gets rough, our best resource is the Guide Himself.

STRONGHOLD

Have you ever stopped to ask a person for directions? He or she tells you to go three blocks north, left at the signal, stay to the right, and go two stop signs to the next intersection—and you're more confused than ever. You wish that person would say, "Follow me. I'm headed in that direction."

Jesus said virtually the same thing in John 14:5-6. Did Jesus say He was only one way among many ways? Or is He the only way? Thank your Lord right now that He does not hand you an impossible creed as a road map for life. He offers you Himself!

Drifting

When I was a child our family always spent summer vacations beach camping near Dewey Beach, Delaware. The crashing waves on that shoreline held no fear for me, and day after day I begged Mother to let me follow my older sisters into the water. Finally giving into my pleas one beautiful morning, she strapped me tightly into my life vest and sternly warned my sisters to keep hold of my hand.

Kathy held me on her hip as we waded through the breakers into the rolling surf. It was quieter there behind the thundering waves, and I giggled and laughed with Kathy and Jay as we rode the roller-coaster swells.

Somehow, at some point, I let go of Kathy's hand. And after the next great swell, it suddenly occurred to me that my sisters were nowhere near. When I saw their faraway heads pop up over another swell, I realized with horror how far I had been carried away.

I was adrift in the wide ocean—and going further from shore.

I don't know how it happened . . . and so quickly! A strong current had caught me, pulling me down the beach. Thankfully, at that moment my mother ran from her umbrella, dove into the sea, and rescued me.

I never realized how far I had drifted until the moment I saw that great distance between me and the others.

Drifting . . . I'm thinking about that today, on this, my thirty-eighth birthday. Birthdays are our special, private marks in time. A chance to glance back over the past year and see how far we've come. An opportunity to take a long, hard look at whether we've wandered off the straight path, meandering into indifference or backsliding into sin. As the writer of Hebrews affirms, none of us can afford to drift.

We must pay more careful attention, therefore, to what we have heard, so that we do not drift away" (Hebrews 2:1, NIV).

Drifting can be dangerous. Always, always, there are currents pulling at us. Always we are swimming upstream, against the tide. There is always the temptation to drift, and we never realize how far we are carried away until we see Christ . . . until we see the others from whom we've parted.

It's possible for *any* of us to drift spiritually or morally. No one is immune. Think of the powerful currents in your own life that can take hold and carry you along unless you make an effort to control the direction. There is the current of social opinion, of fashion or fad. There is a current of personal desire . . . doing the things *you* want to do. Lust is a powerful undertow. Materialism is a relentless tug.

I'm very aware of such currents in my own life. The Bible calls it "walking according to the course of this world." But as I look back over this year—my still-young marriage, my ministry at *Joni and Friends,* my opportunities to write or travel or paint or sing—I realize I must continue to pull on the oars with all the strength God gives me.

Because you see, I'm one of those people who could easily drift, giving myself to whatever current is bearing me along. In order to keep my life from aimlessly coasting, I must make every effort to keep my focus fixed on Jesus. I've got to pull myself in line with God's Word every morning as I begin my day. I need to constantly aim and re-aim my life in a God-honoring direction. I've got to tug at my heart to keep it from wandering off into daydreams or silly temptations.

Following God doesn't come easy for me. It probably never will. But today, on my birthday, I celebrate my recommitment to keep at the oars, rowing against those strong currents. With God's help, next year I will look back on another 365 days of hard-fought, hard-won progress in my walk with Christ.

Let's put our shoulders to those oars together, shall we?

STRONGHOLD

Someone has said, "Sow a thought, reap an action . . . sow an action, reap a habit . . . sow a habit, reap a character." Drifting from God starts in small ways with little thoughts. To keep the current of your thoughts in line, find a King James Bible and look up 2 Corinthians 10:5. Can your thoughts be controlled? Who gives you the power to do so?

Relying on God

While having lunch with a quadriplegic friend the other day, I started talking about the help and encouragement I've received from my relationship with Christ.

My friend, however, wasn't happy at all about that turn in our conversation.

"Jesus can't help me," he frowned. "It isn't Jesus who helps me with this sandwich, it's my friend here," he motioned to the person sitting next to him who was cutting up his food. "And Jesus doesn't put me to bed at night or get me up in the morning or get me a drink of water. Jesus doesn't do that stuff for me. It's *people* I need."

What a shortsighted view this man had of our God. All he could think of was the immediate and urgent needs of his paralysis. He couldn't look past his handicap.

The apostle Paul has advice for people who get shortsighted about their suffering. Bruised and battered, he writes in the second book of Corinthians, chapter one that he was under great pressure, far beyond his ability to endure. Reflecting on those horrendous circumstances, the apostle makes this statement:

But this happened that we might not rely on ourselves but on God (2 Corinthians 1:9, NIV).

Few of us will ever face the sorts of hardships Paul encountered, but his assurance can still be ours. You and I can look at the disappointments which wound and bewilder us and say with resolve that these things have happened that we might not rely on ourselves, but on God.

Being a quadriplegic means I have no use of my hands or legs. Like my friend, I need someone else to floss my teeth or hold a cup to my lips so I can drink. Somebody has to tuck in my blouse when it pulls out of my slacks. If I get too hot someone has to reach for the ice or the fan. Someone has to help me in and out of bed. There's hardly an hour of the day that I don't rely on the willing hands and feet of others.

But I've learned not to be so shortsighted about my disability and the people who help me. It *is* Jesus who feeds me my sandwich . . . after all, He's the one who provides that friend sitting next to me, just as He provides the food. It is Jesus who lovingly works through my husband when he helps me in bed at night. And it is Jesus who brings people to help me in the morning.

No, my hands and legs don't work. But like Paul, I've learned to see that these things have happened that I might not rely on my own meager, personal resources. These things have happened that I might lean my full weight on the power, presence, and provision of my Lord.

I *do* need Jesus. And if I ever ask you to help me with a sandwich or hold a coffee cup for me, I'll smile my thanks at you . . . but give Him the glory.

STRONGHOLD

We often depend on our own skills and abilities when life seems easy, but we only turn to God when we've exhausted other resources. Dependence is not defeat. Dependence is glorious. Read what David, a powerful warrior and king, wrote on the subject in Psalm 62, especially verses 7-8.

Rely . . . lean . . . trust . . . depend . . . count on . . . bank on . . . pin your faith on God. Will you let your problems and pressures today drive you to Him? Rely on God—first!

CHAPTER 25

Lifeline

Those early days when I first got out of the hospital were terrifying. Without the encouragement and perspective of Scripture, I honestly don't know how I would have survived. Like a strong lifeline, God's Word kept me from drowning in my despair.

Several of those "lifeline" passages were from a single chapter in the book of Lamentations. In one verse, Jeremiah wrote:

The LORD is good to those who wait for Him, to the soul who seeks Him (3:25, NKJV).

What else did I have to do but wait? The long, lonely hours in the middle of the night were bearable because of that promise. God would be good. To me. I was waiting, and knew I would see His goodness. The prophet goes on to say:

It is good that one should hope and wait quietly for the salvation of the LORD (3:26, NKJV).

Salvation, deliverance. It was a promise, right there in black and white. And though I had no use of my hands, I clung to that hope with all that was in me. I waited and believed that deliverance (whatever that meant) would surely come.

In the very next verse, Jeremiah says:

It is good for a man to bear the yoke in his youth. Let him sit alone and keep silent, because God has laid it on him (3:27-28, NKJV).

Some things are harder to learn as we get older. Our hearts may be calloused or indifferent. Perhaps age brings about the feeling of being worldly wise . . . we've "seen it all," and there is nothing new to learn. For all the pain of shattered dreams, a yoke is better borne in youth.

As a young teenager, my heart was still at a tender age. I was still hammering out values and principles. There was still much to learn; in my deepest heart I knew that was true. So I gritted my teeth and trusted that it was good to bear such a heavy yoke of disability in my youth.

But the best part of Lamentations 3 was in verses 31 and 32.

> *For the Lord will not cast off forever. Though He causes grief, yet He will show compassion according to the multitude of His mercies* (NKJV).

That verse was like a light at the end of the tunnel for me. To know that things wouldn't be like this forever! Though God had His hand in my injury, He would also show compassion. He had helped me through the long nights. He would be with me during the lonely days of adjusting to my wheelchair.

The yoke? Yes, it's still heavy to bear. But time and again God in His grace has thrown out the sturdy lifeline of His Word just when I felt I was about to go under.

Look . . . there's a lifeline in front of you, too. Grab on like never before. He'll never let you sink.

STRONGHOLD

Lamentations chapter 3 is full of "lifeline" verses, rich with hope, encouragement, and inspiration. Why not investigate them for yourself?

For a little background, Lamentations was the "book of lamenting" that Jeremiah wrote during the crisis of the Babylonian invasion. Tough times they were. Look at verses 22 through 24. How about verse 33 for encouagement? And don't forget verse 40 for a real lifesaver.

Facing tough times today? Grab hold of these lifeline verses.

A Matter of the Heart

Our church has a class for mentally handicapped children and young people. It's a happy group where the students enjoy learning to pray and hearing stories about Jesus, illustrated by puppets and flannelgraphs.

One young girl in the class has been grasping the ideas quickly, thirstily absorbing spiritual content.

Her mother is one astonished lady. She recently called the church elder for special ministries to express her amazement.

"I don't understand it," she said. "My daughter is picking up things I *know* she can't understand. Yet she's learning—far beyond her natural capabilities."

The woman can't believe her eyes and ears. But none of this takes our elder by surprise. For him this is just one more example of the truth in 1 Corinthians 2.

Now we have received, not the spirit of the world, but the Spirit who is from God, that we might know the things freely given to us by God, which things we also speak, not in words taught by human wisdom, but in those taught by the Spirit, combining spiritual thoughts with spiritual words (vv. 12-13).

Time after time he's seen God's Spirit teach mentally handicapped persons truths far beyond their natural capabilities to comprehend.

We tend to think a person needs a super IQ or a Bible college degree to understand spiritual truth. The brighter you are, we reason, the more of God's Word you'll understand.

Not so, this scripture teaches us.

The message of Jesus Christ crucified is not imparted through plausible words of men's wisdom, but "in demonstration of the Spirit and of power, that your faith should not rest on the wisdom of men, but on the power of God" (I Corinthians 2:4-5).

Remember the story of Peter's confession? Late in His ministry, Jesus turned to His disciples with a penetrating question: "Who do people say the Son of Man is?"

"Some say John the Baptist," they replied. "Others say Elijah, and still others Jeremiah or one of the prophets."

"But what about *you*?" Jesus asked. "Who do *you* say that I am?"

"You are the Christ," Simon Peter answered, "the Son of the living God."

Jesus replied, "Blessed are you, Simon son of Jonah, *for this was not revealed to you by man, but by my Father in heaven*" (see Matthew 16:13-17, NIV).

It's interesting Jesus did not commend Peter for his brainpower. Peter's answer had nothing to do with acute observation, logical perception, intellectual prowess, or formal theological training.

Now, you don't have to be mentally handicapped to draw encouragement from these thoughts. Christ's words give comfort to the C-average student who will never achieve beyond a 2.0 GPA . . . to the Bible college flunk-out who just couldn't make the grade . . . to those who never had the opportunity to attend college, or feel their learning capabilities aren't all they could be.

You don't need a seminary degree and an elevated IQ to discern spiritual truth. According to 1 Corinthians 2:16, we have the mind of Christ. Yes, even a mentally handicapped child has the mind of Jesus!

Walking with God isn't a matter of the intellect, it's a matter of the heart.

STRONGHOLD

When it comes to discerning spiritual truth, we are all mentally handicapped apart from the teaching and guidance of the Spirit of God. With this in mind, read John 14:16-17. Will the Holy Spirit ever leave you? Now look at verses 25-27. Exactly what will the Spirit teach you? Take a few moments and thank God for the ministry of His Holy Spirit, a powerful Person who is on your side, working through, for, and with you.

CHAPTER 27

Open My Eyes

Bent on destroying the prophet Elisha, the king of Syria received reliable information that the man he sought was living in the walled city of Dothan.

The king wasn't taking any chances. Rather than sending a couple of hit men to liquidate Elisha, the king mobilized "horses and chariots and a great army" (2 Kings 6:14). The massive Syrian force came by night and surrounded the city, readying for an early-morning assault.

At daybreak, Elisha's servant went out for a casual morning stroll along the top of the wall, pausing to fill his eyes with the tranquil sunrise over the surrounding hills. What he saw must have made the blood freeze in his veins. The morning sun gleamed and flashed from countless shields, helmets, chariot wheels, arrows, and spear tips. A thousand colorful banners fluttered in the soft breeze.

Filled with sheer terror and dismay, the attendant scampered back to the prophet's chamber with the tidings of gloom and doom.

And his servant said to him, "Alas, my master! What shall we do?" (6:15).

If the servant was expecting his master to fly into a panic or tear out what remained of his sparse hair, he was in for a surprise. He was probably even more surprised by Elisha's calm reply:

"Do not fear, for those who are with us are more than those who are with them" (6:16).

Elisha was not afraid of the Syrian king and his intimidating army. For he trusted in One who could not be seen with the physical eye.

But Elisha did more than give a devotional homily to his frightened servant. He prayed for him saying, "O LORD, I pray, open his eyes that he may see." The Lord answered and the servant saw . . .

. . . and behold, the mountain was full of horses and chariots of fire all around Elisha (6:17).

I like that story. Because when we're serving the Lord, fighting off temptation, or making a stand against fear, we may tend to feel lonely on our side of the battle lines. The devil has his troops marshaled against us, and we are too easily overcome with discouragement or fright. After all, look at what we're up against! Bastions of secularism. Strong political lobbies. Pornography running rampant. Racism. Injustice. Stumbling Christian leaders.

At such a time when fear grips your heart and your faith weakens and wavers, pray that the Lord will open your eyes . . . that you may see.

There's no less of a force surrounding you on the front lines of the battlefield as there was in Elisha's day. A host of angels? A legion of saints? A mountain of horses and chariots of fire? Probably. But all you really need is the One who promised never to leave or forsake you—the One who said, "Lo, I am with you always."

You don't need an army on your side when you've got the King of kings.

STRONGHOLD

"Open my eyes that I may see, visions of truth Thou hast for me . . ." I like that old familiar hymn. Oh, that we would be like the two blind men who, when asked by Christ what they wanted, simply replied, "Lord, that our eyes may be opened." Are your eyes open to spiritual reality today . . . or do you feel overwhelmed by the forces that seem arrayed against you? Read Ephesians 1:15-23. What sorts of things should you be able to see when God gives you the "eyes of the heart" described in verse 18?

Secrets of His Character

PART 2

Secrets of His Character

CHAPTER 28

"Surprising" Trials

I just can't get used to trials. Every time I get hit broad-side with a fresh dose of trouble, my first response is, *Whoa! Where in the world did* that *come from? God picked* me *to handle this?*

Like the other day when my van had a flat tire. My first thought was, *God, you've got the wrong person for this one. Remember? This is Joni—the one who's paralyzed. I can't exactly hop out, flip open the trunk, grab the jack and spin on a spare! Good grief, I can't even flag down a passer-by or thumb a ride to a local gas station.*

Frankly, I was surprised.

I would have thought God could have given me a trial more in keeping with my limitations. All I could do was sit helplessly in my van and wait for some kind soul to walk by and give me a hand. And wait and wait and wait.

But guess what verse kept floating its way to the top of my thinking? You guessed it . . .

Dear friends, do not be surprised at the painful trial you are suffering, as though something strange were happen-ing to you (1 Peter 4:12, NIV).

I know I talk a lot about trials, but I don't really think I get an unfair share of them. We all encounter adversities vir-tually every day of our lives. But for as many times as I've fall-en into trials, they still come as a surprise. It seems I would have learned that lesson from reading those verses in Peter so many times. "Don't be surprised . . . as though something strange were happening . . ."

Apparently I'm not the only one who can't get used to trials. Evidently some of Peter's friends couldn't get used to them either.

But James, Peter's cohort, has some sage advice for people like me. "Consider it all joy, my brothers, when you encounter various trials," he writes, "knowing that the testing of your faith produces endurance" (James 1:2-3).

At first glance that passage seems to say, "Hey, jump up and down and shout, 'Way to go' when you encounter various trials." Could James actually be expecting us to paste on a plastic smile when we fall headlong into heartaches? Not at all. James says, ". . . *consider* it all joy." In other words, reckon or regard it; make a conscious acceptance of the fact. The response he is speaking of has more to do with our minds than our emotions.

Why should we regard our problems with joy?

Because we *know* something, says James. We know that those trials are producing endurance in our lives—patience, maturity, and all-around good character.

So why do trials still come as a surprise to me? I'm certain it's because I forget what I should know. Sometimes the comfort of not having trials is a lot more appealing than the character produced by enduring them. When you're comfortable, you don't want to be budged, right? But thankfully, God knows that, in the long run, character is a lot more appealing than comfort.

So the trials come . . . and we get surprised out of our comfortable complacency. Then, later if not sooner, we get around to counting it all joy.

Today—right now—I want to resolve to know something about the intruder that will invariably knock on my door. Before I get up to answer his knock, I want to re-member that this unwelcome visitor, for all his ill manners has come for *my good*, for the good of my character. No mat-ter what my emotions tell me, I want to welcome him in. Why? Because down deep, real character is more important to me than temporary comfort.

Will you resolve the same thing with me today? Let's greet that surprise intruder with a surprise of our own.

Joy.

STRONGHOLD

Paul was a good one for greeting trials with a joyful mindset. Just take a look at Philippians 1:12-18. Even though Paul was writing from prison, his letter is full of joy. In fact, the words *joy* or *rejoice* are used fourteen times in Philippians.

How can you, like Paul, welcome your trials as friends? Try greeting them with God's Word. Take time to memorize Philippians 4:4 and make it your "verse of welcome" when your next trial sneaks up on you.

CHAPTER 29

God's Goodness: Our Response

*Do you show contempt for the riches of his kindness, toler-
ance and patience, not realizing that God's kindness
leads you toward repentance?* (Romans 2:4, NIV).

Contemplating the kindness and goodness of God always leads us to repentance.

I was thinking about that a few days before last Easter.
Like most of you, I read through the story of the crucifixion
to prepare my heart for Easter morning. But I recall spend-
ing more than a few hours deliberating over the words of
Christ when He cried in anguish from the cross, *My God, my
God, why have you forsaken me?*

I have to admit it. The idea that the Father would allow
His Son to suffer the torture of crucifixion is beyond me.
The humiliation of nakedness, the searing pain, the smell of
blood and sweat, the agony of tears, the spit of drunken soldiers, the scorn of a laughing, jeering mob. When the crowd
thinned and the cowards took shelter from the lashing
storm, Jesus was left alone. As tears mingled with blood on
His battered face, He cried out to His Father—the One who
had not once turned away from Him in all of eternity.

The reply was silence. Cold, accusing silence.

Heaven itself accused Jesus of sins in those horrible
moments: lusting and lying . . . cheating and coveting . . .
murder and hypocrisy . . . cruelty and deceit. Of course,
Christ had never been guilty of any of those sins, *but we are.*

And every one of your sins and mine was racked up on His account right there on that cross. As the prophet testified:

It was our *grief he bore,* our *sorrows that weighed him down . . . He was wounded and bruised for* our *sins. He was chastised that we might have peace; he was lashed— and we were healed!* We *are the ones who strayed away like sheep!* We, *who left God's paths to follow our own. Yet God laid on* him *the guilt and sins of every one of us!* (Isaiah 53:4a, 5-6, TLB).

Paul wrote:

He forgave all your sins, and blotted out the charges proved against you, the list of his commandments which you had not obeyed. He took this list of sins and destroyed it by nailing it to Christ's cross. In this way God took away Satan's power to accuse you (Colossians 2:13-15, TLB).

So where was God's goodness in treating Christ so?

Where was the Father's kindness in turning His back on His only Son—while Jesus cried out in horror and grief?

On that terrible, wonderful day, God's goodness and kindness were directed toward you. God forsook His own Son . . . so that He would never have to forsake you! And because of those dark hours two thousand years ago, God can say to me, "I will never leave *you*, Joni, I will never forsake *you*."

As I pondered that amazing thought, I felt ashamed. The goodness of God was, indeed, leading me to repentance. To think that God's anger for my sins was poured out on Christ—and that He has no anger left for me!

You know what that makes me want to do? Praise Him. Thank Him. Honor Him. Obey Him with all my heart and soul and mind. Unlike Christ, I will *never* have to agonize over separation from my Father. And neither will you. God poured the full measure of His wrath—the terrors of eternal hell—on His own Son . . . so that you and I could be adopted into His very family. That's how much He loves you. And me.

His goodness has a marvelous way of pushing us to repentance.

STRONGHOLD

Flip to the end of Matthew's gospel and marvel at the very last verse. Jesus' closing words are the capstone of His entire ministry—and what comforting words they are. The Lord went through heaven and hell to assure you with this last and great statement He made on earth. Let His goodness right now crumble any resistance, any doubt or stubbornness in your heart. Allow His goodness to lead you into a prayer of repentance.

Who Helps the Most?

People will often ask me, "Who helped you the most when you were hurting?"

That's a good question, but I can never seem to come up with a fast answer. I guess that's because there was no one person—no famous writer, no brainy seminary student, no super-sensitive counselor.

No, answers to my questions didn't come from "extraordinary" people. Frankly, when I was first injured in my diving accident and left paralyzed, I wasn't *looking* for wisdom or knowledge.

At first I was just looking for love.

You don't have to have a Ph.D. or a master's from some Bible college in order to give love. Average, commonplace people are just as necessary in the healing process as counselors and theologians. All of us have the capacity to give love to someone who is hurting.

That should be good news to you—especially those of you looking for ways to alleviate the pain of a friend in the hospital or a family member going through a crushing disappointment. If you and I are truly looking for an answer to the question, "How do I help those who are in pain?" we don't have to have a lot of answers. We don't even have to know all the specialized Scriptures or a hundred and one reasons why God allows suffering. All we've got to know is love.

The only Scripture we might need at first is 1 Corinthians 13. We don't have to understand whether or not people in pain want to be cheered up or consoled. We don't have to rationalize, wondering, *What possible good could MY presence do?* We don't have to guess whether somebody wants to talk about his suffering or not. Instead of getting yourself all tangled up in those guessing games, remember . . . the only thing you really need to give is love.

I most appreciated those people who came into the hospital armed with love—and *Seventeen* magazines and Winchell's doughnuts. I appreciated friends dropping by to help me write letters or bringing writing paper and envelopes—even stamps. I was super-impressed when others bought birthday cards for me to send to a friend whose special day was coming up. I especially remember a few girls who made it a weekly ritual to come by and do my nails. What fun!

These were people who helped. They weren't trained counselors. They weren't spiritual giants. They weren't biblical wizards. They weren't Ph.D.'s. They weren't even full of all kinds of knowledge and wisdom. They were just commonplace, everyday sorts of people who gave me what I needed most of all . . . God's love in action.

STRONGHOLD

Love, as it says in the last verse before 1 Corinthians 13, is "the most excellent way" to reach out to someone who's hurting. Why not take this chance to read 1 Corinthians 13 and think of a hurting friend who needs His supernatural love.

I can show *patience* toward my friend who suffers by _____.

It would be a *very kind* thing if I would _____.

Do I *envy* others who seem better able to help? Forgive me, Lord.

Love is not *proud* or *boastful*. Am I that way when I offer a hand? Let me only be proud in You, Lord.

I can avoid being *rude* or *insensitive* by _____.

Why am I helping? What is my motive? Am I *self-seeking*?

If my hurting friend rejects my offers to help, Lord, keep me from becoming *easily angered* or *keeping a record of wrongs*.

How can I help my friend *rejoice in the truth*?

I can *protect* my friend by _____.

I will *trust* God to bless my efforts to help.

I will *hope* for my friend when he or she feels hopeless.

I will *persevere* even though I don't see immediate results.

When God Opens the Shutters

If our happiest moments on earth give us a foretaste of heaven, then the tragic moments make us long for it.

The truth of the matter is I never used to think much about heaven when I was on my feet. It seemed like some vague, distant, misty place where there would be a lot of clouds and harps and we'd polish gold all day—forever! That prospect seemed very unattractive to me—and immensely boring.

Besides, in order to get to heaven, you had to *die*. And at the age of seventeen who wants to think about that?

But heaven is so wonderful, it's just like God to give us a little help to turn our thoughts toward that future reality. And sometimes it takes more than a lovely starlit night or a verse of Scripture to open our eyes.

Samuel Rutherford describes this help in an essay he wrote back in the seventeenth century:

> *If God had told me some time ago that He was about to make me as happy as I could be in this world and then had told me that He should begin by crippling me in arm or limb and removing from me all my usual sources of enjoyment, I should have thought it a very strange mode of accomplishing His purpose. And yet, how is His wisdom manifest even in this. For if you should see a man shut up in a closed room idolizing a set of lamps and rejoicing in their light and you wished*

to make him truly happy, you would begin by blowing out all of his lamps and then throw open the shutters to let in the light of heaven.[2]

That's just what God did for me when He sent a broken neck my way. He blew out all the lamps in my life which lit up the here and now and made it so exciting. To be sure, the dark depression that followed wasn't much fun. But it certainly made the prospect of heaven come to life. My heart leaps to think of the day when I'll have my new body—hands that feel, arms that hold, and legs that run.

One day God will throw open the shutters. The view that fills our eyes in that moment will make us forget all about the lamps in our shuttered room.

Do you find yourself all caught up in the here and now? Do you sometimes feel a slave to a clock? Are you sick and tired of struggling with sin or apathy or the anxieties and sorrows that weigh down your heart? God may be using those very things to turn your thoughts toward your future home . . . and the One who awaits the sound of your steps at the front door.

STRONGHOLD

Read Revelation 21 to help you throw open the shutters of heaven today. Consider verse 21: If the streets of heaven are paved with gold, then it stands to reason that in heaven gold won't have a great deal of value. It's primary use will be paving material for streets! If gold and precious gems won't hold value in heaven, what things will? How can you lay up the kind of treasure which will last for eternity?

Handholds in His Character

When I was emerging from my depression over being paralyzed, I uncovered a promise in the Bible about God's faithfulness. Philippians 1:6 told me to be *confident*, in fact, of this one thing: That He who had begun a good work in me would carry it on to completion until the day of Christ Jesus.

You have to put that promise in the context of my life at that time. For the first time since the accident, I was trying to peer into my future. Yet it seemed as though a thick, black curtain hung just inches in front of my face. The appalling reality of a *lifetime* of paralysis was almost more than I could bear. My faith seemed paralyzed, too. It was hard to imagine how anything good would come out of it. I was convinced I would never smile again.

But then I came across Philippians 1:6. Immediately I grabbed hold of the faithfulness of God. I took hold of His tenderness and His mercy. I quoted the verse to the Lord, asking Him to fulfill His promise of completing a good— yes, a *very good*—work in my life.

And do you know what? I found peace. I was confident that God, in His faithfulness, would hold Himself to His promise.

Charles Spurgeon once said, "You and I may take hold at anytime upon the justice, mercy, faithfulness, wisdom, longsuffering, [or] tenderness of God, and we shall find every attribute of the Most High to be, as it were, a great battering ram with which we may open the gates of heaven."

Obviously Spurgeon wasn't talking about "nukeing" the gates of heaven to somehow overcome God's reluctance or unwillingness. No, God is not an immovable, meditating Mystic who has to be prodded to perform His will. Spurgeon isn't talking about God that way. But I do think that it pleases God when we seek His glory, His will, even His character in a given situation in our lives.

Abraham, pleading with God to spare Sodom, reminded the Lord, "Shall not the Judge of all the earth do right?" (Genesis 18:25, NKJV). Did God need a reminder? "Oh, thanks, Abe. I'd completely forgotten that angle. Thanks for jogging My memory." Obviously, God did not need a nudge to remember His justice. Yet He was delighted that Abraham sought heavenly justice on the merits of the heavenly Judge. Abraham pleaded his case from the platform of God's character.

Habakkuk, too, appealed to God's very nature in his prayer. It was a time of deep national distress in Judah. The ruthless Babylonian army was poised to sweep across the country like water from a ruptured dam. Yes, the prophet agreed with the Lord, Judah was deserving of His judgment. But how could God use a people even more evil than they as His rod of discipline?

> *Your eyes are too pure to look on evil;*
>   *you cannot tolerate wrong.*
> *Why then do you tolerate the treacherous?*
> *Why are you silent while the wicked*
>   *swallow up those more righteous than themselves?*
>   (Habakkuk 1:13, NIV).

David pleaded God's character again and again. Discouraged by his own sins and unfaithfulness, he cried out:

Remember, O LORD, your great mercy and love,
*   for they are from of old.*
Remember not the sins of my youth
*   and my rebellious ways;*
according to your love remember me,
*   for you are good, O LORD*
(Psalm 25:6-7, NIV).

How about you? Do you involve God in your prayer? Do you find handholds and footholds in His character? Do you plead with Him on the basis of Who He is? Consider again His justice, His mercy, His faithfulness, His wisdom, His purity, His might, and His tenderness. If you're hurting or if you're confused, find some attribute of your great God and grab onto it with all your might, asking Him to deal with you accordingly. Humbly hold Him to His promise. God is delighted when you seek His will, His character, His glory—and yes, His heart—in your prayers.

STRONGHOLD

Pick an attribute of God—wisdom, mercy, purity, tenderness, justice, or some other character quality of your Lord. Meditate for a few moments on how marvelously God reveals Himself through that attribute.

In your prayers during the rest of the day—whether for your family or friends, for emergencies or even for incidentals—link all of your requests to that special attribute of your heavenly Father. Not only will your prayers have power, but you will get to know God more intimately.

The Process Is the End

Tens of thousands of students are sweating their way through midterm exams as I write these words. They're thinking about declaring their major, or deciding on post-graduate work. Will it be the mission field? Business administration? Data processing? Journalism? Should they choose a graduate school back East or out West? Where does marriage fit in—if at all?

Their minds are on the future.

It seems everything they do right now has an incredible bearing on where they will be next year. Today's domino is going to fall squarely on tomorrow's.

You and I tend to feel the same way, don't we?

We feel that we're in training for "something in the future." And every decision we make is a link in a long chain of events that will culminate in some final, better situation. Then and only then will we have "arrived." But in the meantime, we've got to do double duty to make certain we're in the middle of God's will. Don't want to take a wrong turn. Don't want to make a second-best decision. After all, everything right now prepares us for that marvelous future—whether it be a career, a marriage, a job, or a ministry.

God, we assure ourselves, is leading us to a particular end, a desired goal. But sometimes the question of *getting there* is merely incidental.

You see, what we call "the process"—the process of getting there—God calls "the end."

Think about it. How much of what you're doing right now is oriented toward some goal? You're in the kitchen only to finish something up and hurry out to the car. You're in the car to rush to the gas station. You're at the gas station only to fill your tank to get to the market. And even when you're at the market, you're already thinking about getting the kids at school. From school to home. From home to church. From church to work the next morning.

Stop! God's training is for *right now*, not for some mist-shrouded future. His purpose is for this minute, not for something better down the road. His power and His presence are available to you as you draw your next breath, not for some great impending struggle.

This moment is the future for which you've been preparing!

James, the Lord's brother, brings us up short in our preoccupation with tomorrow.

> *Just a moment, now, you who say, "We are going to such-and-such a city today or tomorrow. We shall stay there a year doing business and make a profit!" How do you know what will happen tomorrow? What, after all, is your life? It is like a puff of smoke visible for a little while and then dissolving into thin air. Your remarks should be prefaced with, "If it is the Lord's will, we shall still be alive and will do so-and-so." As it is, you take a certain pride in planning with such confidence. That sort of pride is all wrong* (James 4:13-16, Phillips).

In God's economy, it is *today* that is of utmost importance. The way you cling to Christ today, the opportunities you maximize today, the conversations you engage in or the acts of kindness you perform today are the most critical activities of your entire life. And who this side of heaven knows how God may use them?

Oswald Chambers has said, "What you call preparation, God calls the end. And if you have a further end in view, then perhaps you are not paying sufficient attention to the immediate present." If you and I can only realize that obedience right now—this moment—is what is most important, then we'll escape from that terrible "marking time" frame of mind . . . each moment as it comes will be precious.

STRONGHOLD

Let me ask you a question straight out.

Do you occasionally find yourself grasping for the future as though the present didn't quite satisfy? Do you sometimes feel you miss the best of life while looking the other way, preoccupied with shaping your future? Look up Psalm 39:4 and make it your prayer today.

CHAPTER 34

Workmanship

It's so much fun to be a painter.

One of my favorite times of day is when I wheel into the art studio, close the door behind me, and maneuver my chair in front of my easel.

There, a whole world opens up to me.

As an artist, I can express my deepest thoughts and wishes on canvas. I can paint mountains which inspire and elevate the thinking of those who view the rendering. I can evoke calmness and peace with a gently rolling seascape. Through works of art, a painter can teach and inform, encourage and uplift, and communicate all sorts of helpful and positive qualities.

Our great, creative God does the same thing in each of our lives. Listen to Paul's encouraging words to his friends, the Ephesians.

For we are God's workmanship, created in Christ Jesus to do good works, which God prepared in advance for us to do (2:10, NIV).

You and I are God's *workmanship*. The Greek word translated "workmanship" here is *poiema*, which means a work of art or a specially designed product.

Do you see what Scripture is saying?

Each one of us is God's special work of art. Through us, He teaches and inspires, delights and encourages, informs and uplifts all those who view our lives. God, the master artist, is most concerned about expressing Himself—His thoughts and His intentions—through what He paints in our character. Each unchangeable part, each weakness, each strength, is like a brush stroke in the complete composition He has in mind for us. Our master artist takes time to mix the colors He wants to portray through our character.

My art studio would be in chaos if my canvas, paint, brushes, and colors had minds of their own. What a mess that would be!

And listen . . . what an insult to me, as the artist. After all, who's in control?

That must be how God feels when we jump off His easel and start running our own lives—carelessly pushing our own wants, goals, ambitions, and fantasies. As the master designer, God has something so much better in mind . . . if only we'd acknowledge His control.

Ephesians 2:10 reminds us just who the master artist is. We are His workmanship, His *poiema*, His work of art.

Maybe you don't feel much like a "work of art" today. I understand. If you saw the beginning stages of some of my paintings, you'd wonder if anything of beauty could *ever* emerge from such a confusion of colors. Just remember . . . the master artist wants to paint a beautiful portrait of His Son in and through your life. A painting like no other in all of time.

And He isn't finished yet.

STRONGHOLD

As Francis Schaeffer said, "Made in God's image, man was made to be great, he was made to be beautiful, and he was made to be creative in life and art . . ."

Just think! You are a work of art—a painting, poem, symphony, or ballet. Just as the potter will shape and mold a piece of clay into a beautiful vase, God touches your life with His creative genius. Read about it in Jeremiah 18:1-6, and rejoice that He has chosen the perfect design, the best composition just for you!

Medicine for "Midnight Moments"

You punch your feather pillow, pull the quilt over your ears, and scrunch up in your favorite sleeping position. Just as you're going under, a nagging thought props your eyes open.

Did I leave the dog door open?

And then another.

Did the girls remember to lock the sliding glass door when they came in from the backyard?

It's no use trying to reassure yourself. With a sigh, you throw back the covers to go and check. After you've made the tour of doors and locks, you collapse back in bed. But no sooner do you rescrunch yourself under the covers than a whole swarm of thoughts begin to buzz through your mind.

Why am I the only one in this family who thinks about such things? . . . Suppose I hadn't double-checked? . . . My girls, when are they going to learn? . . . Someone, anyone could have slid that door open, slipped into the house and . . . and, oh! . . . Maybe we should get an alarm system . . . Our little dog is useless, perhaps a bigger one . . . I wonder if pit bulls are really that dangerous? . . . What would I do if a prowler really managed to get in . . . ?

There you go again—another night without rest. Sure, you might sleep some. But genuine rest goes beyond slumber. Rest, says Webster is "to remain based or founded; to cause to be firmly fixed . . ."

How many of us experience *that* kind of rest—even when we lie down at night?

I'm one who has a hard time kicking back, turning off the thought machine, and parking my worries somewhere in a back lot. Oftentimes rest and relaxation don't come easy for me. If you're like me, you've probably experienced some of those "mad midnight moments," as C. S. Lewis describes them. You're assaulted with worry and anxieties. You wonder how you'll get through this, how you'll finish that, or how you'll endure the other.

Fortunately, I've found a remedy for those restless, late-night bouts with anxiety. And it's not in a bottle, tablet, capsule, or herb tea bag.

My prescription for tranquility of spirit is simply resting in the sovereignty of God.

When we learn to lean back in God's sovereignty, fixing and settling our thoughts on that unshakable, unmovable reality, we can experience great inner peace. Our troubles may not change. Our pain may not diminish. Our loss may not be restored. Our problems may not fade with the new dawn. *But the power of those things to harm us is broken as we rest in the fact that God is in control.*

There's a big difference between suffering in God's will and suffering apart from that assurance. When you think about it, accepting God's control in a situation shouldn't be all that difficult. After all, God's sovereignty is simply a fact—and facts are hard to deny.

God wants us to lay our burdens on Him and rest in His love. It's *His* responsibility to work out the purpose and plan in our hardships. Only our refusal to trust Him—our stubborn wrestling against the fact of His sovereignty—can hinder His purposes in our lives. When we resist, we make life much harder for ourselves.

Sleeplessness gives way to rest when we relax in God's sovereignty. The one who trusts thinks clearly, while a mind gripped with fear is drained of creative energy. Decisions are better made by minds at rest.

If you're going to work yourself up about anything today, take advice from Hebrews 4:11 and "make every effort" to enter into God's rest.

STRONGHOLD

Read Habakkuk 3. The prophet Habakkuk was shaken to the soul by a God-given glimpse into the future. Israel's existence hung by the thinnest of threads. A cruel and powerful army would sweep in from the north and destroy everything Habakkuk held dear. In his perplexity and sorrow, the prophet bowed before the sovereignty of God, finally yielding the full weight of his worry. His song of trust in Habakkuk 3:16-19 is one of the most beautiful in all of Scripture. Follow this godly man's lead today as you release your fears . . . and rejoice in God's sovereign control.

Comforting Light

I was a child who was scared of the dark.

I didn't like being the first one through the front door to flick on the lights. And things didn't change much even after I became a teenager. I'd come home from a date and dread to see the house dark. Turning the key in the front lock and creaking open the door, I'd call, "Anybody home?"

I'd step into the hall and gasp—was that a man standing behind the living room sofa? On went the lights! Whew . . . it was only a lampstand. And that awful shadow looming outside the window was only the branch of a tree.

In the dark, shapes take on eerie silhouettes. True meanings are obscured. We're frightened by the unfamiliar.

But what a comfort light is! Light reveals things for what they really are. That lampstand was no threatening stranger. That tree shadow was no Peeping Tom. Light takes away the frightening guesswork. It makes reality clear.

As we read Scripture, we realize that it didn't take God very long to "turn on the light." In the second verse of the Bible, the author describes a brooding, primordial darkness. But in the very next verse, God says, "Let there be light."

As I pondered that statement recently, comparing it with other verses in Genesis 1, I discovered that God wasn't talking about the light of the sun, moon, or stars. God didn't form the light-bearing heavenly bodies until later, on creation's fourth day.

So what could He mean? Where was the light coming from?

I checked a couple of cross references and noted this verse in John 1:

In the beginning was the Word, and the Word was with God, and the Word was God (v. 1).

Can you imagine the scene? God is ready to begin creation. The script is written, the play is about to commence. The curtain is closed, the stage is empty, and there's darkness all around. But God, much like the director of a great, moving drama, begins the play. *"Let there be light,"* He shouts, and the central character of creation steps out to take the leading role. Jesus, the light of the world, the Creator and Sustainer of creation, walks out on stage in the middle of His own spotlight.

What a thought! How thrilled I was to see Jesus, the Alpha and Omega, as described in the last book of the Bible, spotlighted in the very beginning of the first book of the Bible.

Truly, God's Word begins and ends with Christ.

Where is He in your life today? Is He at the beginning of your day . . . and the end? Is He on center stage, in the spotlight of your plans, goals, and ambitions? Are you reading His script or somebody else's? Studying His Word or books about His Word?

He who is the Light of creation now says, "You are the light of the world." He has given you and me the responsibility to reveal reality in a dark, sin-blinded world—to show things for what they really are.

People are afraid. People are confused, bewildered, and in despair. It's time to let the Light shine.

STRONGHOLD

Read John 3:16-21. Why do some people refuse to "see the Light"? Think of several unbelievers on your prayer list. Is it possible they may feel threatened by your desire to obey God and do what is right? Perhaps they're afraid the light in you may expose some darkness in their lives. Don't let that discourage you. Keep praying they will come to see how much better it is to live in light rather than darkness. In fact . . . why not pray for them right now?

Love Is Extravagant

I had just finished packing my bags. Ken had packed his things, too, including his rods and reels. We had to be away from one another for several days, I on a speaking engagement, and he on a fishing trip. We knew we'd really miss each other.

Wheeling through the living room that afternoon, I was surprised to see a beautiful red rose in a bud vase on the table. That Ken! So thoughtful. Moving into the bedroom to gather my things, I spotted *another* rose in a bud vase on my dresser. I was shocked. I glanced in the bathroom and to my amazement yet *another* red rose—a fresh, delicate, little bud—adorned the counter.

By the third rose, I have to admit my excitement turned sour. It wasn't that I didn't appreciate his gifts, it was just that . . well, both he and I were ready to leave. Nobody but our miniature schnauzer Scruffy would be in the house to enjoy such lovely flowers. *Expensive* flowers at that, I pointed out.

Ken gave me a big hug that melted my protests.

As I went off on that speaking trip, I thought of the quality that marks the ministry of love. And that is its sheer *extravagance*. Love is extravagant in the price it is willing to pay, the time it is willing to give, the hardships it is willing to endure, and the strength it is willing to spend.

Love never thinks in terms of "how little," but always in terms of "how much."

Love gives, love knows, and love lasts.

And that is what God has given to us. The quality that marks the ministry of God's love for us is the sheer extravagance of giving His most priceless and precious gift . . . His Son. When the Father considered ransoming sinful, wretched men and women such as ourselves, I don't think He thought in terms of how little He should give, but *how much*. Our hearts should—*must*—be overflowing with thankfulness and gratitude for all our Father has given.

When I returned home from my trip, I got an added surprise. Those little buds were in full bloom, brightening my home with their extravagance . . . and a lingering fragrance of love.

STRONGHOLD

Take a few moments to read Mark 14:3-7.

The woman in Bethany did a very extravagant and, in the eyes of some, wasteful thing. Praise is like that. There are *so* many things to pray about, so many needs—the poor, the homeless, the aged, not to mention family and financial problems. If time is short, shouldn't it mostly be spent on praying over these needs?

But Jesus reminds us in Mark 14 that praise—extravagant, lavish, and profuse—comes before any request. There is nothing wasteful about loving praise. Take some moments right now and offer up a "sacrifice of praise" to the One who sacrificed so much for you.

Coming Home to God's Word

My husband Ken came home from a fishing trip last Saturday afternoon and plopped contentedly into his favorite chair.

"This is great," he sighed. "I've looked forward to coming home."

He'll never know how much that little comment warmed my heart. I so much want our home to be a place of refreshment for him, a place where he likes to spend his time.

I think that's what Paul was talking about when he told the Colossians, "Let the word of Christ dwell in you richly" (3:16, KJV). Or, as Phillips translates the verse, "Let the full richness of Christ's teaching find its home among you."

God intends His Word to *dwell* within us, to make its home in us. What a poignant way to put it. Think how well you know your own home—or perhaps the home where you grew up. Visualize its rooms and hallways, its closets and cupboards. You know it like the back of your hand, don't you?

. . . You know what's in the linen closet.

. . . Where the glass measuring cups are stored.

. . . The squeak of the linoleum tile by the washing machine.

. . . The way the rafters creak on a cold night.

. . . Which part of the roof leaks when it rains.

. . . Exactly how many minutes somebody can be in the shower before the hot water runs out.

. . . The way the dining room looks in the moonlight.

. . . The smell of your old cedar chest.

Home. A place of familiarity and relaxation. A place to build memories. The focus for so many of our hopes and longings.

When Paul said, "Let the word of Christ dwell in you richly," he was reminding us that Scripture should find a home in our hearts; that we should live in its light. And, much like any other home, we should know it like the back of our hands. We should be able to place where most things are in between its pages. We should go to God's Word because we prefer it—we're familiar with its commands and we relax in its promises.

I can visualize one dear old saint who has lived comfortably in the Word of God for seventy-five years. He can not only quote chapter after chapter of his old Bible verbatim, he can tell you where individual verses appear on the pages! When it comes to the Bible, this man's at home.

How many of us actually consider God's Word a "dwelling place"? Does it truly *live* in our hearts, or is Scripture something we just kind of visit for occasional refreshment. Like a vacation spot.

God wants His Word to be a home to us—a strong refuge, a warm and restful sanctuary from the bumps, bruises, and perplexities of everyday life.

Let His Word live in you with all of its richness, promises, teaching, and direction. Let it be your retreat from a cynical, pressure-filled world. Let it make you rich in true wisdom.

Wherever life takes you, wherever your road leads, home can be as close as your heart.

STRONGHOLD

Let me guess. You've put it off long enough. Over and over you've been reminded by the Spirit to make a home in your heart for God's Word. And today's reading has only reinforced it. Isn't now as good a time as any to once-and-for-all do something about it?

"But where do I begin?" you might ask. One of the best plans I know of is the *Topical Memory System* published by the Navigators. I've used it and the plan has definitely helped (they're not paying me to say this, either). Why not check it out at your local Christian bookstore?

CHAPTER 39

Loving Our Little Corner

When I was a little girl, my mother would take me to Grandmom's place on housecleaning days. I would help her carry the buckets and mops and the Spic 'N Span. As we began work on the kitchen, Mom would delegate one corner of the kitchen floor to me. Then I'd go to work scrubbing with my little sponge.

That was something I could handle.

Thankfully, Mom didn't expect me to scrub the entire kitchen. That would have been overwhelming. But I did just fine with my corner.

As I grew older, I noticed the size of my "corner" gradually increasing. Finally, the time came when I was expected to clean the entire floor myself—along with the countertops and appliances, I might add.

Looking back on that episode in my childhood, I'm glad my mother never expected me to houseclean to the DEGREE she did. But she *did* expect me to perform that chore in her same MANNER. No, I wasn't expected to scour the entire kitchen, but I *was* expected to do a good job on the tiny piece of floor that was my responsibility.

My little corner was supposed to shine.

That's very much like the way God deals with us. There is no way that I can love in the same DEGREE that God loves me. Or obey to the same degree that Jesus obeyed His Father. It would be overwhelming—demoralizing—if God expected me to sacrifice to the degree that He sacrificed. I can't. I can't love with the same intensity, the same strength as He. The thought of even trying fills me with despair.

Yet if we love God, we are expected to show it as God showed His love to us. John said as much in his first letter:

Dear friends, let us love one another, for love comes from God. Everyone who loves has been born of God and knows God. Whoever does not love does not know God, because God is love. This is how God showed his love among us: He sent his one and only Son into the world that we might live through him . . . Dear friends, since God so loved us, we also ought to love one another (1 John 4:7-9, 11, NIV).

Now granted, we may not be able to love in the same DEGREE as our heavenly Father. But we *can* love or obey or even sacrifice in the same MANNER as He. "Be imitators of God, therefore, as dearly loved children," Paul wrote, "and live a life of love, just as Christ loved us and gave himself up for us" (Ephesians 5:1-2, NIV).

As we imitate our Father, then, we learn to love like Him.

God loves the worthless . . . we are expected to love the worthless.

God loves His enemies . . . we are expected to love our enemies.

The Lord loves in word and deed . . . we are to love in exactly the same way.

He sacrificed . . . we must sacrifice in the same manner.

An overwhelming thought? A demoralizing responsibility? Not at all! With His grace, we can show love in the same manner as the Lord Jesus. As we do, as we are found faithful in our little corners of His kingdom, God begins to slowly extend and expand our love for Him and for others. We find that the older we grow in Christ, the more our little corner begins to widen. Our area of ministry gradually increases. Even the *degree* of our love and obedience and sacrifice will be so much more than we ever dreamed possible.

So how are things in your corner of ministry today?

Do all your efforts seem small . . . perhaps insignificant, compared to others? Don't let it discourage you. Don't worry about the degree of your love and sacrifice and service. That will come in time. Just concentrate on imitating your heavenly Father, on living life as Christ would live it through you. In the same way. In the same manner.

Make your little corner shine. Then watch it grow.

STRONGHOLD

It's exciting to think that as we are found faithful in our little corner of His kingdom, God will begin to slowly extend and expand our love for Him and for others.

Read Matthew 25:14-28 and be joyful about the day God will say to *you*, "Well done, good and faithful servant! You have been faithful with a few things; I will put you in charge of many things. Come and share your Master's happiness!"

But wait a minute. Are you afraid of your little corner expanding and extending? Sound like too much responsibility? Take a closer look at Matthew 25:15, breathe a sigh of relief, and finish off with these questions.

1. The Master divided the money among His servants according to their _____. No one received more or less money than he could handle.

2. Money, as used in Matthew 25, represents any kind of resource we are given. God gives me _____, and _____, and _____. Am I using well what God has given me?

3. The issue is not how _____ we have, but what we _____ with what we have.

Preconceived Notions

Indulge me for a moment with an art question.

Why do we get bored with the beautiful paintings we hang on our walls?

You know what I'm talking about. You position a painting in a certain room and after a few weeks you're oblivious to it. It's as though the painting has become invisible. Mysteriously absorbed by the masonite. Swallowed alive by the wallpaper.

Why is that?

Part of the fault, of course, may be in the painting itself. It may have been poorly composed, rendered with dull colors, or occupied by boring subject matter. But that's unlikely. After all, you loved the painting enough to *buy* it and display it in your home. It must have had something going for it.

The fault may not lie in the painting at all. It may lie with you, and with the way you *view* that piece of art.

You may be simply "using" the painting. Using it to fill up the space on your wall. Using it to accent the color on your decorator couch. Some people treat paintings as launch pads for their own imaginations and emotional activities. They bring their own agendas to the artwork. They *do* things with the painting, rather than laying themselves open to see what the painting might do for them.

Appreciating a given work of art demands that we set aside our preconceptions, prejudices, and mental associations. That's why you see people in art museums sitting for long minutes in front of a Rembrandt. They allow the painting to speak to them.

The first demand any work of art makes upon us is to surrender. We must look, and go on looking until we have seen exactly what is there.

Look. Listen. Receive. Get yourself out of the way.

Only when *our* ideas about Rembrandt are set aside, can Rembrandt's ideas reach us.

That principle of art has taught me something about a principle of Scripture. So many of us come to a biblical passage with preconceived notions and expectations about what we think it ought to say to us. We treat the Bible as a launch pad for our own ideas or desires. We have no intention of *receiving* God's Word . . . only *using* it.

But the first demand the Bible makes on us as we read is to surrender. To lay aside our prejudices, agendas, and pet theories. To read and re-read until we see exactly what is being said.

Only when *our* ideas about the Lord Jesus are set aside, can His ideas reach us.

So look. Listen. Receive. Get yourself out of the way. Don't try to squeeze God's Word into the mold of "the way you see things."

Instead, let God's Word be the mold that squeezes you.

STRONGHOLD

A verse such as John 3:16 is probably old and very familiar territory to you. You may even know it by heart— "For God so loved the world that He gave His only begotten Son . . ."

You've probably read it ten thousand times, but it can still remain fresh for you. How? First, ask the Holy Spirit to help you. Then, read the verse slowly several times, each time placing special emphasis and thoughtful meditation on one word. "For GOD so loved the world . . . For God SO loved the world . . . For God so LOVED the world" . . . and so on.

Prayerfully approach other favorite verses this way and begin to understand God's ideas for you—fresh and new!

CHAPTER 41

The Heart of the Window

Here it is the first of June and I just finished painting one of my premiere designs for the upcoming Christmas season. You heard me right—Christmas!

You see, I have to finish my paintings this far in advance to assure that they will be ready months from now for the holiday season. And I'm really excited about this painting. It's painted to look like a stained glass window, with a figure of Mary holding baby Jesus. A king, one of the magi, kneels on one side of them, and a shepherd on the other.

My window is filled with symbols.

The kneeling figures suggest the Child's destiny as both the Great Shepherd and the King of kings. The lamp at Mary's feet reminds us that He is the Light of the World. Christ is also called "the Rose of Sharon," and I painted a thorny bush of beautiful lavender roses cascading around Mary. A little lamb tucked against the shepherd foreshadows His role as the Lamb of God. The One sacrificed for my sin . . . and yours.

Pulling together all the elements and symbols in this picture was a real challenge. Instead of coming together as a unity, different parts of the picture kept vying for attention—competing with one another. As the artist, it was my responsibility to give these symbols their proper relationship to one another, so that they would complement one another. It wasn't easy!

The king's robe, for instance, was *very* violet. Just too bright. So I had to keep putting on a coat of bright yellow paint, until it was finally subdued. In other portions of the painting the colors were too dull, too weak, and I had to keep brightening them—pulling them forward.

I kept experimenting this way on all the parts of the picture, pulling them into unity, forcing them to cooperate with one another. Finally, all those parts obeyed.

When I looked at the painting, my eye went right to Jesus.

We're like that painting, aren't we?

Instead of being unified as Christians, we vie with each other for special notice. We're all supposed to be adoring Jesus—like the figures kneeling in my window—and we end up muddling the message. Spoiling the focus.

God has to *force* us to cooperate with one another—pulling and pushing us into unity . . . until all the parts obey.

When we finally come to that place, the message rings out loud and clear. When we're unified, when we as Christians are joined together in love, Jesus—and Jesus only—is the center of attention.

STRONGHOLD

The early church had problems being unified, too. Paul exposes the problem in 1 Corinthians 1:10-13. Read it for an eye-opening account of just how destructive it can be when the parts of Christ's church start vying for attention. What advice does Paul give these warring factions? Continue on to 1 Corinthians 3 for the inside story.

Ask yourself: Do I secretly think I'm better than other Christians? How can I better cooperate today with someone I've been competing against? Do I want Jesus to be the focus of my life? Of my fellowship?

CHAPTER 42

God's Power and Compassion

It's easy to picture a kindly, loving Jesus. We've had lots of help on that score from religious artists down through the centuries. But do you find it a bit more challenging to visualize an angry—I mean violently angry—Jesus Christ?

Let's pick up one of the closing scenes of His ministry:

As he entered Jerusalem a shock ran through the whole city. "Who is this?" men cried. "This is Jesus the prophet," replied the crowd, "the man from Nazareth in Galilee!"

Then Jesus went into the Temple-precincts and drove out all the buyers and sellers there. He overturned the tables of the money-changers and the benches of those who sold doves, crying—

"It is written, 'My house shall be called a house of prayer.' But you have turned it into a thieves' kitchen!" (Matthew 21:10-13, Phillips).

This was not the "gentle Jesus, meek and mild." You can probably picture Him kicking over tables, overturning cash registers, grabbing those guys by the scruff of the neck and heaving them out the temple door onto their self-righteous backsides. Matthew even says He drove out all those who were buying and selling there—trashing the booths of the moneychangers and capsizing the benches of the Jerusalem dove franchise.

No one, he asserted, was going to make *His* Father's house into a haven for con-men and rip-off artists. He meant business.

If I had been a moneychanger, I think I would have opted for a career change at that very moment. Anything would have been preferable—selling newspapers in Nazareth, baking bagels in Bethlehem, picking up gum wrappers in the park—anything to get me away from the piercing gaze of this Man of Authority.

His anger and indignation must have been terrible to behold.

But if you want a surprise, catch the very next verse in Matthew 21.

And there in the Temple the blind and the lame came to him and he healed them (v. 14).

Does that hit you the way it hit me? The Lord's angry shouts were still echoing from the temple walls. The dove salesmen were still scuttling away down the alleys like frightened rats. Coins were still rolling around on the pavement. But our Lord doesn't miss a beat. He immediately turns his attention to the blind and lame—releasing them from their physical bondage.

Remarkable! Those hapless, handicapped folks must have been hanging around the temple for who knows how long hoping and praying for some kind of break. Most likely they had done some begging from the temple priests or guards. They would have undoubtedly given anything just to get a word in edgewise with the religious officials. In all of those weary, monotonous years, nobody had paid them much mind. Nobody really took care of their requests or listened to their needs. Perhaps they were even considered second-rate citizens, an embarrassment, a kind of eyesore around the temple courtyard.

The Pharisees never cared about them. The religious leaders had no time for them. The priests could have cared two cents. Yet Jesus, the Son of God, stops right in the middle of bringing down divine judgment on that place, sets aside His anger, and shows tender compassion to that little band of forgotten "nobodies." In the midst of revealing His power and judgment, Jesus paused to display His compassion.

That, to me, is a stunning sketch of our Lord and Savior. And it's one of many in Scripture.

We see His greatness complemented by His goodness.

We see His holiness contrasted by His mercy.

We see His tremendous power balanced by His tenderness and gentleness.

There is no room in Scripture for a one-sided view of our Lord. He points an angry, righteous finger at the hypocrites on one hand, yet reaches down to gently touch the need of the lowly with the other. He turns a face as hard as steel to the religious phonies yet smiles encouragement at those who reach to Him in simple faith.

Do you identify with those weak, overlooked men and women in the far corner of the temple courtyard? Do you feel lonely today—perhaps ignored or devalued? Or maybe you're seeing a different face of God right now—the conviction of His anger with your sin and rebellion.

Remember this portrait of Jesus from the book of Matthew. He's powerful and He's going to deal with your sin. But He's also ready to forgive, heal your wounds, and offer you a fresh start.

Now that's what I call compassion.

STRONGHOLD

Take a look at Romans 11:22 and notice the two characteristics of God. Do you see a balance? Kindness is one characteristic of God. Sternness might be considered its complement. Match a characteristic of God listed on the left with one on the right. Remember, there's no room for a one-sided view of our Lord.

Power	Tenderness
Anger	Approachability
Justice	Forgiveness
Wrath	Meekness
Strength	Mercy
Unapproachability	Gentleness

CHAPTER 43

Is God Proud?

Dorothy's letter was full of sunlight. She penned such glowing words that I was, frankly, a little embarrassed.

Then she made a curious comment.

"Joni," she said, "God is surely proud of you and the way you've overcome your handicap . . ."

I know she meant well . . . but I just couldn't let that sentence go by. Is God "proud" of us when we do something so simple as appropriate His grace? Somehow I can't imagine the Lord inserting His thumbs beneath His suspenders and glowing with pride over my obedience. After all, isn't obedience something you *expect* from servants?

On the other hand, I don't believe our Father in heaven is some frowning, straitlaced God who isn't moved by the sincere submission of His dearly-loved children. I think of what the writer of Scripture said to the Hebrew believers:

God is not unjust; he will not forget your work and the love you have shown him as you have helped his people and continue to help them (Hebrews 6:10, NIV).

Jesus Himself said to the church in Ephesus:

I know your deeds, your hard work and your perseverance . . . You have persevered and have endured hardships for my name, and have not grown weary (Revelation 2:2-3, NIV).

After all, you and I are intended for "the praise of His glory." And every time we step out in obedience, God must take pleasure in our actions, knowing they will result in honor and glory for His Son.

So what is it that makes me a little restless with the notion of God's pride in my response to the wheelchair?

It's simply this: I must never ever think I am doing God a great favor when I obey His Word or follow His commands. If today I have made strides in obedience, such as speaking the truth in love or avoiding all appearances of evil or not leading a weaker brother into sin, I have in no sense climbed higher on a scale of God's favor. I am simply living the life God *expects* me to live. I am being conformed to Christ's image as He intends. I am experiencing the normal Christian life.

If I obey, my perspective ought not to be, *Well, look at this! I'm miles above where I was yesterday!* Once I start thinking that way, humility is out the window—and any degree of gain along with it. No, the more I obey Him, the more I begin to grasp how far I am from His ultimate goal for my life. Like Paul, I would rather look at how far I need to go, rather than at how far I have already come.

> *Not that I claim to have achieved all this, nor to have reached perfection already. But I keep going on, trying to grasp that purpose for which Christ Jesus grasped me. My brothers, I do not consider myself to have grasped it fully even now. But I do concentrate on this: I forget all that lies behind me and with hands outstretched to whatever lies ahead I go straight for the goal—my reward the honour of my high calling by God in Christ Jesus* (Philippians 3:12-14, Phillips).

So, getting back to Dorothy's comment, it would delight me to think that God might be pleased with my life. But neither Dorothy nor I—nor you for that matter—can slack off and assume we've done God a big favor by obeying Him. In humility we can only forget what lies behind and run straight for the goal . . . the high calling of our God.

All of us have a long way to go.

STRONGHOLD

Who is it who feels he has done God a favor by obeying Him? He is described in Isaiah 29:13.

But who is it who obeys God out of humility and sincere submission? Psalm 15 provides a clear snapshot.

Now the question: Which best describes *you*? Make it your prayer today to obey out of humility and submission.

Those "Other" Promises

It gives us a warm, secure feeling to sing "standing on the promises of Christ my King . . ." Some of us have put God's promises on plaques above our fireplace, or stitched them into a needlepoint for the hallway.

Such snug, comforting promises, like . . .

I have come that you might have abundant life.

Or, *He richly gives us all things.*

Or, *Ask and you shall receive.*

Or, *It will be done for you that your joy may be full.*

We claim those promises as believers. We memorize them, meditate on them, make them our own. And rightly so. God intends us to enter into His promises.

But there's a catch. You can't pick and choose. God means for us to embrace *all His promises*—not just some of them. And not all His promises are snug and comfortable.

Some of God's assurances are more easily ignored, aren't they? Especially the ones having to do with pain and hardship. You don't see *those* promises hanging over fireplaces or stitched in needlepoint or penned in the back of Bibles or calligraphically written on parchment paper. We have a way of sidestepping them. Yet if there's one thing the New Testament promises the people of God, it is suffering and tribulation, trials and chastening and persecution. All of these things are promised to true disciples.

Everyone who wants to live a godly life in Christ Jesus will be persecuted (2 Timothy 3:12, NIV).

"No servant is greater than his master." If they persecuted me, they will persecute you also (John 15:20, NIV).

Consider it pure joy, my brothers, whenever you face trials of many kinds, because you know that the testing of your faith develops perseverance (James 1:2-3, NIV).

Blessed are you when men cast insults at you, and persecute you, and say all kinds of evil against you falsely, on account of Me (Matthew 5:11).

Through many tribulations we must enter the kingdom of God (Acts 14:22).

We are heirs—heirs of God and co-heirs with Christ, if indeed we share in his sufferings in order that we may also share in his glory (Romans 8:17, NIV).

To this you were called, because Christ suffered for you, leaving you an example, that you should follow in his steps (1 Peter 2:21, NIV).

No, we'd rather not "name 'n' claim" *those* promises. You won't find 2 Timothy 3:12 gracing many living room walls. You won't spy Acts 14:22 magnetized to many refrigerator doors. Frankly, we'd rather circumvent the suffering. We make every effort to weed out all the discomfort in our lives. We consider trials and disciplines to be rude interruptions in our plans for an easy, comfortable life. We demand miracles of healing and are willing to believe all sorts of wild irrationalities in order to get what we want. We seek to escape the promise of hardship rather than to allow Him to work out His will in our lives through the experience.

I can recall a time when I used to think those promises were more like threats.

Oh, sure, the Bible promises a lot of hardship. Well, with friends like that, who needs enemies? If I break my neck at the age of seventeen, what in the world is going to happen when I reach twenty or thirty? If this is the way God is going to start out discipling me, then I might as well forget it!

I just expected that my life should be easy—as though that were some kind of inalienable right as a human being. Life was supposed to be comfortable, with distress and trouble mere exceptions to the rule.

Yet I really wanted to be a disciple! I really wanted to follow Christ.

Do you see yourself in that contradiction? If we want to know Christ, a casual glance at the New Testament will tell us that God's Son was made perfect by suffering (Hebrews 2:10). And if the Christ of glory came to His glory only through suffering . . . how shall we know His glory any other way? If we want to know Him, and if we want to be made like Him, we can expect a few bumps and bruises along the way.

And that's a promise!

STRONGHOLD

Promises . . . they get broken, forgotten, or ignored. It's unfortunate, but often people don't come through on their promises.

John 16:33 offers a twofold promise. "In this world you will have trouble. But take heart! I have overcome the world." Why is it we can take heart despite our troubles? You guessed it—because Jesus has overcome. How does Jesus help you to overcome?

_____

_____

_____

Take heart. Jesus is a promise-keeper!

CHAPTER 45

A Rendering of God

A little boy pulled out his crayons and sheet of paper one afternoon. Resting his hand on his chin, he thought a few minutes, then picked up a crayon and began sketching.

Noticing his intentness as he worked, his mother asked, "What are you drawing?"

"A picture of God," he replied, without looking up.

His mother smiled. "But honey, no one knows what God looks like."

The boy put down his crayon and rubbed his hands together, still staring at his handiwork.

"Well," he replied, "they will when I finish."

We smile at that little story. On one hand, we can understand the mother's point of view. John 1:18 tells us that no one has seen God at any time. God Himself told Moses, "You cannot see my face, for no one may see me and live" (Exodus 33:20, NIV).

Nobody knows what He looks like.

Yet even though none of us has ever looked God in the face, all of us desire to know something about Him, don't we? We drive up into the mountains, awed by the power displayed in His majestic creation. We sit by the seashore at twilight or early in the morning, and listen for His voice in the roar of the waves.

We long to see God and somehow know Him.

But although John 1:18 reminds us that no one can look on the face of God at any time, that same verse goes on to declare that God's only Son, Jesus Christ, *has made Him known*.

To a bewildered Philip, Jesus replied, "Don't you know me, Philip, even after I have been among you such a long time? Anyone who has seen me has seen the Father. How can you say, 'Show us the Father'? Don't you believe that I am in the Father, and that the Father is in me?" (John 14:9-10, NIV).

Through His life and words and deeds, the Nazarene sketched an unerring illustration of His Father. He drew a picture so that we would have a clear idea of just who our Father in heaven really is.

No man has seen God at any time. Yes, that's true. John tells us that the day will come "when we *shall* see Him—as He is" (1 John 3:2). Not in the reflected glory of burning bush or pillar of cloud, but face to face. Until that time, however, God has already provided a revelation of Himself. Jesus Christ is that perfect expression of the Father.

There should be no confusion, no questions. Our curiosity about God can be satisfied in Jesus.

You and I today are very much like that little boy with his crayons. Through our words and deeds, our everyday conversations, our attitudes and actions, we are sketching an illustration for all to see. Our lives should be a portrayal, a rendering, a picture of what God looks like.

Intent as we are on living for Him, people will inevitably approach us and ask what we're doing. They'll be curious. Looking over our shoulders. Maybe even asking questions. Hopefully, they'll see a beautiful image in us—a clearer picture of just who God really is and what He's like.

No, He's not finished with us yet. But Paul assures us that as we fix our gaze on the Lord Jesus, we will resemble Him more and more with each passing day. "We, who with unveiled faces all reflect the Lord's glory," he writes, "are being transformed into his likeness with ever-increasing glory" (2 Corinthians 3:18, NIV).

So let's pick up our crayons and get to work! We've got a job to do. We've got to show a despairing, cynical world what God really looks like.

If they didn't know before, maybe they'll know when we're finished . . . or, rather, when *He's* finished.

STRONGHOLD

People have painted pictures of the Lord Jesus throughout the centuries. But these capture only a frozen image, a stiff and motionless representation. God wants us to be "living pictures" of Him. Read 1 John 4:7-12 and think of ways you can color other peoples' impressions of God. Say to yourself: "What I do and say will give people a clearer impression of Jesus than any painting ever could!"

Don't Touch the Tar-Baby

Do you remember the Uncle Remus story of B'rer Rabbit and the tar-baby?

I can close my eyes and see old tar-baby sitting on a log near the dear old brier patch and B'rer Rabbit's front door. Someone had plunked a hat on his head, stuck a pipe in his mouth, and there tar-baby sat, waiting for an unsuspecting passer-by to come along and give his hand a shake. And then that poor somebody—I suspect B'rer Fox laying a trap for B'rer Rabbit— would be hopelessly stuck to that sticky, icky black tar. Everybody, if they knew what was good for them, should have avoided that tar-baby.

I once read an article in which the author gave fresh meaning to that old story. He asked. . .

Do you know any tar-babies—people better avoided, loaded down with problems? Folks you'd rather not approach or come near?

Any tar-babies in your church? I keep thinking of a pretty tar-baby named Carol.

Carol and her family are members at a prominent evangelical church. She is an outstanding senior at a Christian high school. Everyone was stunned to hear that she had become pregnant. Her school refused to let her continue her education. The whole family is hurting as I write these words, in desperate need of somebody who will just mingle some tears with their tears—even in their disgrace.

But the church stands awkwardly by, shuffling its feet, not knowing how to mix reproof and correction with love and encouragement.

Is it possible that we're so anxious to protect our spiritual reputation—or the reputation of our church—that we deliberately avoid the "contamination" of helping people in deep spiritual trouble?

Do we think they will somehow tempt us to sin, too?

Do we suppose that an "example" should be made of a wrong done?

Do we fear that our loyalty to somebody in trouble tars us with their disgrace?

No, we certainly do not need a casual attitude toward sin. And yes, we should deal with wrongdoing in a straightforward way. But we need to couple that direct approach with love and comfort to those who are broken apart by the shame and humiliation of a sin.

People in trouble should not be viewed as tar-babies, waiting to glue others into the sticky mess they've made of themselves.

Paul had a better idea. He wrote to the church at Galatia: "Even if a man should be detected in some sin, my brothers, the spiritual ones among you should quietly set him back on the right path, not with any feeling of superiority but being yourselves on guard against temptation. Carry each other's burdens and so live out the law of Christ. If a man thinks he is 'somebody' when he is nobody, he is deceiving himself" (Galatians 6:1-3, Phillips).

Paul is saying that hurting, stumbling people are not tar-babies. To deliberately look the other way and give them a wide berth is not "discipline." It is spiritual snobbery—and a direct affront to the law of Christ.

Has someone come to your mind as you've read these words? Can you visualize his face, feel his shame and hurt? Take the apostle's advice. Restore that person . . . quietly, gently. Today. Mingle your tears with his. Touch his disgrace. Just as Jesus touched yours.

God forbid, but there may come a day when the tar-baby's shoe is on the other foot.

STRONGHOLD

It's easy to pray with compassion and empathy for those we love or respect. It's harder to pray for people in trouble—a neighbor with AIDS, a church member who's schizophrenic, or a homosexual struggling to change his lifestyle.

Take five minutes right now to pray for an individual who comes to mind. Still fighting spiritual snobbery? Try using Colossians 1:9-14 as a prayer guideline for that person, paying special attention to all the good things you're praying for him.

Against You, You Only . . .

It hit me like a sudden shaft of sunlight piercing the clouds.

"Against You, You only, have I sinned, and done this evil in Your sight."

I'd been reading Psalm 51 and came across the anguished words of David in verse 4.

I felt a pang as I whispered the words aloud. *"Against You, You only . . ."* How often did I really consider whether my sins, big or small, offended God? Wasn't my attention more on myself, or on those I might have offended, than it was on the Lord?

Let me explain. There are countless times when I get impatient with my husband, Ken. Usually it's over small things. Like when he dumps food down the garbage disposal and walks away from the kitchen sink without turning the disposal on. Okay, so it's no big deal. But it always irks me.

And then I get angry. Angry at him, but also angry at me for allowing myself to become so irritated over something so trivial. When, I ask myself, am I going to quit attaching such ridiculous importance to such small things?

There's that phrase again . . . "small things." Perhaps that's why I don't feel as though I've sinned against God when it involves small things that I can sweep under the carpet of my conscience.

An immoral thought allowed to linger on the screen of my mind.

A sarcastic remark about a co-worker over the telephone.

A slight—but conscious—"exaggeration" of the truth.

A twinge of jealousy allowed to become bitter on the edges.

An extra minute or two of an indecent TV program after the Spirit of God has whispered "Turn it off."

A surge of self-pity coddled instead of rejected.

A conscious neglect of prayer and Bible reading.

Little things, right? No great transgressions. No major felonies. Just everyday slips and stumbles. Easily brushed aside. Hardly worth taking the time to confess or pray about.

Somewhere I've come up with this idea that God is there to handle the big things—the major struggles with the big temptations—but it's up to me and my self-control to deal with the little things.

I have a feeling quite a few people handle sin in much the same way. Our problem is that our attitude toward sin is more *self*-centered than God-centered.

Jerry Bridges, in his book, *The Pursuit of Holiness*, agrees: We are more concerned about our victory over sin than we are about the fact that our sins grieve the heart of God. We cannot tolerate failure in our struggle with sin chiefly because we are success-oriented, not because we know it is offensive to God.

Now you might say that "small" sins of disobedience or neglect don't really *offend* God, that He is quite content to have you sweep little things under the carpet. Not so. Perhaps half of the problem is that we do not take sin seriously enough—that we have mentally categorized sins into those which are unacceptable and those which may be tolerated.

When you come right down to it, we never see sin in its true perspective until we see all of it lined up against a holy God. *All* of our sin drove the nails into Jesus' hands and feet. *All* of our sin caused the Father's white-hot wrath to fall across His shoulders.

Big things . . . or eensy weensy small things . . . we must understand that in all things it is wise to say with the psalmist, "Against You, and You only have I sinned, O Lord."

STRONGHOLD

Read 2 Samuel 11 to get an inside look at the way David kept trying to sweep his sin under the carpet. One thing piled on top of another until Nathan confronts him in the next chapter. Finally, David breaks. His heartbroken confession is recorded in Psalm 51.

What "little sins" in David's life might have led to his great fall? What "little sins" frequently go unconfessed and unrepented in your life? Stop and put your finger on them now. Sweep them out from under the carpet of your conscience and present them in confession before God.

Our Highest Good

Benjamin, my friend Bonnie's young son, waited patiently for his turn to pray. It was family devotional time and he listened, head bowed, as someone intoned, "Jesus, we just want to know You better."

When Ben's turn came up, he put forth his petitions then closed by saying, "And Jesus, I hope You get to know me better, too."

I can identify with Benjamin's concern. Years ago, while still very young in the faith, I too struggled with some things everybody else seemed to take for granted. Before long, I had cultivated a kind of twisted, upside down view of God's glory.

Sitting in Sunday School, I listened to all of those stories of how Jesus moved among the crowds—how He was always walking here and there with multitudes of people at his heels. I wondered why.

I found myself slightly repelled by the paintings and drawings of Jesus I saw on the walls and in the Bibles. They always made Him look like some sanctimonious saint—you know, somebody with His head way up in the clouds.

As a youngster I fostered the idea that God was on an ego trip, always telling people how wonderful He was. Telling men that they should get to know Him. Calling lots of people to follow Him. I got the impression that God just *had* to be worshiped—that somehow He had to have a big crowd of people adoring Him.

Maybe you'd never admit it out loud, but have you ever found yourself thinking thoughts like those? Do you ever feel like God is making a bit much of all this stuff about His glory? Do you ever wonder if all this attention He is getting is simply satisfying His ego? Do you ever question exactly *why* God wants us to get to know Him?

If we're going to wrestle with questions like these, we had better stop using human logic. With God's help, we need to view these mysteries from His perspective.

In my earlier book, *A Step Further*, I tried to do that: Suppose you, like God, were the most true, just, pure, lovely, and praiseworthy being in existence. And what if everything else in the universe that had any of these qualities got them from you? Because they reflected, to some extent, you? For that matter, suppose that without you, these qualities would have never existed?

> *If that were the case, then for anyone around you to improve in any way, they would have to become more like you. For you to ask men to think about these good qualities would be to ask them to think about you. Their ego trips would be wrong, for then they would be centering their thoughts around sin and imperfection. But your ego trip would be glorious. Indeed, it would be the only hope for mankind, for your so-called ego trip would revolve around perfection.*
>
> *So when God asks us to think about Him, He asks us to think about everything that is true, just, pure, lovely, and praiseworthy . . . He knows how desperately we need His qualities to become ours.* [3]

God knows that the more we get to know Him, the more we will know of life—real life—the life we were created to experience. HE IS LIFE.

He understands that by walking with Him, we will better comprehend what genuine love is all about—how it differs from the tawdry imitations put forward by the world. HE IS LOVE.

By focusing our thoughts on Him we will grasp more fully His goodness and be all the better for it. HE IS GOOD-NESS.

Our minds will begin to blossom as we feed on the truth of His Word—pure truth, unadulterated by prejudice, politics, or impure motives. HE IS TRUTH.

We'll come to see how much we really do depend on Him for *everything*, from salvation . . . to strength for each day . . . to the next breath we draw into our lungs.

God wants us to get to know Him—not because He needs our worship, but because we need His strength. It has nothing to do with satisfying His ego, but everything to do with our hope of making sense out of life today and finding eternal life in the future.

"God's glory," someone has said, "is man's highest good." He knows that we'll be all the better for just getting to know who He really is.

STRONGHOLD

Don't we have a great God? Just take a look at Acts 17:24-28. If the person being described were anyone other than God, you might think he was on an ego trip. But God's ego trip has a very special purpose. Locate God's purpose in this section of Scripture and make it your personal prayer today.

CHAPTER 49

God and Our Questions

One of the first places I turned after my diving accident was to the Book of Job. As I lay immobilized in the hospital, my mind swirled with questions. When I learned that my paralysis was going to be permanent, it raised even more questions.

I was desperate to find answers.

Job, I reasoned, had suffered terribly and questioned God again and again. Perhaps I could find comfort and insight from following his search for answers.

Frankly, it's ironic that many Christians turn to Job for help and comfort. In reality, the book raises more questions than it answers.

You'll look in vain through its pages for neat, compact theories on why people suffer. God not only refuses to answer Job's agonizing questions, He also declines to comment on all the tidy theological theories offered by Job's erstwhile friends.

And make no mistake, Job's questions to God weren't of the polite Sunday school variety. They were pointed, sharp, and seemed at times on the border of blasphemy.

Why didn't You let me die at birth? (3:11)
Why didn't you dry up my mother's breasts so that I would starve? (3:12)
Why do You keep wretched people like me alive? (3:20-22)
How do You expect me to have hope and patience? (6:11)

What do You think I'm made of, anyway? Stone? Metal? (6:12)

If life is so short, does it have to be miserable, too? (7:1-10)

Why don't You back off and quit hurting me for a while? (7:17, 19)

What did I ever do to You that I became the target for Your arrows? (7:20)

Why don't You forgive me before I die and it's too late? (7:21)

How can mortal man be righteous before a holy God? (9:2)

Why do You favor the wicked? (9:24)

Since You've already decided I'm guilty, why should I even try? (9:29)

You're the One who created me, so why are You destroying me? (10:8)

Why do you hide Your face and consider me Your enemy? (13:24)

Why don't You let me meet You somewhere face to face so I can state my case? (23:3-6)

Why don't You set a time to judge wicked men? (24:1)

Tough, searching questions. Job's friends were horrified. They half expected lightning to fall and fry the suffering man on the spot.

But the lightning never fell.

And that, to me, is the comfort of the book of Job. What meant the most to me in my suffering was that God never condemns Job for his doubt and despair. God was even ready to take on the hard questions. Ah, but the answers? They weren't quite the ones Job was expecting.

Likewise, when it comes right down to it, I'm not sure if it would have sufficed to find "the answers" to all of my questions, anyway. What if God had suddenly consented to answer all of my queries? Could I have even begun to handle it? It would have been like pouring million-gallon truths into a one-ounce container. Dumping a water tower into a Dixie cup. My poor pea brain wouldn't have been able to process it.

For some odd reason, however, it comforted me to realize that God did not condemn me for plying Him with questions. I didn't have to worry about insulting God by my outbursts in time of stress and fear and pain. My despair wasn't going to shock Him. God, according to the book of Job, is never threatened by our questions.

And so . . . did I find answers? Answers for the deepest, darkest questions about a life of total paralysis?

Just one. But it is enough. I think I'll let Paul put it in his words:

> *Oh, the depth of the riches of the wisdom and knowledge of God! How unsearchable his judgments, and his paths beyond tracing out! Who has known the mind of the Lord? Or who has been his counselor? Who has ever given to God, that God should repay him? For from him and through him and to him are all things. To him be the glory forever! Amen* (Romans 11:33-36, NIV).

STRONGHOLD

I knew a disabled person who once said, "I used to have a million questions and no answers. I still don't have the answers. But you know what? I don't have the questions, either."

Come up with one question for God you've been putting on the back burner. Now read Romans 8:38-39. Commit yourself to read and meditate on those two verses every day for the next week.

CHAPTER 50

Keeping God's Attention

There's nothing more frustrating than trying to keep someone's attention. I went through that game as an immature teenager, desperately seeking to impress the captain of the football team from our neighboring high school.

I vividly recall those ridiculous mental gymnastics I went through . . . trying to dress right . . . combing my hair just so . . . losing those few extra inches around my waist . . . working so hard to impress . . . striving to pique his interest with my witty conversation. I felt that his fondness for me waxed and waned according to how clever and cool my overtures were.

What a disaster that relationship was! Frankly, I got plain worn out trying to hold his affection. He dumped me and I deserved it. Through it all, however, I learned something that's stayed with me through the years.

I'm reminded of that frenzied high school relationship every time I catch myself trying to keep *God's* attention. Have you ever thought of it in those terms? When illness comes, when anxiety threatens, when conflict disturbs our friendships, we may conclude that God has gotten bored looking after us and has shifted His attention to a more "exciting" Christian.

"Look over there, archangel Gabriel. Now, that young woman has possibilities. She's a climber. So responsive! So disciplined and faithful! On her way up in the kingdom. Too bad about Joni. I think we've invested more than enough time and energy in her for a while."

Or we imagine that God becomes disgusted with our meandering obedience and decides to stand us up, leaving us to fend for ourselves for a while. ("I'll teach *her* a lesson!") We're afraid that if we don't keep in God's spotlight, He'll get too busy juggling galaxies or fulfilling prophecy in the Middle East. Or worse yet, we're afraid we might so exasperate God that He won't take the time to sort out the complicated mess we've gotten ourselves into.

If you ever find yourself thinking thoughts like these, run, don't walk to the book of Psalms. Get alone for a few uninterrupted minutes with Psalm 121. Open your heart and let the Spirit of God bring those words home to you in a very personal way. It won't be long before those feelings of discouragement and inner turmoil begin to fade like a bad dream.

Down in a valley, in desperate need of encouragement, the psalmist looks all around him—north, south, east, and west. From where will his help come? Only from the Lord, the very creator of those intimidating mountains and hills that surround him (vv. 1-2). With his eyes focused on this mighty source of strength, the singer's spirit begins to bubble over with assurance.

This caring, concerned God, he tells us, "will not let your foot slip." Twenty-four hours every day, seven days a week, He will keep watch over you. He is a shade to you through long, weary days and a guardian through the darkest of nights (vv. 3- 6).

Does anyone *really* care about your life?

The Lord God does. "He will watch over your life." As a matter of fact, "the LORD will watch over your coming and going both now and *forevermore*" (vv. 7-8, NIV).

Oh, please don't make the mistake of supposing God's interest in you waxes and wanes in response to your spiritual temperature. God's love doesn't vacillate according to how many victories you have over sin or how many times you use His name in your prayers. His love for you goes deeper than mere affection or surface infatuation.

Your God will never be fickle. He will never give up on you. He will never become distracted. His interest will never cool with the passing years. You don't have to worry about trying to impress Him in order to catch His eye.

Read Psalm 121 and let the matchless love of God sweep away your doubts and fears. You already have God's attention and you will never lose it. The real question is, how will He keep yours?

STRONGHOLD

As you read Psalm 121, personalize it by inserting your own name in each verse, just to see how personally God involves Himself with your life's details.

CHAPTER 51

Glory: The Everyday Word

"Glory."

That's one of those lofty, in-the-clouds words, isn't it? Difficult to visualize. Hard to get in focus. The meaning is either so heavy we can't keep a grip on it—or so high above our heads that we can't even reach it.

We hear people talk about God's grace, righteousness, redemption, and glory and we nod our heads. Sure, all of those things are important, but sometimes the meaning seems a little, well, *distant* from our daily lives. What does God's glory have to do with finishing a report for school, changing the oil in the car, or getting the laundry folded?

At one time I felt "glory" must mean some kind of cosmic brilliance or blinding light. Images of long-ago Bethlehem would play on the screen of my mind, with magnificent heavenly beings shouldering back the night and shouting out, "Glory to God in the highest!"

In recent days, however, I've learned that "glory" comes closer to home than that. Much closer.

Glory, I've learned, is what God is all about. His essential being. Whenever you talk about His character or attributes—like holiness, love, compassion, justice, truth, or mercy—that's God's glory. And when He reveals Himself in any of those qualities, we say that He is "glorifying Himself."

In times past, He revealed those qualities in both places and people. He still does.

Not long ago I entered a friend's home and immediately sensed the glory of God. No, that impression was not based on some heebie-jeebie feeling or super-spiritual instinct. And it had nothing to do with several Christian plaques I spotted hanging in the hallway. Yet there was a peace and orderliness that pervaded that home. Joy and music hung in the air. Although the kids were normal, active youngsters, everyone's activity seemed to dovetail together, creating the impression that the home had direction, that the kids really cared about each other, that the parents put love into action.

We didn't even spend that much time "fellowshiping" in the usual sense of the word—talking about the Bible or praying together. Yet we laughed. And really heard each other. And opened our hearts like family members.

After dinner I left that home refreshed. It was a place where God's essential being was on display. His kindness, His love, His justice. It was filled with God's glory.

So how is it that you and I can glorify God? It happens every time we reveal His attributes in the course of our daily lives. Every time you share the good news of Christ with another. Every time you reflect patience in the middle of an upsetting or perplexing problem. Every time you smile from the heart or offer an encouraging word. Whenever those around you see God's character displayed in your attitudes and responses, you are displaying His glory.

So you see, God's glory isn't reserved for a temple of stone or some heavenly vista. It can shine out clearly while you're changing a flat on the freeway . . . or counseling an angry co- worker . . . or lying in a hospital bed . . . or balancing two crying babies in the church nursery.

Exciting as all of this is, Paul has news that's even better still.

But we all, with unveiled face beholding as in a mirror the glory of the Lord, are being transformed into the same image from glory to glory, just as from the Lord, the Spirit (2 Corinthians 3:18).

The more we look to the Lord Jesus throughout the hours and days of our lives, Paul is saying, the more we begin to actually resemble Him!

Far from being some spacey concept out of a theology text, *glory* is as close as your next breath, as real as a smile on a dark day, as warm as the clasp of a caring hand.

STRONGHOLD

Think of all the different kinds of mirrors you have around your house—everything from the large beveled mirror in your living room to your little, round, compact mirror. Mirrors may come in different sizes and shapes, but they all do the same thing—reflect!

Now take a closer look at 2 Corinthians 3:18. Have you ever considered that you are a mirror which reflects the glory of the Lord? No matter how big or small you see yourself in God's family, God wants you to reflect His Son's image.

People usually see the Lord glorified in my life when I am able to _____.

CHAPTER 52

God of the Little Things

Is God concerned about the details of your life?

Does He care about the "little things"?

Maybe you've shaped words like those in your heart—if not on your lips—during the course of a busy day at home or the office.

Piles of dishes need to be done. The typewriter runs out of ribbon. The washer leaks a big soapy puddle on the floor—and you've got people coming in an hour. Your best friend seemed cold on the phone and you can't figure out why.

Little things.

Nobody else seems to notice or pay that much mind . . . so why should God? After all, isn't He the God of the BIG things? Isn't He the One who spoke swirling galaxies into the vast frontiers of space?

Isn't He the One, as Isaiah wrote, who

has measured the waters in the hollow of His hand,
And marked off the heavens by the span,
And calculated the dust of the earth by the measure,
And weighed the mountains in a balance,
And the hills in a pair of scales? (40:12).

Why should this great, awesome God notice the tears that came to my eyes this morning at breakfast—when no one else noticed? Why should the Creator of the universe care about the worries that kept me awake until 2:00 A.M.? Why should the mighty Sovereign of eternity be concerned about the fact that I'm late for an appointment and can't find a parking place?

Sure, the Bible says He has compassion for His people. But isn't that sort of a "general" compassion for mankind? Isn't that an arms-length kind of compassion? Like a multi-millionaire might feel when he writes out a check for an anonymous poor child living on the other side of the world.

Just how intimately is God involved in our small, petty problems?

Again and again I go back to David's words in Psalm 103:

Just as a father has compassion on his children,
So the LORD has compassion on those who fear Him
(v.13).

This verse gives us an idea just how and in what way God expresses His compassion. It isn't the compassion of a distant king . . . or a distracted executive. The kind of compassion God has is the intimate, heartfelt compassion of a *father*.

I remember my father having that kind of compassion with me. Often when my dad would be busy at his easel, mixing oils and painting on his big canvas, I'd be sitting on the floor at his side with my crayons and coloring book—working just as hard as he was. Even though he was intent on his work, he'd look down at me and smile. And sometimes he'd set his brushes aside, reach down and lift me into his lap. Then he'd fix my hand on one of his brushes and enfold his larger, stronger hand around mine. Ever so gently, he would guide my hand and the brush, dipping it into the palette, mixing the burnt umbers and raw siennas and stroking the wet, shiny paint on the canvas before us.

And I would watch in amazement as, together, we made something beautiful.

I look back on that scene, even these many years later, and find myself warmed by the intimate, emotional compassion my father had for me.

This is the kind of love our God has for us. Fatherlove. The kind, gentle compassion of a dad who deeply cares for his sons and daughters. Maybe you never had a dad like that . . . but you do have such a Father.

No, God is not so preoccupied with the running of His big universe that your problems—even the little ones— somehow escape His notice. The Lord Jesus assured us that "every hair of your head is numbered." So if your problems today are piling so high that you feel ready to stumble beneath the weight of them, stop and take Peter's good advice:

Cast all your anxiety and care upon Him, because He cares for you (1 Peter 5:7).

Let God's big hand close gently over yours. With His help, even the discouraging crayon scribbles of your life can become a masterpiece.

Nothing would delight a father's heart more.

STRONGHOLD

Have you ever borrowed a tool from a neighbor and had it break in your hand? A small inconvenience to most, but quite a big concern for you! Does God care about such little annoyances? Just in case you doubt, read 2 Kings 6:1-7.

God's Secrets

Lean a little closer to the page for a moment. Can I tell you a secret?

Hang around a little longer and I just might! That's something I would very likely do if you and I became close friends. I'm a people person, and it just comes naturally to confide in a friend, seek sympathy when I'm hurt, or look for approval if I complete a painting I'm especially pleased with.

Almost everybody engages in those sorts of social bonds. A rainbow of personal dynamics flow between us. We develop frank habits in our relationships . . . action and interaction. Even our trustfulness, our eagerness to find some ear for our most sacred secrets demonstrates that we're people-dependent. The satisfaction we find in sharing our hopes and cares and wrongs with those who care about us is a sign we are finite and frail . . . so very, very human.

God, on the other hand, is a mystery.

He holds back many things to remind us of His unapproachable majesty and perfection. Unlike us, He often remains silent. A silence that tells us He is totally self-sufficient. He doesn't need our help. If He so chooses, God can accomplish all of His desire without the slightest cooperation of a single one of us. "Whom did the LORD consult to enlighten Him, and who taught Him the right way?" asks the prophet Isaiah. "Who was it that taught Him knowledge or showed Him the path of understanding?" (Isaiah 40:14, NIV).

The answer, of course, is no one.

But here's the marvel. Although God is totally self-sufficient, He *chooses* to involve Himself in our lives. There's a little verse in Psalm 25 which astounds me everytime I think of it.

The LORD confides in those who fear him; he makes his covenant known to them (v.14, NIV).

Other translations say, "The Lord is intimate with those who fear Him." He doesn't need to, but *He shares His secrets with me*. He gets personal and intimate. He lets down His guard. He draws me into quiet conversation. He invites me into His confidence. *Me!*

God doesn't need little old me. He certainly doesn't require my advice. He doesn't need my attention, emotional support, or listening ear. He can go about His business as though I never existed. (He seemed to manage just fine before I was born.) He doesn't have to stoop so low as to use a broken, earthen vessel such as myself. It is only by His unbelievable grace that He calls my simple labor an actual service to Himself. He permits, and even solicits, my help.

And to think He would even whisper the secrets of His heart in my ear!

But here's the catch. Usually we reserve our secrets and confidences for those with whom we are especially buddy-buddy. Not so with God. God reserves intimacies for those who *fear* Him. Those who hold Him in awe and deep respect. Those who revere His name.

I'm overwhelmed at His great glory, His total self-sufficiency, His holiness and completeness. But I'm even more overwhelmed when I consider that God, by His own choice, makes His covenants known to you and me. Insecure, frail, stumbling you and me.

That's a secret I can hardly keep to myself.

STRONGHOLD

Has God taken you into His confidence lately? Has he revealed some special truth to you? Something about His love that before seemed incomprehensible, or His plans that formerly seemed an enigma? If so, take a moment to praise God for choosing to be intimate with you.

If you haven't heard any good secrets lately, remember this: "Blessed is the man who always fears the Lord . . ." When you fear the Lord, it's like cupping your ear so you may hear Him!

God's Humility

When I ponder the marvelous attributes of my God, there's always one quality which moves me above all the rest.

The humility of our Savior.

Contrasted against His glory and greatness as the Creator of the universe, His humility is all the more striking. Scripture tells us that through Christ:

> . . . *all things were created: things in heaven and on earth, visible and invisible, whether thrones or powers or rulers or authorities; all things were created by him and for him. He is before all things, and in Him all things hold together . . . for God was pleased to have all his fullness dwell in him . . .* (Colossians 1:16-17, 19, NIV).

Now ponder, through this poem, the *humility* of Jesus.

The Hands that shaped the flaming spheres
  and set them spinning, vast light years
  away from Planet Earth,
have laid aside the Robes of State,
donned human likeness by the great
  indignity of birth.
The hands, responsive to Love's Plan,
that formed the God-reflector, Man,
  of dust and destiny,
outstretched—by Man's fierce hate impaled—
wrought life anew, Love's Plan unveiled
  upon Golgotha's Tree.

The Hands that found it nothing strange
to pucker up a mountain range
   or ladle out a sea,
that balance Nature's systems still,
and shape all History to His will,
   hold, and are molding, me! [4]

For me, the supreme demonstration of the nature and character of our great God was when He laid aside His divine splendor, took upon Himself the form of a servant, and died a martyr's death for us. Since God has done *that*, surely He has proven His intentions.

His humility, gentle and unpresuming, shouts to us of His glory and greatness.

STRONGHOLD

Open your Bible to 2 Corinthians 8:9. I challenge you to spend at least five minutes today pondering what the Lord Jesus gave up to become your Savior. Let your thoughts and meditation bring you to your knees in adoration of this great God who humbled Himself . . . for you.

Secrets of His Grace

PART 3

Secrets of His Grace

In the Family

Let me tell you about my big sisters.

You've heard the phrase, "Blood is thicker than water." When I was a girl an expression like that would have sounded gross. But I instinctively understood its meaning. For even though I loved my friends, there was nobody who could match the importance of my three older sisters.

Sure, we had our share of scuffles—which occasionally erupted into screaming, full-scale, hand-to-hand combat. Just routine sibling rivalry, right?

We'd fight over the craziest things . . .

Why didn't you hang up my blouse?

It's YOUR turn to dry dishes.

I don't care if you DO tell Mom . . . I've got some stuff I could tell, too!

Get your grimy hands off of my diary!

You said WHAT to my boyfriend?

Ah, but as much as I squared off with my sisters, I was always glad to be paired off with them. I took special pride in being the youngest of four girls. I loved posing for photographs with them. Inwardly, I was tickled with their achievements. And I glowed with pleasure when they'd say something nice about me. Their opinions meant much more than even my best friend's.

There's something wonderful about sharing the same genetics with another person—the same parents, roots, background, memories, history, and, in a sense, flesh and blood.

I was reminded of that "blood-is-thicker" expression just recently as I read in the book of John.

Throughout the course of His life on earth, the Lord Jesus had special names for those who followed Him. He called them His servants, His sheep, or His beloved. He seemed to have special nicknames for at least several of them. At the last supper, He must have encouraged His men mightily when He named them "friends."

You are my friends if you do what I command. I no longer call you servants, because a servant does not know his master's business. Instead, I have called you friends, for everything that I learned from my Father I have made known to you (John 15:14-15, NIV).

It wasn't until after His resurrection, however, that Christ referred to His disciples as His *brothers*.

One of the first things Jesus said after He rose from the dead was, "Mary, go to My brothers and tell them that I am returning to My Father and your Father."

Even though He was as close as a good friend could be to the men and women who followed Him through His earthly ministry, He couldn't call them blood relatives until after He paid the penalty for sin and welcomed them into the family. Christ's death and resurrection opened the door for men and women to share the same genes, so to speak, with the Son of God. To share the same Father and family.

That thought stirs me so! I think how proud I was to be identified with my sisters and call them my family. What must Jesus have felt to utter for the first time the word, *brothers* to us?

Blood *is* thicker than water. And if you have found salvation through Jesus Christ, you can never be an only child. You're in the family of Jesus.

Let me tell you about my big Brother . . .

STRONGHOLD

How does your big Brother, the Lord Jesus, feel about naming you as one of the family? Flip to Hebrews 2:5-15 and take a little pride in the way Jesus speaks of His relationship to you.

Verse 11 affirms that the Son of God is "not ashamed" to call us His brothers and sisters. What reasons does the passage give for our Brother's decision to "share in our humanity"? Think on that . . . and take some time before you get into bed tonight to tell Him what that decision means to you.

Grace: Fresh Daily

Not long ago I was looking through a *National Geographic* magazine and came across an article on the Sinai wilderness. It was enough to send me to the refrigerator for a Pepsi.

Page after page showed photos of a dry wasteland. Vegetation amounted to a few scrub bushes here and there and an occasional lonely palm. It certainly didn't seem like a place where anyone would want to live, let alone wander about aimlessly for forty years.

But it prompted me to look up a few more facts regarding the wilderness journeys of the nation Israel after the exodus from Egypt. It seems that the main staple of their diet was a flaky foodstuff called "manna." It wasn't exactly *coq au vin* or caviar. In fact, it must have looked something like those dried mashed potato buds that come in a box.

The Bible tells us that they ate that stuff for forty years. Can you imagine? They must have outdone Julia Child in thinking of 101 ways to make manna taste good. I imagine they broiled it, baked it, maybe fried it, and—who knows— even scalloped it. Yet it was food. It was life. And it was necessary for them to gather it fresh every morning before it could melt away in the heat of the noonday sun.

It was this provision—this manna—which kept them strong and fit to meet the challenges of daily life out in that trackless desert.

Now there is a lesson in all this talk about manna and the wilderness. A few years ago I found myself in a wilderness. I wasn't camping in Death Valley or trekking across the Utah salt flats. I was in bed . . . for three long months . . . with a pressure sore that refused to heal.

For me, remaining down for those months, unable to get up, was a real wilderness experience. There were times during that twelve-week stay in bed that I wondered how I would continue. I'd get depressed just thinking about the remaining weeks I needed to stay out of my wheelchair. Plans were interrupted, paintings were postponed, and I discovered that there are only so many books, tapes, or TV programs you can endure for that length of time flat on your back.

It's been said that grace is the desire and the power to do God's will. Well, I lacked both. It was clear that this grace, this gift, was going to have to come from God. And as a gift, it's something for which I had to *ask*.

James tells us that the asking must be done in humility. "God opposes the proud," he writes, "but gives grace to the humble" (4:6, NIV).

At that point I wasn't having trouble with pride. I had come to a place where I was broken, humbled, even humiliated by my lack of ability. Yet my mind was locked up with worry over the future.

Perhaps my days of boredom will go on forever . . . perhaps my sore will get worse and worse . . . perhaps I will forget how to write or paint . . . perhaps my friends will forget about me . . . perhaps I will get another sore!

Numb with anxiety, I finally came across three verses from Lamentations 3 which unlocked my spirit.

This I recall to my mind,
Therefore I have hope.

The LORD's lovingkindnesses indeed never cease,
For His compassions never fail.
They are new every morning;
Great is Thy faithfulness (vv. 21-23).

In other words, the grace God gives you today is sufficient *for today only.* Like manna. And as much as I needed that daily manna of God's grace, it wouldn't be mine until I sought it. Just like the Israelites, I had to wake up in the morning, go out and gather a day's supply. It was no good trying to stockpile grace for the long, hungry days ahead. Grace, like manna, can't be stored. It is "new every morning."

Do you find yourself wrestling with a worry just over the horizon? Do you have a hard time imagining how in the world you're going to cope if this or that comes to pass? God is telling you not to worry, just like He told me. Jesus made that clear when He said, "Do not be anxious about tomorrow; for tomorrow will care for itself. Each day has enough trouble of its own" (Matthew 6:34).

God will give you the grace to see you through *this* day. But remember . . . go to Him bright and early tomorrow morning and He'll be waiting there to give you more grace—a fresh and ample supply for whatever that day will bring.

The manna will be fresh at sunrise. There is no better time to gather it in.

STRONGHOLD

You've sung it scores of times in church, but have you put it to memory? And remember to sing it through the day when the worries of next week tempt you.

> *Great is Thy faithfulness! Great is Thy*
> *faithfulness!*
> *Morning by morning new mercies I see;*
> *All I have needed Thy hand hath provided;*
> *Great is Thy faithfulness, Lord, unto me!* [5]

With the idea that grace is the desire and power to do God's will, look more closely at Philippians 2:12-13. What do we call that work of God in our life? You guessed it—*grace.*

Dying of Thirst

Johan is young, tall, blond, and Dutch. I got to know him through my cousin, who attended the same Bible school in England. Gifted and handsome, Johan could have carved out a comfortable youth ministry in his native Netherlands—or most anywhere in the world, for that matter.

Comfort, however, isn't one of Johan's major goals. He chose to take the gospel of Christ to the bedouins and nomads near Israel's desolate Sinai desert. A forgotten people in one of the most desolate corners of the world.

Johan works by an oasis near the sea, attracting travelers and bedouins by offering hot meals, clothing, and first aid. Following this hospitality, he tells Bible stories and gives a simple testimony of his faith in the One who walked the same sandy waste, two thousand years ago.

The work isn't easy. Loneliness stalks those sun-scorched regions. Bibles and other supplies are few and far between. But Johan's desire to proclaim Christ is greater than all these obstacles. He has a message to offer—and considers it every bit as valuable as the life-giving water he ladles out to his guests.

From the bedouins, Johan learned it is considered worse than murder if you know of a water source and yet neglect to tell your fellow man.

Few of us will ever live in a wilderness like the one where young Johan has pitched his tent. Not many among us will ever proclaim salvation to desert nomads. But all around us, no matter where we reside or work, there are thirsty men and women. The neighbor down the street, the man at the service station, the boy who carries our groceries, the secretary who types and files, or even the distant aunt who occasionally comes by for visits.

If these people don't know Christ, they're going to die of thirst.

In John 4, Jesus had a conversation with a thirsty woman. It was a hot, dry day in a town near the edge of the desert. Sitting on the edge of an ancient well, He talked to the woman about two kinds of thirst: the immediate physical sort, and a deeper, more profound thirst of the soul.

"Everyone who drinks of this water shall thirst again;" He told her, "but whoever drinks of the water that I shall give him shall never thirst; but the water that I shall give him shall become in him a well of water springing up to eternal life" (vv. 13-14).

The woman left her waterpot unfilled and hurried back into the city. Yet her thirst was quenched that day as never before. She had found a deeper well than the one in the village square. She had found the Source of living water and didn't waste a moment in telling everyone in town.

Do you know the Source of living water? If you do, please don't withhold a drink from somebody who is thirsty.

It's not just a matter of hospitality. It's a matter of life and death.

STRONGHOLD

Read John 7:37-39. Can you grab the meaning of those powerful words in the context of the climate in which these people lived? The abundance or lack of water was a life-or-death issue. Why do you think Jesus used the analogy of a *river* instead of a "lake" or "pool" or some other body of water? What does that imply about the nature and quality of the life He offers to those who place their trust in Him?

CHAPTER 58

Feeling Sorry for Yourself

Have you ever reached into your freezer, grabbed that carton of chocolate chip ice cream and said, "I deserve this"?

Or do you go on a shopping spree and buy that expensive blouse because you've been under a lot of pressure lately or feel misunderstood by your kids or your husband? If you're a guy, maybe you retreat deep into a shell of silence, splurge on fishing equipment, or lose yourself in a football game.

Am I describing anybody that lives at your house? Somebody with a grocery list of complaints tallied and checked off? Add them up and the grand total tells you life has handed you the short end of the wishbone, right? You have a first-class, blue-ribbon right to feel sorry for yourself. You've earned the right to be miserable and no one is going to take it away from you!

Don't look now, but you have lots of company.

Self-pity is such a—well, *comforting* feeling. It's so hard to deal with because it's so easy to justify. Our human logic constructs an internal scale of balances, and by the time we've piled up all the little aggravations and thrown on a couple major frustrations, life seems weighted against us. So the ladies escape to the soaps on TV, go on an eating binge, storm the malls, or just have a good cry. And the guys slam their fist into a wall, ram the accelerator to the floorboard, or paste on a touch-me-not frown.

But underneath it all is raw self-pity.

As I've said, we who pity ourselves have a lot of company. You might be surprised to find some of that company in the Bible. At one despondent moment in his life, the great prophet Elijah crawled under a broom tree in the desert and asked God to kill him.

"I've had enough," he told the Lord. "Take away my life. I've got to die sometime, and it might as well be now" (1 Kings 19:4, TLB).

Later, still in the midst of a pity-party, he told the Lord:

"I have worked very hard for the Lord God of the heavens; but the people of Israel have broken their covenant with you and torn down your altars and killed your prophets, and only I am left; and now they are trying to kill me, too" (19:10, TLB).

Can you identify? "Lord, I've worked so hard for you but I'm the only one who really cares. Everyone else is blowing it and they're all against me!"

Or how about old Jonah? The Lord had sent him to preach his heart out over the wickedness of the city of Nineveh. How Jonah hated these enemies of Israel! He was just itching to see God scorch them off the face of earth. But then the Ninevites spoiled everything by repenting and turning to the Lord! In His mercy, God decided to spare them and that made Jonah *really* upset.

This change of plans made Jonah very angry. He complained to the Lord about it. "This is exactly what I thought you'd do, Lord . . . I knew how easily you could cancel your plans for destroying these people. Please kill me, Lord; I'd rather be dead than alive [when nothing that I told them happens].

So Jonah went out and sat sulking on the east side of the city, and he made a leafy shelter to shade him as he waited there . . . (Jonah 4:1-3, 5, TLB).

But if anyone in the Bible had the right to feel sorry for himself, it was the apostle Paul. Tucked away in 2 Corinthians chapters 11 and 12 is a long list of complaints. The apostle had been bullied by a bevy of so-called supersaints. He gave and he gave, and what did he get from these guys? Nothing but insults and slaps in the face. (See 2 Corinthians 11:1-15.)

Ah, that would be bad enough. But it was only the beginning. Since his foes were playing the "can-you-top-this?" game, Paul played along with a list of his own.

I have worked harder than any of them.

I have served more prison sentences!

I have been beaten times without number.

I have faced death again and again.

I have been beaten the regulation thirty-nine stripes by the Jews five times.

I have been beaten with rods three times.

I have been stoned once.

I have been shipwrecked three times.

I have been twenty-four hours in the open sea.

In my travels I have been in constant danger from rivers, from bandits, from my own countrymen, and from pagans. I have faced danger in city streets, danger in the desert, danger on the high seas, danger among false Christians. I have known drudgery, exhaustion, many sleepless nights, hunger and thirst, fasting, cold and exposure.

Apart from all external trials I have the daily burden of responsibility for all the churches (2 Corinthians 11:23-29, Phillips).

Whew! Suffice to say, all these circumstances brought this battered missionary to the point of despair. But what was Paul's response? Self-pity? Well, maybe he was tempted. *But he didn't give in!*

In chapter 12 verse 10 he declares:

Therefore I am well content with weaknesses, with insults, with distresses, with persecutions, with difficulties, for Christ's sake; for when I am weak, then I am strong.

He could say *that* because just a verse earlier, the Lord had told him *this*:

"My grace is sufficient for you, for [My] power is made perfect in weakness" (12:9).

"Okay," I hear you saying. "That's fine for Paul. But what about me? Is self-pity all that bad? Is it really that much of an offense to God?"

There's no doubt about it. Self-pity is a *sin* and it cuts us off from the sufficient grace God promises to provide. Allowed to fester in the secret places of the heart, it spreads a poison through the whole of your life (Hebrews 12:15). It colors your vision, warps your thoughts, distorts your face, darkens your hope and—worst of all—neutralizes the power of God's Spirit in your life. Ironically, it cuts us off from the very thing we crave most: the love and compassion of God and our loved ones.

I have battled this frightful monster again and again, and let me tell you . . . self-pity isn't worth the price, no matter how "comfortable" it feels.

So remember: If you feel inclined to open the freezer and grab that carton of chocolate chip pistachio double fudge . . . God's grace is sufficient.

And it isn't even fattening.

STRONGHOLD

For a closer look at how Jesus handled self-pity in the life of one of His disciples, read John 21:20-23. Why was Peter so jealous of John? How did this magnify his own self-pity? Most importantly, what was Christ's response?

Make this your prayer:

Father, when I compare myself to others it only magnifies my misery. I've even doubted Your good plan for my life when I've been in tough times. Help me to listen when I hear You say, "What is that to You? You follow Me!" And most of all, help me to follow.

CHAPTER 59

Part of the Family

Those of us who love God's Book find in its pages people with whom we identify.

Strong, mission-minded believers find a champion in the apostle Paul. Young pastors feel a strong kinship with Timothy—a green pastor with a "problem" church and a queasy stomach! Single girls swoon over Ruth's love story. Harried homemakers identify with Martha—but long to be more like her sister, Mary. Teens see themselves in the youthful David on his lonely, nighttime vigils. If children don't picture themselves with the little ones gathered at Jesus' feet, they may sympathize with young Samuel who had to leave his mom and dad to live in the temple.

I don't know too many stories of people in the Bible whose spinal cord was injured. But there is one name I do remember from my Sunday school days—one disabled individual with whom I can identify.

Mephibosheth, son of Jonathan.

Prince Jonathan had died in battle along with his father, King Saul. Before his death, the prince and the fugitive David had been the closest of friends—though by all logic they should have been bitter rivals. When David ascended to the throne after the death of Saul and Jonathan, he wondered how he might honor the memory of his dear friend. So he summoned one of Saul's former household servants to the palace.

The king then asked him, "Is anyone left from Saul's family? If so, I want to fulfill a sacred vow by being kind to him."

"Yes," Ziba replied, "Jonathan's lame son is still alive." "Where is he?" the king asked.

"In Lo-debar," Ziba told him. "At the home of Machir."

So King David sent for Mephibosheth—Jonathan's son and Saul's grandson. Mephibosheth arrived in great fear and greeted the king in deep humility, bowing low before him.

But David said, "Don't be afraid! I've asked you to come so that I can be kind to you because of my vow to your father Jonathan. I will restore to you all the land of your grandfather Saul, and you shall live here at the palace!"

Mephibosheth fell to the ground before the king. "Should the king show kindness to a dead dog like me?"

. . . From that time on, Mephibosheth ate regularly with King David, as though he were one of his own sons (2 Samuel 9:3-8, 11, TLB).

It's no easy thing to be disabled, even in *this* day and age, but it was immeasurably more difficult in those days. Not only was medical care all but nonexistent, but the disabled person had to endure the stab of pity and prejudice. Believe me, nobody cared about accessibility back then! People who were lame or blind were either relegated to back bedrooms or forced to beg on city streets.

That was the kind of future faced by Mephibosheth, whose feet were lame.

But all of that changed when King David found the young man and summoned him to his throne. Lame, considered worthless, an embarrassment even in his own eyes, the son of Jonathan was bidden by the king to come and dine.

As an heir to the throne, Mephibosheth deserved banishment. Now the new king wanted to dine with him? What had Mephibosheth done to deserve this great honor?

Absolutely nothing.

When Mephibosheth asked the king the reason for this extraordinary compassion, David explained, "I will surely show kindness to you for the sake of your father" (9:7).

It was because of David's great love for Jonathan that Mephibosheth was welcomed into the king's presence. Disability or no, he was now part of the family and enjoyed all the privileges of a king's son.

Isn't that the way God deals with us? We were alienated, crippled by our sin. Our disability was our ignorance and fear of the God who had every right to snuff us out in His righteous anger. As Paul put it:

> *You were spiritually dead through your sins and failures . . . and obeyed the evil ruler of the spiritual realm . . . being in fact under the wrath of God by nature, like everyone else* (Ephesians 2:1, 2, 3, Phillips).

Like Jonathan, the best thing we could have expected from our King was permanent banishment or a swift execution. But no. Because of Jesus, we are invited to become the very sons and daughters of God.

> *In love he . . . adopted us as his sons through Jesus Christ, in accordance with his pleasure and will—to the praise of his glorious grace, which he has freely given us in the One he loves. In him we have redemption through his blood, the forgiveness of sins, in accordance with the riches of God's grace that he lavished on us.*

> *Consider the incredible love that the Father has shown us in allowing us to be called "children of God"—and that*

is not just what we are called, but what we are (Ephesians 1:4,5-8, NIV, 1 John 3:1, Phillips).

Through Jesus' provision, we can now draw our chairs up to the King's table. We are welcomed. In spite of our spiritual disabilities—whatever they are—we are part of a family. There is no reason to fear. The King has called us into His intimate family circle, as His own sons and daughters.

Remember that, if today you feel unworthy to come into the King's presence . . . if, like Mephibosheth, you sense that somehow you could never fit in.

Come anyway, says the King. No matter what your weakness, handicap, or disability.

Come and dine.

STRONGHOLD

To dine at the King's table is a special privilege. God even has a banquet prepared—for His Son, the King, and for us. Read about it in Revelation 19:6-10 and rejoice that you're on the invitation list!

Fingers of Love

Can you hear the voice, the words—somewhere in your memory?

"I know it hurts . . . but remember, God screens the suffering that comes into your life. He filters it through fingers of love, giving you only that which works for your good and will point you toward Him."

Have words like those, spoken with kindness and deep concern, ever sifted down and settled into your mind—perhaps through a cloud of pain or grief?

They are good words, and true. It's an incalculable comfort to know that God won't let trials pour on top of us like sand slipping carelessly through His fingers.

We know better. We know He is aware. We know He is in control. We know He is concerned beyond our comprehension. We're confident He handles everything that touches our lives, measuring it out, sorting it carefully, sifting it through a sieve of His providence and protection.

Makes you feel special and close to Him, doesn't it?

But let's take that hopeful thought a quantum leap further.

True, God filters everything through His fingers. But did you ever stop to consider *that you are one of His fingers?*

Paul states it point blank in 1 Corinthians 12:27

Now you are the body of Christ . . . each one of you is a part of it (NIV).

Wow. Now that's a different proposition altogether. Talk about feeling special and close to Him! That's as close as you can get. The Lord Jesus is our head, and you and I make up His body here on earth. There could be no more intimate linkage.

In a real sense, we *are* His fingers. That image of sand trickling down from a great distance and piling high around us isn't accurate.

We are much closer than that.

We are His body. We make up the hands and the feet and the eyes and the ears—and fingers, too—just as Paul affirmed.

"As the human body, which has many parts, is a unity, and those parts, despite their multiplicity, constitute one single body, so it is with Christ . . . Now the body is not one part but many . . . God has arranged all the parts in the one body according to his design . . . you are together the body of Christ" (1 Corinthians 12:12, 14, 18, 27, Phillips).

God would never do anything to harm His body. What foolishness to suggest He would do Himself purposeful and deliberate injury.

Yet some of us seem to think just that.

It shows in our reactions and attitudes. Embittered, thoughtless reactions tell the world we don't trust God when He allows pain or problems to touch us. In a way, when we grumble and complain against the hardships, we are saying that God is thoughtlessly harming His own body.

To correct that kind of thinking, we need to see ourselves intimately linked, actual members of Christ's body—a body God would never do anything to harm. The Spirit of God can teach us this truth, when we are ready to listen.

Our Father doesn't simply filter our sorrows and setbacks through His fingers, we *are* those fingers. Don't allow thoughtless voices or the Enemy himself tell you differently!

STRONGHOLD

Here's an additional thought. If God filters trials and disappointments through His fingers, and we are those fingers, it gives us some real responsibililty toward one another. If suffering and discouragement are besieging your life, what can I do—as the very fingers of Jesus Christ—to protect you, to push away the harm, to wipe away your tears, to hold your hand or clasp your shoulder? To whom can you be the fingers of the Lord Jesus today?

Taking the Initiative

It's a good thing I can't knot my hands into a fist. Because if I could, I'd probably punch things when I get mad. Ken, for instance.

Wait—don't take me too seriously. I doubt that our disagreements would ever get that furious, even if I had use of my hands. About the most violent we've ever gotten was the time I got so mad at Ken I tried to skim his shins with my wheelchair.

Thankfully, I missed. Anyway, if I *had* managed to run over Ken's toes, he probably would have let the air out of my tires.

I say all of this to let you know that my husband and I are like every other couple you meet. We argue. Now, we try not to quarrel—quarreling is a lava of boiling words that spew out of your mouth. Rather, we *argue*, carefully observing a couple of basic rules, like letting the other person have his say without interrupting, promising to listen, and so on.

Yet even when we argue with the best of intentions, we *still* come up against barricades. Attitudinal roadblocks. I get stubborn and refuse to compromise. Or I get resentful because I feel like I have to give in more than *he* does in order to resolve the conflict. Do you get the picture?

When Ken and I reach one of those impasses, we sometimes sit for long minutes in belligerent silence. And as I sit there, I secretly resent the demands of marriage. I find I have a reluctance to give away any more than absolutely necessary. I feel a temptation to pull back from the full intensity of my relationship with Ken and settle for the "basic requirements."

But in the middle of all that stubbornness, Ken is usually the first to break the silence and take the initiative. Unaccountably, he will begin to show forgiveness and love. That *shocks* me. It catches me up short. Ken doesn't wait around until I am repentant or promise to change my ways. He loves me . . . icky, argumentative person that I sometimes am. And that makes me love him all the more right back.

That's exactly what God has done for us.

The Father didn't wait around until He had an apology before He sent Jesus. He took the initiative. He didn't fold his arms and tap His foot, waiting until we "came around," until we shaped up and changed our ways.

No, God caught us up short in that "while we were yet sinners, Christ died for us." I can't resist such love. It amazes me that the Lord loved me long before I promised to give Him my life or change my ways. The result is just as the apostle John predicted: I find that I love Jesus Christ "because He first loved us" (1 John 4:19).

That's called taking the initiative. It's not only a principle God uses with us, it's also a plan of action we, in turn, need to implement with each member of our family . . . and God's family.

Don't sit there and stew in your stubbornness. If you want to heal what's hurting, either in your life or in the life of another, take the initiative.

Like Christ.

STRONGHOLD

Are you aware of a hurt today that could be healed if only you would take the initiative? What does Matthew 5:23-24 indicate about the practice of waiting for the other person to "come around"?

CHAPTER 62

"But I'm So Small . . ."

Last week Ken and I pitched a tent underneath some tall, straight Sequoias near a mountain creek still flowing swiftly with melted snow from the high Sierras. Mornings were crisp—almost cold—and that made the aroma of fresh mountain trout sizzling on the breakfast campfire smell even better.

We don't do anything fancy on our camping trips. For me, it's a flannel shirt, dusty jeans, no makeup, and a bandana over dirty hair. But we start our day early so we have lots of time to fish or wander around a trail or two, or read a book in the sun.

One morning we rented a boat on a lake laden with trout. The scenery was enough to suck the breath out of your lungs. It made me feel so small, drifting around in that little rowboat, surrounded by soaring mountain peaks, wide blue water, and blustery winds. Like being in some vast cathedral. I felt like whispering.

I thought of Job as we drifted in the morning stillness. He too, must have felt so very small that day when the Almighty came down to question him.

"Where were you," God asked, "when I laid the foundation of the earth! . . . Who set its measurements . . . or laid its cornerstone, when the morning stars sang together and all the sons of God shouted for joy?" (Job 38:4-7).

Watching those high mountain glaciers, I thought of how God went on to query Job about forming the ice and snow.

Have you entered the storehouses of the snow, Or have you seen the storehouses of the hail? (38:22)

No, Job must have whispered in his heart. *Those places are higher than me—higher than I can ever go. I am small and bound to the earth.*

God questioned him further.

Can you lift up your voice to the clouds . . . can [you] count the clouds by wisdom? (38:34, 37)

Watching the windswept cloudscape brush across the tips of the peaks, I felt sure of Job's answer. *No, Lord, my voice is weak, and my wisdom is, too. I couldn't begin to count Your mighty works.*

Once again, God spoke to his trembling servant.

Is it by your understanding that the hawk soars, stretching his wings toward the south? Is it at your command that the eagle mounts up, and makes his nest on high? (39:26-27).

I thought of those words as I watched an eagle leave his nest in one of the rocky crags and sweep over our lake in search of a fish for breakfast.

Yes, the mountains, the snow, the hawks and eagles, the clouds and wind all have a way of making me feel so small . . . almost insignificant . . . just as Job must have felt. And a camping trip up into the Sierras has a way of reminding me of the measureless greatness of God.

But before I begin to think of myself as a tiny-nothing-of-a-speck in God's fathomless universe, there is another side of the story to consider . . .

As marvelous as the mountains are, the proud eagles, the ancient glaciers, and the mighty panorama of wind and clouds, lake and sky, I am not so small that God did not strip

Himself of all His divine trappings and humble Himself to save me. As Paul wrote:

> *Christ Jesus himself . . . he, who had always been God by nature, did not cling to his privileges as God's equal, but stripped himself of every advantage by consenting to be a slave by nature and being born a man. And, plainly seen as a human being, he humbled himself by living a life of utter obedience, to the point of death, and the death he died was the death of a common criminal* (Philippians 2:5-9, Phillips).

He became small in the eyes of the world . . . He became insignificant in the sight of men . . . He even made Himself lower than the angels . . . for me. To lift me up.

Have you been overshadowed by some larger-than-life realities around you lately? Are there times when you cringe with Job, thinking that you are so small, so . . . so nothing? Please don't stop there. Don't be overwhelmed. Recognize that this same God who towers around you also humbled Himself and became a man. He lived and died and came out of that grave for you. To lift you up.

There's nothing small or insignificant about that.

STRONGHOLD

Do something small today. Listen in on a conversation between two grade schoolers. Read a chapter from *Little House on the Prairie*. Wind up a music box and hum along with the tune. Delight yourself in little, seemingly insignificant things.

And in case you think you're above such things, read the account in Matthew 19:13-14 of Jesus, the great Creator of the universe, enjoying time and small-talk with children. Was anyone too small in His eyes?

Dubious Roots

Not long ago my sisters and I followed an intriguing branch of the Eareckson family tree.

On a crisp morning in early winter, we crossed Chesapeake Bay Bridge and made a right turn onto little Kent Island. Armed with an old family map, we set out to locate the original Eareckson homestead somewhere near Bat's Neck Creek at the bottom end of the island. After asking at a few farmhouses, we were directed down a lonely dirt road.

There it stood . . . an old, colonial, two-story brick home surrounded by woods and barren fields. Nobody was home.

We drove past the house out into the back field. According to our map, the little family graveyard was nearby. Where the field crested slightly at the horizon, we spotted a large spreading oak surrounded by a plot of scrub brush. A likely spot.

Kathy poked around the base of the tree with a stick, pushing aside the ivy and tangled brush until she struck rock. There it was—a moss-covered stone with a crudely chiseled name:

BENJAMIN EARECKSON.

And then another,

ELIZABETH EARECKSON.

We were thrilled—you'd have thought we'd found gold. I can't describe the feeling of elation that filled me to find those links in the family tree.

On our way back to Baltimore, we invented stories about Benjamin and Elizabeth. Struggling against the elements. Pushing back the frontier. Planting the Eareckson banner in the American soil. They were probably early settlers from Scandinavia. Farmers, perhaps. Or maybe fishermen, since their home was on the edge of a creek leading to the Bay. They must have made friends with the Indians. Swapped stories with the oystermen. Their sons probably went to Baltimore and became shipbuilders, or went to Washington and became lawyers.

I was bursting with pride and I didn't even know those people.

My pride deflated a few months later when I happened to look through a detailed record of our family history. There I noticed the mention of slaves. Benjamin not only kept slaves, but willed them to his son. A postscript added that the Eareckson family dealt kindly with their slaves, but I was hurt, nonetheless.

None of us enjoys discovering blight on our family tree.

I wonder how the Lord Jesus felt about His human ancestry. Have you thought about that? A careful study reveals a few rather remarkable characters up in the limbs of His family tree. Kings and poets. Saints and sinners. Jews and Gentiles.

Look, for example, at the five women mentioned in His genealogy.

There was Tamar . . . the widow of an evil son of Judah. When Judah failed to honor custom and give her his next youngest son as a husband, Tamar disguised herself as a harlot and seduced her own father-in-law.

There was Rahab . . . not only a pagan Canaanite, but one of Jericho's best-known prostitutes.

There was Ruth . . . a foreigner and stranger to the nation of Israel; a former resident of Moab, a nation that fell under God's curse.

There was Bathsheba . . . who yielded to a lustful King David and committed adultery. Afterwards, when she realized she had conceived, David had her gallant husband murdered and Bathsheba moved into the palace. While not ignoring this tragedy, Matthew's genealogy makes this unadorned notation: "David was the father of Solomon, *whose mother had been Uriah's wife*."

God included all of these women in the royal line of the King of kings—an example of His grace that crosses even racial and national barriers.

The presence of these women listed in the genealogy of Jesus speaks of the extent of God's mercy. It shows how great God's forgiveness really is, how wide His grace. God identified with forgiven sinners, even to the point of including them in His Son's human ancestry.

What does that say to you and me? You may feel like an outcast, an outsider. You may feel shame over your family background. You may still ache over the consequences of past sins and failures. Could God's mercy really be available to you? Could He actually love you and use your life for His glory?

Take heart from the stories of Tamar, Rahab, Ruth and Bathsheba. God not only forgave them, He even exalted them to a place of honor in His Son's family tree.

No matter who you are, where you've been, or what you've done, you can be a member of God's royal family. No matter what your background, parentage, or track record, you can hold an honored position in the service of the great King. And that . . . is grace.

STRONGHOLD

God is pleased to have your name included in His Son's family tree. In fact, look at 1 Corinthians 1:21. What exactly is God's attitude when it comes to your salvation? Why is He pleased to have you join His family?

Do a little investigation on your own family tree. How many relatives do you have who you hardly ever see? They may not know it, but they need prayer . . . your prayers. Why not list in your mind names of distant or close relatives and bring them before God in prayer today? Who knows? Through your prayers, some of them may one day end up on a limb of the family tree of Jesus as well!

CHAPTER 64

Washing

The young wife tenderly leaned over her husband in the wheelchair. Her husband, severely brain damaged as a result of an automobile accident, lifted his head slightly and smiled. The woman straightened his collar and smoothed his shirt as she talked.

"I used to have a hard time accepting Bob's injury," she said, smiling as she leaned around and looked at him. "And the hardest part was bathing my husband, wasn't it, honey?"

His eyes rolled slightly and he smiled as if to say, "You bet!"

She straightened and fought back tears as she continued. "He would stand in the shower and hold onto the towel rack while I scrubbed his back. All the while my tears mingled with the running water. My big, strong, handsome husband . . . now he couldn't do for me, I had to do for him. To the point of washing him even."

The man shifted his weight in his wheelchair, unable to speak, only to listen.

"But all that changed when I realized that Jesus did the same—no, I take that back . . . He did *much more* when He washed me of the dirt and filth in my own life. Now I count it a privilege to give Bob a bath."

As I listened to this woman's story, reflecting on my own humbling experiences with bathing since paralysis, I was reminded that we're washed every day as believers. The apostle

John assures us that "if we confess our sins, He is faithful and righteous to forgive us our sins and to cleanse us from all unrighteousness" (1 John 1:9).

In John 13, the Lord got on His hands and knees and washed the dirty feet of His own disciples.

In Psalm 51 David pled with God to wash him. "Wash me thoroughly from my iniquity," he prayed, "and cleanse me from my sin . . . wash me, and I shall be whiter than snow . . . create in me a clean heart" (Psalm 51:2, 7, 10).

I wonder if David had always had that attitude. I wonder if he ever felt a reluctance about being bathed by somebody else—even if that somebody was God. He may have thought that personal cleansing was something he would have rather done for himself. After all, it could be humiliating to have somebody else take on such private routines. There came a day, however, when King David had no hesitations. He was so soiled, so thoroughly stained by sin and guilt that he fell from his throne and on bended knees cried out to God for cleansing.

The disciples got the picture, too. Even though Peter initially objected to the idea of divine footwashing, he quickly changed his tune as Jesus spelled out the implications. "Then, Lord, not just my feet but my hands and my head as well!" (John 13:9, NIV).

The young woman with the brain-damaged husband began to change her attitude toward washing as she realized what her Lord was doing for her every day. God was cleansing away a great deal more dirt and filth from her life than she ever had to face when approaching her husband with a washcloth in hand.

Now, you may not be in a nursing home having to go through bed baths every day. You may not be in bed or ill while others take care of those very intimate needs. But you may be in need of someone—besides yourself—someone who can give you a real cleansing.

If your feet are dirty or your hands are soiled from the everyday contact with this world, let God wash you, making you whiter than snow, and let Him create in you a clean heart.

STRONGHOLD

Jesus talks a lot about cleansing and washing during His ministry on earth. In fact, washing His disciple's feet was the last act of service He performed before He went to the cross. Read about it in John 13:1-17. Notice our Lord's words in verses 14-17. How can you "wash the feet" of a friend or family member? How can you refresh and invigorate them? What should your attitude be?

CHAPTER 65

Threshing

My friend Bev took a unique vacation recently.

Shunning Disneyland and the High Sierras, she, along with her husband and kids, drove back to the family farm in North Dakota to help with the wheat harvest. Can you imagine? Hundreds of acres of wheat. Big combine tractors. An old farmhouse. A skyscraping windmill. Doesn't it sound like fun? Actually, as Bev recounted their experiences, she reminded me that it was a lot of work . . . but good, hard, family-fun work.

Since I don't know much about wheat, I asked her to describe just what goes on at harvest. Bev recounted how the big combines come lumbering through the fields, raking the furrows of freshly cut wheat into the machine. The combine head, which resembles a rotating blade, then beats or *threshes* the stalks of wheat. The ripe grain is shaken loose and sucked into a large bin at the back of the combine. What's left, the straw and chaff, is spit back onto the ground, fodder for the next gust of prairie wind.

Since my conversation with Bev, I've learned that the biblical word *tribulation* has its root meaning in the word "thresh." What I've just described to you, believe it or not, is a process that applies to believers as well as wheat.

In Romans 5:3, Paul tells us that "tribulation brings about perseverance." If I were to sit down with you today over a cup of coffee, I have a feeling you could put very personal words around that experience. A few of those big combines have most likely lumbered across the field toward you within the past year . . . perhaps within the past *week*.

Tribulations. Those big unavoidable trials that threaten to cut you down and beat you back and forth. Being threshed is never easy. Never pleasant. But Romans 5 goes on to assure us that perseverance, the fruit of tribulation, yields a crop of "proven character" (v.4).

God is after something precious in your soul. Just like that North Dakota farmer, He's after a harvest . . . the golden grain of patience, perseverance, and strong character. And how is that grain harvested? Only through threshing . . . through tribulation. The farmer doesn't thresh weeds, does he? He wouldn't waste his time. He threshes the wheat which yields grain from the chaff. That priceless, blessed grain.

I know it's hard to picture "results" or the "yield" when you're going through so much testing. It's hard to imagine how God might be pleased or how you might be benefited. But splendid spiritual grain is to be found only in the lives of those with noble character—character gleaned through threshing.

Shortly before His betrayal and death on the cross, the Lord Jesus turned to Peter and said, "Simon, Simon, Satan has asked permission to sift you as wheat. But I have prayed for you, Simon, that your faith may not fail. And when you have turned back strengthen your brothers."

Jesus predicted that Peter was about to get mowed down by one big threshing machine of a trial. Yet the Lord never said He would pluck Simon out of the path of that trial, only that He would pray that Simon's faith would not fail—in spite of the threshing. Christ was after lasting fruit in Simon's life—patience, yes, but perseverance even more so.

"You did not choose me," Jesus said in John 15:16, "but I chose you to go and bear fruit—fruit that will last." I'm glad that the grain, the fruit in our lives, will last.

Somehow that makes the beating and the flailing of a threshing trial worthwhile.

STRONGHOLD

Read Romans 5:1-5 and ask yourself this: What wonderful benefit grows out of "proven character"? As you come before your Lord in prayer today, ask Him to help you keep the perspective of these verses as pressures and problems enter your life in the coming week.

Inside Pain

Which pain is worse, physical or emotional?

I have personal opinions on that question. Like you, I've faced both kinds. Physical pain can almost be measured by degrees. Some have developed a remarkably high pain tolerance. Others have learned to distract themselves from thinking about, say, the pain of a sprained ankle or bruised thigh. If worse comes to worse, certain pain medications allow us to block insistent pain messages.

We can sometimes succeed at pushing physical pain right out of our thoughts by crowding our time and attention with other matters. Even those of us in wheelchairs devise clever ways to forget about our paralysis.

But *inside* suffering . . . ah, that's a different matter.

Mental anguish, resentment, bitterness, or even dryness of soul can hound us. And it isn't so easy to put those feelings behind.

Those sorts of hurts—pains of the heart and mind and spirit—create an emptiness, and seem to put us in a spiritual vacuum. We can describe physical pain to a doctor or nurse, but inside pain can only be known—really known—by God.

I think God permits this kind of inner anguish for a good reason. Physical hurt is almost outside of us, something we can drive from our thoughts. But inside pain is *within* our thoughts, and forces us to cope with the problem.

God may allow it because He knows this kind of suffering can be more purifying than any other kind of pain. We're forced to face it and deal with the situation at hand.

When I'm in physical pain from my wheelchair, I can usually block it out. Maybe lie down for a while and rest, or take a couple of aspirin. But if I'm hurting on the inside because of an argument with my husband or a disagreement with a friend at work, I can't push it aside. I'm *miserable*. Anxiety nags me. And that compels me to do something. It forces me to go to my husband and ask forgiveness, or to resolve that conflict at work.

God says that inside anguish can be purifying. In 2 Corinthians 10:5, we're told that we can take captive every thought and make it obedient to Christ. What a promise! The anxiety, the worry, even the resentment or spiritual dryness can be used to make us deal with the issue at hand. And that means obedience.

Perhaps today you're feeling some inner hurt that refuses to be blocked out or forgotten. If the pain is due to a situation over which you no longer have control, commit it to the Lord right now in prayer. Don't carry it alone. Peter urges you to "cast all your anxiety upon Him, because He cares for you" (1 Peter 5:7). If, on the other hand, the pain is a reminder of unconfessed sin, an unresolved conflict, or an unrepentant attitude, then get to the root of the problem. Deal with it. Don't languish another minute in your mental suffering. Not when you don't need to.

The pain clinic in your city may offer high-tech alternatives to deal with physical hurts, but only Jesus Christ can offer a cleansed heart and a clear conscience.

"Peace I leave with you; my peace I give you. I do not give to you as the world gives. Do not let your hearts be troubled" (John 14:27, NIV).

STRONGHOLD

There is One who can enter your pain. The solitary Man, a man of sorrows who was acquainted with grief. Keep a bookmark in this page so you can refer to William Bathurst's fitting poem when pain knocks on your door in the coming days.

Lord Jesus, King of Pain,
Thy subject I;
Thy right it is to reign:
Oh, hear my cry,
And bid in me all longings cease
Save for Thy holy will's increase.

Thy right it is to reign
O'er all Thine own;
Then, if Thy love send pain,
Find there Thy throne,
And help me bear it unto Thee,
Who didst bear death and hell for me.

Lord Jesus, King of pain,
My heart's Adored,
Teach me eternal gain
Is Love's reward:
In Thee I hide me; hold me still
Till pain work all Thy perfect will.[6]

Seek God's Face

When I was little I remember secretly opening a small chest that belonged to my mother and taking out her diary. I don't remember if I was even old enough to read—and I certainly can't recall having learned anything shocking about my mom. But I do remember that panicky sense of excitement as I hid behind the living room piano and delicately turned each page as though it were forbidden treasure.

After finishing, I carefully placed the diary back into the chest, situating it just so. I went out to play, the whole time thinking of my mother's diary . . . and feeling worse and worse about seeing her at dinnertime.

Mom rang the dinner bell at the back door and we kids came running. I busily filled the supper table with a lot of anxious chatter, trying hard to act normal.

Finally Mom asked what the matter was. And you know something? I couldn't look her in the face. She'd catch my eyes for a moment and then I'd quickly look down at my plate. Guilt prevented me from looking straight at my mother and answering her questions.

That little story is repeated in the lives of thousands of children and millions of adults. Looking another straight in the eyes has always been a test of truthfulness.

God knows that. In 2 Chronicles 7:14, He says, "If my people, who are called by my name, will humble themselves and pray and seek my face and turn from their wicked ways, then will I hear from heaven and will forgive their sin and will heal their land" (NIV).

How I love that verse. But especially the part about seeking God's face. Just as I had to make things right with my mom before I could have eye-to-eye contact with her, I have learned that God wants me to seek His face in the same way. He desires to have eye-to-eye contact with me— transparent, truthful, lacking any guilt, guile, or sin. But that means confessing sin—my responsibility. No use filling my prayers with a lot of anxious chatter, trying to fake it with the Lord or lie to myself.

If you have a hard time gazing straight into the face of the Lord today, then you know you've got some confessing to do. God wants you to seek His face. There's nothing like eye-to-eye contact with our loving Father.

STRONGHOLD

Don't you love the clean-clear-through feeling of being able to look someone straight in the eyes? You don't feel insecure or fearful. You only feel the transparency of sheer confidence. Joy flows, not only from your heart, but toward the heart of your friend.

It's no different when looking into the face of God as we pray. Eye-to-eye contact is still the best test of confidence and transparency in any relationship.

Try looking up these three "face" verses—Psalm 27:8-9, Psalm 31:16, and Psalm 67:1—and then top it off with that joyful reminder in 1 John 3:2-3. One day we shall see Him face to face!

How clean-clear-through do you feel as you pray to God today?

CHAPTER 68

Mary ... or Martha?

*Jesus loved Martha and her sister [Mary] and Lazarus
... (John 11:5, NIV).*

No doubt they made up a very ordinary family. Like most families, there were certain differences among the members. Mary, it seems, was the most heavenly-minded of the three. She, after all, was the one who sat at the feet of Christ and anointed His feet with costly perfume, even wiping them dry with her hair. She hung on the Lord's every word, weighing all the things He said.

Martha had her own way of trying to please her Lord. Making the house tidy, scurrying to get things in order, running to do the shopping, racing to prepare the meals. And although she was distracted and anxious by all her busy serving, she probably assumed this the best course of action.

Yes, the family members had their differences. Lazarus may have had serious physical problems. Martha was gently chided by the Lord for allowing the details of homemaking and hospitality to divert her from fellowship with Him. Meditative Mary, on the other hand, received the Lord's commendation. She, said Jesus, had chosen what was better (See Luke 10:38-42).

Yet John 11:5 tells us that Jesus loved them all.

That's good news. Not only to those who are strong, but also to the weaker members of the family of faith. Perhaps you fall into the latter group.

"Me? I'm no great saint. I'm not a Paul or John, and I'm certainly not a Mary. I have a hard time getting into the Bible. I can't pray out loud. I don't seem to understand spiritual things the way others do. I guess I'm kind of feeble in my Christian life—and sometimes I wonder if Jesus really cares for me as much He does for those who have it all put together."

If you see yourself like that, as a Martha, perhaps, take heart. For just as a mother loves all of her children, even the weak and less gifted, so Christ cares for those who are weak in the faith . . . who wrestle with heavy burdens and temptations . . . who struggle with nagging doubts and fears . . . who find themselves distracted from their walk with God by the everyday pressures.

What an encouragement to remember that He loves us all!

If, on the other hand, you're one of the Marys, a real pillar of faith, please remember the counsel of Romans 14:1, to "Accept him whose faith is weak."

So many of us don't. We're quick to judge and criticize those who are groping or slipping and can't seem to make the pieces fit. Few of us are willing to humble ourselves to help those who are weak in faith.

You might be a real Mary—memorizing your third chapter in the book of James, leading a Bible study, and waking up at 5:30 every morning for daily devotions. Then again, you might be Miss Martha—collapsing in bed after a busy day, apologetically mumbling your evening prayers as you sink into sleep.

Whichever you are, and however you fit into the family— strong or weak—please know that Jesus loves you. He's reserved a special spot at His feet with your name on it.

He's ready for a closer relationship . . . whenever you are.

STRONGHOLD

Families are complex, their relationships intricate and involved. Some members fall apart in a crisis, others rise to the occasion and take charge.

It can be fascinating to take a close look at the way family members relate to each other. Take sisters, for instance—the way they talk together, the way they deal with problems, the way they laugh, cry, or get angry with each other.

For an inside look into Mary and Martha, find time today to read John 11:17-44. Notice how differently these sisters face the death of their brother . . . and the delay of their Lord. Which sister seems stronger? Who seems to take charge? Who is noted as crying?

Picture yourself at the scene—perhaps as a member of the family. How do you see yourself responding?

CHAPTER 69

My Father's Creation

When we go camping with my parents, my elderly father is a wonder to watch. While others busy themselves with tents and stoves, ice chests and lanterns, he's out quietly gathering chunks of wood.

He'll come back to the campsite with an armload—trunks of gnarled redwood, juniper, or perhaps some pine that's had time to harden in the weather. Piling this trove near a comfortable rock, he sits down, pulls out his knives and begins whittling away the crusty bark and dead, dry, twigs. He scrapes off the dirt and any soft or decayed wood in the cracks of the stumps.

People who pass by our campsite have wondered why this little old man is so captivated by pieces of dirty, gray wood. Yet he works on with deliberation, obviously with something very special in mind.

I've often wondered at Daddy's work myself. Some of the pieces he selects look utterly unredeemable. The weather has blasted and twisted them. Insects have gnawed and ravished them.

But Daddy works on.

Before you know it, there's a mound of bark, dirt, and twigs piled at his feet. A lovely piece of carved wood rests in his grip, shiny from the oil on his hands and smooth from the cut of his knife. The heart of that wood reveals a beautiful grain when the bark is chipped away. These lovely pieces are then fashioned into lamps, tables, chests, or stools.

Once while watching Daddy at his work, I did some work of my own—a charcoal sketch of him toiling away with his knife, cutting into a piece of work. I entitled the rendering, "My Father's Creation."

I wanted to parallel the charcoal drawing with the idea that our heavenly Father is hard at work in each of His children, creating something beautiful in us with the knife of His Word. The Holy Spirit peels away the crusty, dead layers of our old nature. He cuts out the decayed areas of habitual sin and lops off the dead or dying branches that don't produce fruit. Slicing away the diseased and damaged layers, His work reveals a changed heart, beautifully transformed by His sharp Word and His skilled hands.

"If anyone is in Christ," writes Paul, "he is a new creation; the old has gone, the new has come! . . . For we are God's workmanship, created in Christ Jesus to do good works" (2 Corinthians 5:17, Ephesians 2:10, NIV).

There isn't one of us who doesn't feel the encrusted weight of our old nature. We long to have stubborn sins stripped away and the worthless preoccupations and dead, earthbound things sloughed off.

God in His Word can do that. Yes, the cut of the knife will be sharp, often painful. In our foolishness and fear we will want to cling to some of those dead, fruitless branches. But God works on with deliberation, obviously with something very special in mind.

Christ Jesus in you.

STRONGHOLD

Just think—in Christ you are a brand new person on the inside. You're not simply a rehabilitated, shaped-up version with a couple of Band-Aids stuck on to cover the old self. You haven't merely turned over a new leaf. You are a new creation, living in vital union with Christ.

Turn to Romans 6:11. What does it mean to reckon, or consider, or count yourself dead to sin but alive to God? For a deeper look at these thoughts, read Romans 6 all the way through. Colossians 2:9-13 offers some exciting insight as well.

CHAPTER 70

Grace on Display

The jade was exquisite. Smooth, glossy, and finely carved. Delicate gold chains cradled the light and returned it, ripe and mellow. Translucent opals graced their settings with milky fire.

Yes, I confess. I've been window shopping in the mall. I was only going to linger at the jewelry store window a moment, but the artistry of those precious stones held me a bit longer than I'd intended.

The diamonds, set against a black yard of velvet, were radiant—breaking the light into flashes of color. It seemed as though the contrast between the black velvet and the diamonds made those gems all the more brilliant. No other color cloth would have done—no blues, no grays, no pinks.

Midnight velvet produced the best contrast.

No, I didn't buy a diamond that day. But as I wheeled back through the parking lot to my van I kept thinking about that jeweler's display. It struck me as just one more illustration of how God works in our lives.

It seems God best displays the brilliance of His grace against the backdrop of our dark and even blackest moments. Somehow, His grace is made all the more glorious when people see it at work in the lives of those who suffer.

Paul expressed a thought like that in a letter to the church in Corinth.

For God, who said, "Let light shine out of darkness,"
made his light shine in our hearts . . . We have this trea-
sure [that is, the brilliance of God's grace] in jars of clay
to show that this all-surpassing power is from God and
not from us (2 Corinthians 4:6a, 7, NIV).

I don't know how often you're prone to stop by display
cases of jewelry stores. And I'm not sure if you've ever
thought about why they display those precious stones the
way they do. But as you read these words, you may feel as
though your life is blanketed by blackness. Maybe you don't
see much rhyme or reason behind that dark curtain of discouragement or grief right now. As difficult as this thought
may be to understand, God may want to use your life as a display case for a time. He wants your life to be a setting where
He can display His grace for all to see.

The contrast between your suffering and God's grace is
going to catch people's eyes—believe me. Your life will be set
apart from the rest of the ordinary stones and settings around
you. Believers and unbelievers alike will be drawn to you. To
observe the dark backdrop? No, not at all. But rather to
wonder at the beauty and radiance of God's grace in your life.

You will discover that God's power shows up best
against your weakness.

STRONGHOLD

Contrasts. A black night seems to make the moon
brighter. Purple irises brighten yellow daffodils and a
dark gray Kansas sky makes the wheat look truly golden.

The Bible talks about contrasts in 2 Corinthians 4:7-12.
Ponder Paul's words and then consider this: The su-
premely valuable message of salvation has been en-
trusted by God to you, a frail and fallible human being.
You are holding this precious treasure in your body, a
weak and perishable container. How does your life contrast—that is, show up best—the light and power of
Christ within you?

CHAPTER 71

Mind Games

I've got a problem with my prayer life. Perhaps you can identify with it.

Let's say I've been disobedient . . . maybe lax in reading the Word, grumpy with Ken, or feeling just plain lousy, dull, and dried out.

I know that prayer is a big part of the answer. So I begin to talk with God. But then this problem crops up. No sooner do I begin to pray than my mind starts playing games . . .

"Father, You are so full of mercy, so good. I agree with You that what I told that person was a half-truth—no, a lie. Thank You for forgiving me. I'm glad that's all behind me now, and I can go on . . ."

Oh, come on now. God wants to see a little bit of repentance before He helps you out of this mess.

"Well, uh . . . I know You are faithful and just to forgive me of my sins . . ."

Yes, but you're not feeling sorry enough. Are you?

"But I am. I truly am sorry for my sin."

Well, let's see a little bit more emotional involvement then! How long has it been since you've shed some tears? How much do you REALLY care?

"I care. I care! God . . . You told me to acknowledge my sins, and I've done that. I confess I may not be in tears over that lie, but—"

Oh what's the use with you! God is probably so sick and tired of you piddling around with your Christian walk— like it was some kind of plaything—that He's probably hidden Himself from you anyway. If that's all the remorse you can drum up, just forget it!

Does that sound vaguely familiar? You know as well as I that if you wrestle with those mind games long enough, you'll throw in the towel and quit praying, more discouraged than before you started.

When that happens, I do my best to remember two important verses out of the book of Isaiah. Perhaps you'd do well to remember them also.

In Isaiah 30:18 we read:

The LORD longs to be gracious to you;
*   he rises to show you compassion.*
For the Lord is a God of justice.
Blessed are all who wait for Him!

(NIV)

That's a favorite of mine when I feel discouraged in prayer. That God can be the God of justice and at the same time long to show graciousness and compassion is a wonderfully comforting thought.

Then there's Isaiah 45:19.

I have not spoken in secret,
*   from somewhere in a land of darkness;*
I have not said to Jacob's descendants,
*   "Seek me in vain."*

(NIV)

When we truly desire mercy, God is ready to be found. There need be no cat-and-mouse mind games when we approach Him in prayer.

If we seek Him, He promises it won't be in vain.

If we desire grace, He longs to give it to us.

If we want comfort, He rises to show compassion.

As you pray today, remember those unchangeable truths about our Lord. Push aside the mind games and push through to Him, our God of compassion and love.

STRONGHOLD

"We can perhaps understand a God who would forgive sinners who crawl to Him for mercy," says Ken Taylor, "but a God who searches for sinners and then forgives them must have extraordinary love!"

This is the kind of love that prompted Jesus to come to earth to search for lost people and save them. This is the kind of extraordinary love God has for you. If your prayer life has been a trap of "mind games," if you feel far from God, don't despair. Take comfort by reading Luke 15:3-10. God is searching for you!

CHAPTER 72

His Finishing Touch

It was my first recording session. I had studied for days, memorizing all the melodies.

But what really excited me was the thought of hearing it all put together—violins, piano, horns, and harps. All the tracks blending into one beautiful expression.

To get an idea of how it was done, I went down to the recording studio several days in advance, just to listen to the musicians lay down the orchestral background music. They gathered in a little studio, representatives of the musicians union, some of the top professionals in the country.

The arranger put the score sheets before them and—believe it or not—after one rehearsal they were ready for a take.

I was stunned that these people could just walk right in and play a very complicated score—full of sharps and flats, minor and descant chords—all on sight.

The sound they created was breathtaking. Absolutely beautiful.

But do you know what happened after they went through it once and got it down on tape? Many of them left their seats and went on break, milling around the rooms of the recording studio, sipping on Cokes or coffee. They seemed totally detached from the beauty of the music they had just had a part in creating. Only one or two bothered to listen to the playback.

I couldn't believe it! How could these people create something so extraordinary and then . . . just walk away from it, not wanting to hear its final form?

Since that experience, I've thought about God's joy in creating something beautiful in us. Philippians 1:6 tells us that, "He who began a good work in you will *carry it on to completion* until the day of Christ Jesus" (NIV).

In other words, He will develop that good work that He has begun in your heart and life. He will perfect it and bring it to a full and satisfying completion.

You see, God doesn't walk away from His creation. He doesn't take coffee breaks. He's not off somewhere relaxing between jobs, sipping on some refreshments. He's never nonchalant or aloof about the work of His hands. He's creating something beautiful in us—far more beautiful than a symphony.

For Him it's not simply another job that needs to be done. His reputation is at stake and His Son's image is the model. It's perfection that God has in mind—maturity in Christ, that's the end result.

God is always finding new ways of refining you and changing you and improving upon the score He's written with you in mind. He's at work in your life today. He's not on a break, no matter what your faltering faith or weary emotions might tell you.

He's going to stick around. He's going to be there for the finishing touches. When it comes to the tracks of your life, He's going to be involved with the blending and sorting. And on the day of Jesus Christ, He'll be there with you for the playback. All of heaven will be stunned to see and hear what His marvelous work has created in your life.

STRONGHOLD

When King George II attended the London premiere of Handel's *Messiah*, it is said he was so touched by the "Hallelujah Chorus" that he rose and remained standing until its end. Of course, when the king stood up, the rest of the audience did, too. Since that time virtually all audiences have done the same.

Handel said that while composing the chorus, "I did think I did see all Heaven before me, and the great God Himself." It is one of the most glorious of all musical moments!

God, like a great composer, has you in mind as He composes the entire score of His kingdom. You are in His thoughts as He blends the parts into one great symphony. Want to hear what it's going to sound like? Turn to Revelation 5:11-14 and imagine yourself joining in the chorus of millions of angels.

Now, how about putting Handel's *Messiah* on the stereo and singing along? It's a great way to praise God!

CHAPTER 73

A Friend

I was sitting at my friend's coffee table, wrestling with whether or not I should tell her about the depression that had gripped me for several days. I decided to open up. I told my friend I needed to share a problem . . . did she have time to listen?

"Sure," she said, and promptly rose to retrieve a whistling tea kettle from the stove. As she poured, I took a deep breath and started to unfold my problem.

"Milk in your tea?" she interrupted.

"Uh, sure," I said.

"Now, what were you saying?" she asked, sipping her tea.

I went on with my story. Midway, the phone rang.

Her daughter called from the next room. "Mom! It's Dad at the office."

My friend sighed. "I'd better take that. I'll be right back."

I waited, occasionally glancing at my watch. The longer she took, the more my hurt festered. When she came back into the kitchen, she babbled on about her phone conversation.

"Shall I warm your tea?" she asked, before sitting down.

Now it was my turn to sigh. No, I didn't want more tea. I just wanted her to listen. But at that point I wasn't so sure I wanted to talk.

You've had it happen. You'll be going through a heartache or a period of loneliness and you'll want to tell a friend. Your phone calls, however, are persistently interrupted—or never returned. Or worse, you've drawn a friend aside to describe some of the things you've been going through and you get the distinct impression your friend is distracted, only half listening. You get little eye contact, and only a few vague, mumbled words for a reply.

Longing for counsel, you ask for advice and receive a shrug of the shoulders or a pat on the back and a "cheer up, chin up" kind of reply.

And you wonder, *Does anybody really care about what I'm going through? Will anybody listen?*

Jesus had the same thing happen to Him. In Matthew 20:17-28, He and His disciples were on the road to Jerusalem. It would be His last earthly journey. He knew full well what awaited Him at the end of the road.

Betrayal. A shameful trial. Cruel humiliation. Brutal torture. A bloody cross. A lonely death on a dark afternoon. The sins of the world, of all time, dumped on His shoulders. Broken fellowship with His Father.

The dread of it must have weighed heavier on His heart with each step.

He stopped and turned to His friends. He poured out His heart to them, telling them exactly what was going to happen to Him when He passed through those city gates.

Talk about unkind ears! The disciples not only ignored His troubled words, they turned right around and began arguing about who was going to be tops in the coming kingdom, who was going to get the head honcho job or the hotshot seat near the throne. Two of them even sent their mother over to Jesus to argue their case. Unbelievable!

No kind words. No helpful advice. No sympathetic ears or compassionate hearts. The disciples, distracted and called away by their own ambition, were only half listening.

That may be the loneliest part of loneliness. Knowing that no one else really understands—or even cares—what you're going through. Knowing that your burden of pain is yours alone.

That's the way it is sometimes, isn't it? Friends won't always be there. Or if they are, they may not always see past the surface. Others may be busy—justifiably so—or simply unavailable.

And there you are, carrying it all by yourself.

Thankfully, Jesus has been through it, too. He understands. He, too, knows what it feels like to have friends who can't, or perhaps don't always care. So He's the one who lends the sympathetic ear. His eye contact never falters. He will not be distracted from your cry. His heart is with yours in the middle of your pain.

"There is a friend," Scripture says, "who sticks closer than a brother" (Proverbs 18:24).

I've never had a brother, but I have the Friend. His name is Jesus. He listens and He cares.

STRONGHOLD

It breaks my heart to think of those unsympathetic disciples in Matthew 20 turning a deaf ear to Jesus at His deepest point of need. If I had been there, I would like to think I would have held my Lord's hand, looked straight into His eyes, and said, "Please . . . tell me all about it." That's what friends are for.

But do I—do you—*really* treat the Lord as a treasured friend?

Think of all the special things friends share—heart-to-heart talks, the sacrifice of time, wants and needs, joys and sorrows, love and companionship. Jesus covers His side of friendship with you in John 15:15. As you read those words, and then read through that whole chapter, ask yourself, *How can I be a better friend to Jesus?*

CHAPTER 74

You're Not Alone

Ever feel like you're the only one holding it all together?

Nobody seems to be worried about the things that worry you. If you didn't make that call or write that note, who would? The co-chairman of your committee is more than content to bask in the glory—and leave all the work to you. The dog would starve if you didn't feed it. The cat would despair of ever escaping the house unless you took action. The goldfish would strangle in a toxic waste dump if you didn't clean its bowl. The kitchen trash would overflow into the dining room unless you prodded and pleaded. You strongly suspect that the whole house (or church, or office, or Bible study, or carpool) would fall apart were it not for you, holding together all those loose ends by your fingers and toes.

You're not alone. In fact, you've got Somebody on your side who's taking more than His fair share of the load.

Look with me for a moment in the ninth chapter of John. Jesus is having a conversation with not only His disciples, but a man who had been blind from birth. The disciples opened the dialogue with a question:

"Rabbi, who sinned, this man or his parents, that he was born blind?"

"Neither this man nor his parents sinned," said Jesus,

"but this happened so that the work of God might be displayed in his life" (vv. 2-3, NIV).

And then Jesus said a very curious thing.

"As long as it is day, we must do the work of him who sent me. Night is coming, when no one can work" (v. 4).

Who was Jesus talking to? I can't be sure . . . but I have a strong feeling He was looking directly at that disabled man.

"We . . . *we* must do the work of Him who sent Me."

I choose to think Jesus was reminding that blind man that he was not alone. He was not alone in his disability. He was not alone in his despair. The works of God were about to be displayed through him. The Lord wanted this man to know that God Himself was standing by his side, taking on more than His fair share of the load.

Jesus went on to actually heal the man, of course, but I think the Lord's words alone must have thrilled him beyond telling. Jesus was siding up with him to do the work of God. He was choosing him, saying, "We, my friend, must do the works of God. Together."

It awes me to think that Jesus wants me to help Him get the work of God done.

I'm not in it alone.

I don't have to weaken under the pressure.

It doesn't all fall on my sagging shoulders.

Christ stands with me—just as He stood with the blind man that day. And He's standing with you today, too. Especially if you feel you're desperately holding together all the loose ends. It won't all fall apart without you. Jesus is saying to you, "We—WE must do the works of God."

Jesus and you. Together. You couldn't be on a better team.

STRONGHOLD

If you want an idea of how the Lord takes on His fair share of your load, read Matthew 11:28-30. Jesus had in mind a double-yoke, two oxen sharing the weight of the same burden. It was also the practice to put a younger ox in a yoke with an older, stronger, more experienced ox.

As you "plow" through a heavy, frustrating schedule yoked with Jesus Christ, which one of you will take most of the weight? From where does the "rest" come?

CHAPTER 75

Enlightened . . . but Not Lit

I'm sure you know people who have edged awfully close to the kingdom. In fact, you may have thought for sure they were Christians. They knew the right language, the right songs, the right tone of voice, the right facial expressions. They could recite the Four Spiritual Laws, pray with passion, and maybe even tell others about the Lord Jesus.

But then, mysteriously, they simply dropped out of sight.

Poof. They're off the edge of the world. Spiritually speaking, they're no longer among us.

If you asked them today whether or not their commitment was real, they'd just shrug their shoulders and say they really don't care.

I knew someone like that in high school. We went to the same Young Life weekend camp and even made a profession of faith in Christ on the same night. He wrote in my Bible and I wrote in his. We prayed together and talked about trusting and obeying.

I don't know what happened, but somewhere along the line, the light went out. As I think back on that young man, the words of Hebrews 6 come to mind. The writer speaks of those who have been "enlightened," who go so far as to "taste the heavenly gift," share in the Holy Spirit, and taste "the goodness of the word of God"—and then fall away!

It's a mystery to me—and a scary one at that—how a person could be so close to Jesus Christ, so close to heaven, and then turn his or her back and walk away.

But Scripture says it can happen. Just look at the parable of the seed in Matthew 13. The thorns either choked out the seedling or the hard ground dried it up. But in each case, there was some sort of evidence . . . some sign that the seed had almost, but not quite, taken root.

How could that be?

You could compare it to almost—but not quite—lighting a candle. If you hold a match near the wick of a candle, the candle itself almost glows, doesn't it? The wax has a luster. It shines. And all around the wick there's a kind of halo of illumination. You could say, in fact, that the candle is enlightened.

But it's not lit. The flame, though very close, has not ignited the wick. And there's quite a wide gap between being "enlightened," as Hebrews puts it in chapter 6, and actually being lit by the Spirit of God. A gap as wide as heaven and hell.

So let me ask again. Do you know someone who has slipped away? Has it made you question the security of your own salvation? Please don't let it. There are people who are genuinely enlightened, exhibiting all the evidences of close contact with the Spirit of God. But close only counts in horseshoes and hand grenades. It does not count when it comes to having one's name written in the Lamb's Book of Life.

Some people are enlightened. But only Christians are lit. And once ignited, nothing in all the universe can put out that flame.

STRONGHOLD

As you read this, you may find yourself unsure of whether or not you're "lit." Perhaps you're uncertain you are truly a child of God.

Put to rest your doubts, once and for all. Quietly ask God to forgive you of all your sins. Accept the fact that the Lord Jesus Christ personally paid the penalty for your sins on His cross. Now ask Him to not only be your Savior, but Lord as well, believing He will give you His powerful Spirit to help you trust and obey Him.

Now, take out one of your dinner candles and light it.

Do you have the assurance that you are "lit," and not simply "enlightened"? Take a look at 2 Peter 1:5-11 and rejoice in the fact that you will one day receive a rich welcome into the eternal kingdom!

Truths Once Despised

The blind man felt the warm strength of the Carpenter's hand.

He had come to the one called Jesus for healing. Now the two of them were walking, hand in hand, toward the edge of the village.

Yes, there was the familiar little dip in the road. And there—the rustling of leaves in the olive grove. Now they were stopping. The teacher was turning to face him. What would He do?

Jesus spit on the man's eyes.

To me, that's one of the most curious things Christ ever did in touching the life of a disabled person. Mark, chapter 8, records the whole incident for us.

When he had spit on the man's eyes and put his hands on him, Jesus asked, "Do you see anything?"

He looked up and said, "I see people; they look like trees walking around."

Once more Jesus put his hands on the man's eyes. Then . . . his sight was restored, and he saw everything clearly (vv. 23-25, NIV).

The healing isn't the curious part. After all, the Lord Jesus performed many such miracles. What's curious is the *way* in which He performed this particular miracle. The Lord spit in the man's eye!

He didn't use myrrh or frankincense, common remedies in those days. No powders or drugs. Just spit.

Now you and I naturally associate a man's spit with . . . well, despicable things. Spit, we would all agree, is rather disgusting . . . even humiliating . . . especially when somebody else's spit ends up on you. Not to mention on your eyes!

But this was no ordinary man's saliva. And perhaps in employing this strange method of healing, Christ had teaching on His mind—an important lesson for all of us.

Consider this thought. *It is possible that God will bless you by the very truth you once despised.*

Let me explain. When I was first injured and in the hospital, a well-meaning Christian friend stood by my bed and said:

"Remember, Joni, God is sovereign. God is in control."

It felt as though that friend had just spit in my eye. I was disgusted with the idea that God was in control. It turned my stomach. I despised a doctrine that told me God *could* have prevented my injury, but chose not to.

How sickening. How unthinkable.

In time, however, I was to discover the healing influence of that marvelous doctrine. What was at one point a repulsive thing miraculously became my greatest comfort. As the months and years went by, I was able to praise God that He was in control. That there were no accidents in my life. That all things were fitting together for good. That He had reasons—and good ones—yet to be revealed.

It *is* possible that God will bless you by the very truth—or person, or turn of events, or circumstance—you once despised.

Do you feel today as though God has spit in your eye?

Do you feel betrayed, disgusted, and perhaps even tempted to despise your Lord for allowing such awful things to come into your life? Remember, it could be your very cure . . . as hard as that may be to believe or even stomach right now.

Give Him time. Circumstances may make no more sense to you now than trees walking around. But if He has touched your life once, He will touch you again.

The spit from His mouth may be the means of opening your eyes.

STRONGHOLD

Do you feel confused, even betrayed by some sad series of circumstances in your life? Each of the following verses is like a spoonful of strong-tasting medicine, yet can be a healing influence in your life today. At first glance, the three verses will seem hard to fathom, but allow God to minister each as a dose, a healing balm to help soothe away the confusion and sense of betrayal.

"Blessed is the man whom God corrects; so do not despise the discipline of the Almighty" (Job 5:17, NIV).

"Come, let us return to the LORD. He has torn us to pieces but He will heal us; he has injured us but he will bind up our wounds" (Hosea 6:1, NIV).

"It was good for me to be afflicted so that I might learn your decrees" (Psalm 119:71, NIV).

When God Stood Still

He felt the excitement before he heard the sound.

Something—someone—was coming down the highway. The noise of a crowd boiling out of the city gates. It was like a wave, about to break over the top of him. He was that close.

"What is it?" he shouted. "What's coming?"

A voice answered him from the darkness—the perpetual, all-encompassing darkness he had always known.

"Jesus of Nazareth is coming this way."

He started yelling. Yelling like there was no tomorrow. Yelling until he thought his throat would split.

"JESUS! Son of David! Have mercy on me!"

A cuff came out of the darkness. A kick. Harsh, grating words.

"Hush, you fool!"

"Shut up!"

"Hold your tongue!"

"Can't someone silence that man?"

He paid them no mind, no mind at all. He only shouted all the more.

"Son of David, have *mercy* on me!"

The Nazarene stood still and ordered the man to be brought to Him. When he came near, Jesus asked him, "What do you want me to do for you?"

I've always loved that portion of Mark, chapter ten. There have been many times when I've felt just like Bartimaeus, the blind beggar at the gates of Jericho.

Somehow I've aimlessly wandered off the path God has put me on. I've sinned—maybe deliberately, perhaps thoughtlessly. And I feel so far from God. I picture myself lost in a crowd, pushed to the side of the road, groping in the dark. I want to find my way back to the right path but sometimes feel too ashamed or discouraged to even approach God in prayer.

I foolishly imagine God is busy somewhere else, tending to the prayers of other people who are more sincere, more valuable to the kingdom.

When things get that way, I picture poor Bartimaeus—lost and going nowhere. And sometimes, even though I don't shout, I feel like whispering the words.

Jesus, Son of David, have mercy on me.

And somehow the hustle and bustle of the crowd stops. The Lord hears the call.

I love those two little words that describe the action that Jesus took.

"And Jesus stood still" . . . (Mark 10:49, KJV).

The Lord actually stopped what He was doing. The God of the universe stood still and beckoned the poor beggar to be brought to Him . . . simply because he asked for mercy.

I've wondered why the Lord was so moved with this one man. Surely there were other beggars in the crowd, just as lost, going nowhere. But this man had cried out from his heart. He wanted mercy. And sincerely believed that Jesus could deliver him.

That's what I need to remember when I've wandered away from the path God has put me on . . . when I've carelessly ignored the truth.

Hebrews 4:16 says that when we approach the throne of grace with confidence, we do so that first we may receive *mercy*. Only after that, we'll find grace to help us in our time of trouble.

We needn't fear that Jesus is busy elsewhere in His vast universe. Or tending to the prayers of the "super-saints." Right now if you sense a deep spiritual need, if you feel the weight of guilt or regret crushing your shoulders, remember that Jesus of Nazareth is passing by.

Call out for mercy. And for you, God will stand still.

STRONGHOLD

The dictionary will tell you that to show mercy is to "refrain from harming or punishing an enemy . . . or to show kindness in excess of what may be expected . . . or to give compassionate treatment or relief of suffering."

For another story of God's mercy toward those who need it most, read Matthew 9:9-13 and ask yourself these questions:

1. What did our Lord mean when He said He came to help the sick and not the healthy?
2. How has God shown unexpected kindness to me this week?
3. How can I show mercy to one of my "enemies" today? Or compassion to one who is hurting?

God's Best Secret

Webster defines "secret" as something beyond normal comprehension . . . something obscure, hidden from view, concealed from knowledge.

In light of that, it's curious that in Philippians Paul says he has learned the "secret" of being content in any and every situation (Philippians 4:11-12).

Have you ever wondered what "secret" Paul was talking about?

The New Testament word translated "contentment" in our English Bibles means *sufficiency*. I've been told that Paul uses the same Greek root here in Philippians that he does in 2 Corinthians 12:9, where he says God's grace is sufficient.

Perhaps Paul's secret of learning to be content was *simply learning to lean on God's grace*.

What a secret, this working of grace in our lives! Beyond our normal comprehension. Hidden from our view. Hard to explain. Impossible to pinpoint. Difficult to understand.

A friend of mine named Susan recently experienced unbearable pain with the sudden, unexpected breakup of her marriage. Even after a year, she's still picking up the pieces, the few fragments her husband left her when he broke their marriage vows for another woman. I watched Susan go through months of agony, struggling against rejection and just plain nausea. But God's grace sustained her in a startling way. In fact, she commented to me just the other day that she believed the hardest thing to explain was how grace was at work in her life. To her, and to those of us who watched the tragedy, the sustaining, preserving, uplifting power of God's grace was truly a mystery. A wondrous secret none of us could understand.

All we could say was that God's grace was working. It was sufficient. For Susan, Jesus was enough.

Paul learned the secret of contentment. Susan is still learning the secret. How about you? Are you struggling today with discontentment, frustration, disappointment, or downright irritation? Take a moment to quiet your heart and listen to God's best secret . . . it's called grace, and it sounds like this:

Have hope. Take hold. He is sufficient.

STRONGHOLD

Learn some more secrets about grace!
Locate Ephesians 2:8-9 and learn that grace is a _____ of God.

Read Titus 2:11. Who is grace for? _____

Second Peter 3:18 says you can _____ in grace.

What does God require of us in 1 Peter 5:5 in order to receive grace? _____

There's one drawback, and it's listed in Hebrews 12:15. Grace can be _____.

Who Hurts the Most?

A father warns his child time and again to stay away from all those bottles and containers underneath the sink. But then one day it happens. Dad walks into the kitchen and in one horrible moment, sees his little boy, pale and unconscious, on the floor.

Somehow the boy managed to pry the lid off that old bottle of insecticide and . . .

The paramedics arrive and, after a few anxious moments, revive the child. Yet in the coming days, the tragedy continues to unfold. Doctors report that the little boy will never be the same. He will be permanently impaired with a mental handicap.

Tell me something . . . who do you think hurts the most?

The young son? Certainly he's been hurt—terribly. But in a strange way, almost like a hidden blessing, he will never fully understand the consequences of his actions. He has no concept of what life could have been if he had not disobeyed.

How about the father? I imagine he would be the one who would really suffer. *I kept telling him time and again—even after pushing the bottles to the rear of the cabinet. Why didn't he listen?*

That father will carry the pain of his son's disobedience for the rest of his life. It is he who must bear the hurt of awareness—fully knowing the consequences of that bad decision.

Let's apply this story to our relationship with God. Just who felt the deepest hurt back in the Garden of Eden? Adam and Eve? Yes, they must have suffered dreadfully as they began to live out the consequences of their disobedience. How could they begin to reckon with the fact that their sons and daughters—throughout the long ages—would never, could never, be the same?

Impaired by sin, our first parents were probably only dimly aware of what consequences their tragic decision had unleashed on the world.

Murder,
   pain,
      deceit,
        rape,
          warfare,
            abortion,
              nuclear war,
                homosexuality,
                  pollution,
                famine,
              disease,
            divorce,
          incest,
        sorrow,
     fear,
   cruelty,
  holocaust,
 injustice,
greed . . . no, they couldn't have known. They didn't begin to understand.

And neither do we. Blinded by our fallen nature, we have only the vaguest notion of what consequences our disobedience and sinful choices are causing in our life and the lives of others.

But how about God the Father? He has complete understanding. He is totally aware. He can see not only what is and will be, but also *what might have been*. He knows the full impact of our permanent impairment by sin.

And does He grieve? Does the God of the universe sorrow over man's sin and the terrible effects he brings on himself? Scripture indicates that He does feel anguish—deeper than you and I could ever understand.

> *The LORD saw how great man's wickedness on the earth had become, and . . . was grieved that he had made man on the earth, and his heart was filled with pain* (Genesis 6:5, 6, NIV).

> *He [God] could bear the misery of Israel no longer* (Judges 10:16).

> *How can I give you up, O Ephraim?*
> *How can I surrender you, O Israel?*
> *My heart is turned over within Me,*
> *All My compassions are kindled*
> (Hosea 11:8).

> *As [Jesus] approached Jerusalem and saw the city, he wept over it and said, "If you, even you, had only known on this day what would bring you peace—but now it is hidden from your eyes . . . O Jerusalem, Jerusalem, you who kill the prophets and stone those sent to you, how often I have longed to gather your children together, as a hen gathers her chicks under her wings, but you were not willing!"* (Luke 19:41-42, 13:34, NIV).

> *And do not grieve the Holy Spirit of God, by whom you were sealed for the day of redemption* (Ephesians 4:30).

Our Father, much like the dad in our story, carries the pain of complete awareness. He knows as we will never know . . . and He grieves.

But listen—there is a piercing shaft of hope in these dark reflections. A miracle drug has been applied. Christ's blood on the cross is an antidote for the awful impairment of sin. Though we can never flee from the consequences of our sin, we can be restored. It's deadening effects can be reversed. We can, in a sense, get back into the Garden.

Yes, it hurts to know that we have brought pain to the heart of God. It hurts to realize that we continue to grieve Him when we turn from His counsel and go our own way. But Scripture tells us that "if we walk in the light as He Himself is in the light, we have fellowship with one another, and the blood of Jesus His Son cleanses us from all sin" (1 John 1:7).

We who have brought such grief to the heart of God can also bring joy and delight and companionship as we accept His cure and walk with His Son.

STRONGHOLD

Take a look at the word *poison* in the dictionary and it will tell you it's a substance which, even if taken in small quantities, can cause illness or death.

Do we have even the vaguest notion of how our disobedience acts like poison—not only in our own lives but the lives of others? Hebrews 12:15 reads like a doctor's diagnosis and prescription: "Be careful that none of you fails to respond to the grace of God, for if he does there can spring up in him a bitter spirit which can poison the lives of many others" (Phillips).

Do a little self-diagnosis. What poison is there in your life for which the antidote of God's grace can be applied?

In prayer, ask God to apply His healing balm, His love and grace.

"Life Would Be Great If Only . . ."

What do quadriplegics daydream about? Running a marathon? Ballroom dancing? Climbing a mountain?

Not necessarily. Many of us have scaled down our fantasies.

Life would be great if only I were a paraplegic . . . then I could use my hands.

I can't tell you how many times I've thought that. Times when I'm feeling sorry for myself. Times when I'm battling a big inferiority complex. I see these paraplegics who can transfer themselves out of their wheelchair into their own bed, reach for things in the refrigerator, wash dishes at a sink, quickly sort through the mail . . . and the old feelings of hurt and despair start to slink back into my heart.

Disabled people who have use of their hands have it easy. Yes, I actually think thoughts like that when my self-image is at a low.

But I don't think I'm alone. Even able-bodied people make the mistake. We look at others who seem more attractive, smarter, richer, healthier. People who seem to get all the "breaks" in life. Then, when we look back at ourselves, our minor defects begin to look like deformities.

Fortunately, the Bible has good advice for people like me when we get down on ourselves. In Colossians 2:10, Paul tells us that we have been given "fullness in Christ." In other words, we are COMPLETE in Him.

Peter agrees. In his second letter, the apostle writes:

His divine power has given us everything we need for life and godliness (2 Peter 1:3, NIV).

Once we comprehend this amazing truth, our minor— or major—defects become reminders of how complete we really are in Christ. The inferiority complex begins to release its grip. The bad self-image fades like last night's bad dream.

And I'm content.

Content to be disabled rather than able-bodied.

Content to be a quadriplegic rather than a paraplegic.

To stay that way, I weave the contents of 2 Corinthians 12:9—back and forth, back and forth—through the fabric of my spirit:

But he said to me, "My grace is sufficient for you, for my power is made perfect in weakness." Therefore I will boast all the more gladly about my weaknesses, so that Christ's power may rest on me (NIV).

It's true. Because I don't have use of my hands, I need Jesus and His grace all the more. Perhaps some paraplegics get a little confident, maybe a little over-secure since they have use of their arms and hands and fingers. Maybe some are tempted not to rely as wholly on God and His strength.

But not having hands? Well, God knows I need an extra measure of His grace . . . since I can't do my own wheelchair transfers . . . or reach for things in a refrigerator . . . or quickly sort through my mail.

One of these days it's going to sink into my thick skull that *I wouldn't be happier* if I were a para rather than a quad. I am complete in Him. The fullness of Christ dwells within me. Because of that, I am lacking nothing. In fact, I have everything to gain. The power of Christ rests upon me because of my infirmities. Therefore, I will gladly boast as a quad.

You can't improve on "complete."

STRONGHOLD

Is there anything you honestly lack? Are you convinced God truly supplies all of your needs? Are you sold on the fact that you are complete in Him?

If there's a shade of doubt, turn to Psalm 23 and zero in on the very first verse. You've read it scores of times before, but it will help you to read it one more time today.

Think of at least five ways of saying, "The Lord is my shepherd, I shall lack nothing."

CHAPTER 81

Responding to Your Accusers

Imagine you're being set up. Framed. And you know it. You're about to be accused of some terrible wrong you had nothing to do with. Trumped-up charges are bouncing around at your office. Malicious gossip circulates wherever you go. Whispers and nudges and cold shoulders.

What would you say to the people who connived those awful things?

Or, let's say you're about to face your boss because of such charges. Your enemies have spread more lies and swayed the opinions of even your best friends. People turn the other way in the lunch room. You've been deserted and you're left alone to make your own defense.

What words would you have? Not only for your accusers, but your friends? How would you feel . . . what would you do?

Or in school. You're in the middle of a classroom controversy. And your buddies? They say bye-bye. Innocent though you may be, they won't touch you.

What's your attitude? Resentment? Anger and bitterness? Even spiteful revenge?

Many of us have been in situations just like that. Maybe not that bad, but similar.

Jesus found himself in that exact predicament. The night He was having an intimate dinner with His disciples was the very night the plot to betray Him was revealed. He knew His accuser was right in the middle of the fellowship. He also knew that at that very moment, His critics were trumping up charges against Him. He knew people would say all sorts of false, slanderous things against Him. He even knew that His dearest friends, Peter and John, would abandon Him like some sort of leper. They would desert Him that very night.

What could He say at such a moment? What would He do?

John 13 verse 4 says that He got up from the meal, took off His outer clothing, wrapped a towel around His waist . . . and began to wash His disciples' feet.

Don't you find that incredible? Those disciples He humbled Himself to serve would be the very ones who hours later wouldn't want to be seen within ten feet of Him. And He knew that.

But there's an extra twist to this story. Jesus also washed the feet of *Judas*. Ever thought about that?

Jesus was perfectly aware of what Judas was up to—his hypocrisy, his evil scheme of betrayal. Jesus knew there was a lot going on behind His back.

What would you have done if you were the Lord? I probably would have grabbed Judas by the scruff of the neck and said, "See here, jerk, I'm up to your evil tricks. There's no way you're going to get away with this." Then I would have punched him in the jaw.

What did Jesus do? He washed the man's feet.

If that weren't enough, Christ goes on in that same chapter to remind us, "I have set you an example that you should do as I have done for you. Now that you know these things, you'll be blessed if you do them" (vv. 15, 17 NIV).

I can't say how all this might work itself out in your situation. I can't tell you the course of action God might lead you to take. But Scripture is clear about the attitude of your heart in the face of unfairness and betrayal. You are to be humble, not angry.

Can you do it? Can you wash the feet of the ones about to double-cross you? Can you give loving service to those who prejudge you or falsely accuse you?

Yes, you can. Because whatever He asks you to do, He will empower you to do.

May God give you grace to respond in humility, like Jesus.

STRONGHOLD

Jesus set us an example to follow in 1 Peter 2:23. So how do we follow an example like that? The advice is short and to the point in 1 Peter 3:8-9.

Stepping on God's Heels

Like to hike?

No, you don't have to be a back-to-nature zealot or a starry-eyed mountain climber. How about a Sunday amble down a country road . . . or an October stroll through a park, kicking the leaves?

When I was on my feet, hiking was one of the finest things I could anticipate. And we were blessed having a big state park backed up against our farm. Oh, there were countless streams to follow and trails to explore!

My dad was a great hiker. Even when we were as young as five or six years old, my sisters and I would line up behind him as he led the way. We never knew where we were going, but with my dad in charge, striding out in front of us, we were convinced it would be an adventure.

Because of my excitement to always see what was just around the corner or over the next hill, I was constantly stepping on my dad's heels, bumping into his back every now and then. Not that I dared run ahead of him . . . I just knew that his trail was hot. He was going places! And as long as I hiked right behind him, I'd be able to keep up and not miss a single thing he wanted to show us.

Funny thing. Seasoned hiker that my father was, he never seemed to get irritated at us girls for following too closely. Even though we occasionally stepped on his heels, or telescoped into his back when he stopped, I think he took

delight in our excitement to stay so close . . . to stick together
. . . to follow him on the trail.

Don't you wish for that kind of excitement when following the Lord Jesus? Wouldn't it be glorious if we could always
look at our Christian walk as a great adventure?

When I read Psalm 119:133, "Direct my footsteps according to Your word," I like to think I'm on an adventurous
journey with Christ as leader. And you know something? I
would also want to be the sort of follower who is constantly
stepping on the Lord's heels, bumping into His back . . . excited to see what lies over the next hill.

No, I don't want to detour around God. I don't want to
run ahead of Him. I just want to stay close behind Him in my
Christian life. I want to know the trail is fresh. I don't want to
miss a thing He might want to point out to me.

"My soul follows close behind You," sang David, "Your
right hand upholds me" (Psalm 63:8, NKJV).

And how does our heavenly Father feel about our tag-
ging along so closely? *Delighted.* Nothing could please Him
more than when we, His children, desire to stay close. It
brings Him great joy when we stick together and follow Him
on the trail.

> *You have made known to me the path of life; you will fill*
> *me with joy in your presence . . . You chart the path ahead*
> *of me, and tell me where to stop and rest* (Psalm 16:11,
> NIV, 139:3, TLB).

So let me ask you again. What do you think about hiking? And for that matter, how do you view the path you are
trekking through life?

Would to God that we all could keep stepping on the
heels of the Lord Jesus, bumping into His back every once in
awhile. How wonderful if we would make it our goal to follow Him and His leading that closely.

"The steps of a man are established by the LORD," David assures us, "and He delights in his way. When he falls, he shall not be hurled headlong; because the LORD is the One who holds his hand" (Psalm 37:23-24).

Today, let's make sure we keep on His heels.

STRONGHOLD

What do you think it means to "step on God's heels"? To get your imagination going, read Proverbs 3:5-6.

Did you catch that phrase, "In all your ways acknowledge Him . . ."? To "acknowledge" God is to step on His heels! If you want to follow God that closely it might mean

> . . . being *instant* in obedience
> . . . being *absolute* in your trust
> . . . praying *immediately* over a concern, or
> . . . responding *quickly* to a suggestion from the Holy Spirit.

Can you think of more ways you might "step on God's heels"? As you encounter twists and turns in your path today, acknowledge Him. And don't forget His promise . . . "He will make your paths straight."

CHAPTER 83

Coming Attractions

I remember those still, chilly nights when I was a kid and I'd step outside, feel the crunch of snow beneath my feet, and look up through the tree branches at a canopy of blazing stars.

It makes me cold to even think about it. Maybe southern California has thinned my blood!

But long ago and far away, on one of those wintry nights on the farm, my sister and I bundled up and stepped outside to gaze at that beautiful nighttime sky. It was one of those nights when the air is sparkling clear and the sky is ablaze with God's light and glory.

I remember that particular night so well because Jay and I started talking about heaven. As we stood together, our breath making little clouds in the night air, one of us reminded the other of James 4:14:

What is your life? You are a mist that appears for a little while and then vanishes (NIV).

Trouble is, you and I don't think of life down here on earth lasting "a little while." Until circumstances forcibly confront us with reminders of our own mortality, we tend to think and act as if this life will go on forever.

But it won't.

This life is not going to go on forever—nor is it the best life we will experience. The good things down here on earth are merely images of the better things we'll know one day in heaven.

It's like my paintings. I like to go out into the countryside to paint and sketch landscape scenes, examples of God's creation. Using the best techniques I know, I seek to imitate the panorama before me. But those drawings are, at best, only a feeble, sketchy attempt to mirror what I see. With the limited capacity of brushes and acrylics, I approximate what God has painted in an infinite array of colors. My works, however, will always be bounded by the edges of the canvas. They can never fully portray God's limitless handiwork above and beneath and around me.

This earth that we know is a rough sketch—a kind of preliminary rendering—of the glory that will one day be revealed.

It's like stealing a tiny sip of stew before dinner. You haven't had a meal, but you have a little foretaste of what to expect when you get to the table. The happiest, most joyous moments of your life are God's way of whetting your appetite for even greater joys, greater fulfillment to come.

So let's not get too settled in, too satisfied with the fine things down here on earth. They're only previews of the coming attractions.

The main feature is only moments away.

STRONGHOLD

Read Psalm 90 and gain a bit of the perspective that Moses had on life. In view of the brevity of life, what was Moses' prayer in verse 12? Carry that verse on a file card today and take time to ponder its meaning. Ask the Lord to grant you His perspective on time and life as you seek to make the most of today's opportunities.

More Than Meets the Eye

The physics teacher was explaining to his twelfth grade class how orderly and full of design the universe is. To illustrate his point, he gave a demonstration that at least one girl in the class would never forget.

The girl was me. And this is what I've remembered.

First he took a flat piece of metal—and sprinkled *salt* across its surface. The sheet was welded to a metal rod, which he held like an umbrella. Holding the rod, he raised the sheet and we all crowded around to see what he might do next.

He took a violin bow and gently stroked the edge of the metal. A note of music resounded throughout the classroom. But something else was happening on top of the vibrating metal sheet. Incredibly, the salt crystals began to arrange themselves into little patterns. Tiny quadrangles!

He stroked the bow at a different angle and new patterns formed—perfect little hexagons—as the crystals responded to the music.

We all stood around with our mouths open. Our teacher smiled, not even needing to add to the lesson from nature. Even *music* had a kind of mathematical design and visible order that we had never even thought of—or dreamed of. Which reminds me of the words of Paul to the Corinthians:

No eye has seen,
no ear has heard,
no mind has conceived
what God has prepared for those
who love him

(1 Corinthians 2:9, NIV).

That little example was something that my eyes did see and my ears did hear—and it will remain in my heart for a long time to come.

Can you think how incredible, though, it's going to be when we meet Jesus and get to see and hear and know things that we can't even dream of down here on earth? Spiritual things, yes, but also knowledge about the order and design of this universe— physics and music and geometry. We're going to learn things that Einstein never considered in his wildest imagination.

God has prepared all this and much, much more . . . for those who love Him. Here and now, these thoughts remind me how deeply I need to lean on the wisdom and counsel of the Holy Spirit as I move through the "mundane" activities of my day. Each day of living has eternal dimensions we can't begin to imagine in our limited minds.

There is more to life than meets the eye—or ear!

STRONGHOLD

For those who belong to the heavenly Father, scientific demonstrations can refresh a sense of awe and wonder within us. These are not simply "patterns of nature," they are the designs of a master Designer! Read Job 28:20-28. What does Job say about wisdom in the creation around us? What is the essence of wisdom? Write Job 28:28 on a three-by-five card and read it several times today.

Grace for Today . . . Only

Some days I can handle only so much.

Living in a wheelchair has a tendency to make even ordinary days seem like a big burden. My weak shoulder muscles ache from holding up my heavy head (notice I didn't say *big* head). My back gets tired from sitting in one position. My neck gets a crick in it from looking up at everybody standing around me.

On days like those I wonder how I've managed twenty years with total paralysis.

I was sharing some of these thoughts recently with a group of prisoners at a maximum-security facility. Gathered around me were seventy to eighty men who had come to Christ in that prison. I was asked to give them a few words of encouragement. As I looked into the eyes of those brothers, I spoke about the sustaining grace of our Lord Jesus—how His power shows up best in our weakness. The men all nodded and said their "amens."

I asked several of them how much time they had yet to serve. Some had only a few months, others many years. I identified more with the guys who had another twenty or thirty years stretching out ahead of them.

Then I confessed something very personal. I told them, rather hesitantly, how weak-kneed I sometimes get when I think about living twenty, even thirty more years in a wheelchair. A number of the men nodded silently. Looking down at my wheelchair, I told them I had my own bolts and bars to live with. And yes, it was frightening to think of another *twenty years*.

No doubt, those prisoners get a little weak-kneed themselves thinking about decades behind bars and barbed wire. Even though they've accepted their circumstances, it's tough to face a future of confinement and limitations.

Before I left them, I related a simple, yet very special secret that helps me face the future with confidence. The secret is simply this: God does not expect me to accept what may or may not happen to me twenty years from now.

God does not give me grace for those future uncertain years. He doesn't give me grace for next year's headaches—or even next month's heartaches. He won't even loan me enough grace to face the prospects of tomorrow! God only gives me grace for today. He expects me to live *this* day in His strength, leaning on His wisdom, drawing on His presence and power.

And that's what He expects of you today. To live one day at a time. To redeem each hour. To make the most of the moment. To live richly and abundantly by His grace. He doesn't expect you to handle the burden of next week or next month or next year. So whether you're in pain . . . in prison . . . in a hospital . . . in a difficult marriage . . . in a deteriorating financial situation or a devastating family crisis . . . wherever you are, by God's grace make the most of today. And leave the future to Him.

Therefore do not worry about tomorrow, for tomorrow will worry about itself. Each day has enough trouble of its own (Matthew 6:34).

STRONGHOLD

Read Hebrews 4:16. Let's dissect the verse, asking the standard "five W's and an H" questions.

To WHOM is the verse written?
WHAT is promised?
WHERE do we find grace?
WHEN do we receive it?
WHY was it given?
And HOW do we ask?

Secrets of Praise

PART 4

Secrets of Praise

Sunday Morning Hassles

It's almost predictable. In the Sunday morning rush to get up, scarf down breakfast, gather notebooks and Bibles, and warm up the van . . . somebody's bound to get irritated.

Ken and I aren't always quick to detect a problem, but when a frosty silence descends inside the van on a sunny California morning, it's obvious one of us has a problem. Oh, we may sing hymns or read some Scripture—our usual practice of preparing for worship—but sometimes it sounds a little stiff, a little restrained.

Invariably one of us pipes in with, "Okay, what's the matter?"

"Nothing," comes the reply. "I thought something was the matter with *you*."

Once we're in church, the irritation often melts away. We both apologize and affirm our love for each other. But then we get into trouble all over again if, on the way home, we try to pinpoint the source of the original irritation.

Recently while driving alone in the van I tuned in James Dobson's "Focus on the Family" broadcast. I was just in time to hear the good doctor interviewing a group of mothers about life at home on Sunday mornings. Now that grabbed my attention!

To my surprise (and relief!) Dr. Dobson mentioned he and Shirley have had their worst arguments on the way to church on Sundays. He felt there was real satanic pressure put on believers on the Lord's day morning.

I got home, pulled into the driveway, and as Ken came out the kitchen door to meet me, I said, "Guess what! Jim Dobson says that Sundays are the pits for him and Shirley at times. Isn't that great news?"

A slow and surprised smile spread across Ken's face. "Really?" he said.

Sometimes we feel we're the only people who could possibly experience such strain on Sunday morning. We don't have any children, but still, Ken has to help me get ready and then get himself ready. No time to clean up. No time for a decent breakfast. Just rush, rush, fly out the door, and "get me to the church on time!"

Once in a while when we've had a hassle, we've almost been tempted to turn the van around and head for home. But at least we know that worshiping God is a must on Sunday mornings. So even if we do get disgruntled at one another, we make it a priority to get it resolved before wheeling through the front doors of that church.

It may mean sitting in the church parking lot for extra minutes . . . praying or reading a psalm of repentance. Sometimes we pray with Romans 8:26-27 in mind—realizing the Spirit helps us in our weakness when we don't know what we ought to pray. That silent stillness before the Lord does wonders to humble Ken and me.

If the words *praise* and *worship* share anything in common, it is this: When we praise and worship God we are doing the most unselfish thing we could possibly do. True praise and worship permit no self-centeredness. We must step outside of our own complaints, irritations, and desires, focusing instead on the greatness of God.

Perhaps that's why the devil makes the extra effort to entangle us in quarrels on Sunday morning. He hates praise. He despises our worship of God. He will go to any length to thwart that purpose. And the Enemy succeeds when we allow self-centeredness to consume us, entangling us in our complaints rather than focusing on our Lord.

Now, I'm not saying that every Sunday morning we come out of our corners with our gloves on. But I am saying that on those occasional Sundays when we feel the pressure rising, we both know the battle is not so much with each other as with the forces of darkness. My adversary is never my husband . . . it's always the devil. Just knowing Satan has his extra legions working overtime on Sundays helps Ken and me to understand what the battle is all about. Like Paul, we are concerned "that no advantage be taken of us by Satan; for we are not ignorant of his schemes" (2 Corinthians 2:11).

Well, Sunday's a-coming. Are you alert? Aware? Prepared? Let's not allow the Enemy to rob us of the privilege of worship.

STRONGHOLD

There are some important and specific ways you can prevent those Sunday morning hassles. And it can begin on Saturday night.

1. Lay out clothes for the morning.
2. Set the table with cereal bowls and juice glasses. Set the timer on the coffee brewer *or* leave for church early and enjoy breakfast at a drive-thru.
3. Read several psalms of praise and worship before retiring. God can work on your heart, mind, and emotions through the night—just take a look at Psalm 16:7.
4. Go to bed a little earlier!
5. When you wake up Sunday morning, spend a quiet moment in prayerful preparation before you even get out of bed.

CHAPTER 87

"Can't Say Enough . . ."

When I was working on my third book, *Choices . . . Changes*, there was one episode I especially enjoyed writing. You guessed it. It was the last episode, about my husband.

It was great fun to sit at the computer with my friend and describe Ken Tada. How he looked the first time I saw him . . . how he talked . . . how he smiled . . . how he carried himself . . . how he moved when he played racquetball. The words about our dating days flowed effortlessly. Writing about our wedding day and marriage was pure joy. Obviously, I didn't need a Thesaurus to think of adjectives. I wanted to go on and on.

And sometimes I did! My friend would have to say, "Uh, Joni, don't you think you've talked enough about Ken's muscles?" Or, "Joni, that's the fourth time in this chapter you've told us how handsome Ken is."

Isn't that funny? I just couldn't say enough good stuff about my husband.

I'll bet it's the same with those you love, too. You want others to know how special that person is—whether it's your mate, your friend, your child, your niece, your nephew, or your grandchild. The best part is finding someone genuinely interested in *listening* to your glowing descriptions. It actually multiplies your pleasure.

Listen in as the author of Hebrews talks about his best Friend, Jesus. It's as if someone had approached him and said, "You seem to put a great deal of stock in this Person, Jesus Christ. Just who is He, anyway? Why are you so excited about Him? Can you describe Him?"

Could he ever! Finding a listening ear, the writer can't say enough. Look at the seven descriptive phrases he uses in the first four verses of his book.

Jumping right in, the writer tells us Jesus is the *appointed heir of all things*. Right off the top He lifts Jesus to where He belongs—over all things.

But that's only the beginning. Next the writer reminds us that through the spoken word of Jesus the universe was created.

Warming to his subject, the author declares that Jesus is the very *radiance of God's glory*. Just as the brilliance of the sun cannot be separated from the sun itself, Jesus cannot be separated from the glory of the Father—He is God Himself.

Not only does Jesus share in the glory of God, He is *an exact representation of God's being*. Like a stamp that leaves its impression on warm wax, Jesus is the exact representation of the character and nature of God.

The writer can't stop. Superlatives keep pouring from his pen. He affirms that this mighty Son of God is *sustaining all things by His powerful word*. He created the world by the word of His mouth, and now He holds it all together.

But Jesus Christ is more than some awesome, distant Deity, the writer hastens to add. He took notice of our helpless plight and became our Savior. *He provided purification for sins* through the sacrifice of His life on the cross. By His death, Christ paid the incalculable penalty for our sins and satisfied every just demand of a holy God.

His work of redemption complete, Jesus *sat down at the right hand of the Majesty in heaven*.

With the ink flowing fast on his parchment, the writer goes on and on. Chapter one, chapter two, chapter three, chapter four . . . Jesus, Jesus, Jesus, Jesus.

How is it with you? Are you looking for listening ears, anxious to go on and on about the Lord Jesus and what He means to you?

If you find you don't have enough adjectives to describe Him, I'd like to introduce you to the author of Hebrews. Sorry I can't give you his name, but he got so excited about his Subject he forgot to introduce himself. Maybe the two of you can get away together for a few minutes today.

There's nothing that excited writer would love more than a listening ear.

STRONGHOLD

This evening just before bed, brew yourself a cup of tea, find a quiet corner and curl up with today's reading and your Bible. Take fifteen minutes to slowly meditate on these descriptions of Jesus, thanking Him for who He is . . . in your own words.

A Star . . . Numbers 24:17
Man of Sorrows . . . Isaiah 53:3
The Ancient of Days . . . Daniel 7:9
Servant . . . Matthew 12:18
The Holy One of God . . . Mark 1:24
Dayspring . . . Luke 1:78
Teacher . . . John 3:2
I Am . . . John 8:58
Rock . . . 1 Corinthians 10:4
The Indescribable Gift . . . 2 Corinthians 9:15
Chief Cornerstone . . . Ephesians 2:20
Our Hope . . . 1 Timothy 1:1.
The Man . . . 1 Timothy 2:5-6
Heir of All Things . . . Hebrews 1:2

Your First Response

Since my hands don't work, typing always involves a team effort here at Joni and Friends. When Francie and I sit down at the computer, her fingers can barely keep up with my thoughts as they come. I talk, she types. In fact, that's exactly the way I've written this book.

This morning we were really humming. For some reason, the ideas seemed to flow with ease. The right Scriptures were on the tip of my tongue. Phrases fell into place like jigsaw pieces. It all came together. I was so delighted with the results that I immediately asked Francie to print out a hard copy of our labors. Which button should she push, Francie wondered. *That* one, I assured her.

Then—in an instant—*ffzzzzt!* The wrong key! All of our morning's work blipped into the twilight zone. Gone! Irretrievable!

I bit my lip. I felt like complaining loudly and bitterly. But instead of committing myself to a bunch of words I might regret, I simply screamed. In fact, we both looked at each other and screamed!

Screaming might not reflect your particular personality, but if you'd like to try an enlightening experiment, I have an idea for you. The next time you unexpectedly come up against an unpleasant surprise, irritation, or frustration, try to make a mental note of all the exclamations or expletives that came out of your mouth. I did that last week and was surprised at how quick I was to voice my complaint. Nothing vile or off-color, you understand—that's not my background. But every time something went awry, it seemed as though I had to say *something*, some expression of disgust or frustration.

Try it sometime. Like me, you may be very surprised at your first reaction to prickly problems.

I thought of that recently as I was reading in the book of Acts. Peter and John had been thrown into prison. Nothing unusual about that. Just like we get pelted with hardships, getting jailed became one of those everyday annoyances to the apostles.

The next day they were hauled before Israel's religious and political hierarchy and severely reprimanded. They were told that any further teaching in the name of Jesus would mean harsh repercussions. The authorities meant it. This was the same group that had Jesus crucified.

What then, was the church's response when Peter and John returned to the fellowship and reported all these things? Acts 4:24 records the first comments out of their mouths:

"Sovereign Lord," they said, "you made the heaven and the earth and the sea, and everything in them" (NIV).

Sovereign Lord, we hear them say. Not "Oh no" or "Oh darn" or "I can't believe it" or "Why us?" We don't hear them say anything of the kind. Instead, we hear them exclaim the joy of their conviction—that God was in control, that God was sovereign, that there was a plan and a purpose and all they had to do was acknowledge that wonderful truth.

In short, they worshiped.

In verse 28 they went on to acknowledge that the authorities had only done what God's "power and will had decided beforehand should happen." They ended their prayer with a plea for confidence and boldness to faithfully proclaim the message of Christ.

Be honest. How many times in this past week have words like that come out of your mouth? Or out of my mouth, for that matter. You're busily making last-minute preparations for dinner, juggling plates and catsup bottles and salt and pepper on the way to the table—and the phone decides to start ringing off the hook. Or you take your super shortcut to work with no time to spare only to run into a terminal traffic jam.

Well, a word to the wise. No matter how irritating the moment, or maddening the circumstance, whatever the problem, we need to learn to bridle our tongues and *think* before we speak. Those first words out of our mouths really do say something about the way we handle trials.

Let's let our apostle friends, Peter and John, set the tone for the rest of our week. When you get up on the wrong side of the bed, choose the wrong route to work, or push the wrong button, be ready with a word of worship.

Sovereign Lord, do whatever You like. You are in control. Grant me the courage to bear up and speak Your name with confidence.

STRONGHOLD

Let's be real. Do not-so-nice words trip off your tongue when your day goes haywire? For that matter, are there other quirky things you do when frustrated—slam your fist, hit a wall, or bang your steering wheel?

Take a look at Daniel 6:6-12 for a glimpse at a man whose first response always seemed to be the right response. When Daniel got wind of the awful decree, what was the very first thing he did? Notice verse 10 and the fact that Daniel prayed in full view of the town. What do you think was on his mind?

Make an exchange! Trade those not-so-nice words and actions for words of thanks and actions of obedience.

What Ever Happened to Palm Wednesday?

They brought the donkey and the colt, and put their cloaks on them, and Jesus took his seat upon them. Then a vast crowd spread their cloaks on the road, while others cut down branches from the trees and spread them in his path. The crowds who went in front of him and the crowds who followed behind him all shouted, "God save the Son of David! Blessed is the man who comes in the name of the Lord! God save him from on high!" (Matthew 21:7-9, Phillips).

Shouting their joyful hosannas, the people shared their expectation of Jesus as the coming King. This was the one who would throw the Roman oppressor out of the Holy City. He would release them from the terrible burden of taxes. He would feed them, provide for and protect them, and give them national dignity once again.

But as the week wore on, the mood of the crowd changed.

Why wasn't the Nazarene making His move? Sure, He continued to heal and teach in the temple. But He remained aloof and reclusive, retreating to a nearby village every night, spending time with His disciples outside the city walls. When was He going to *do* something? When was He going to take control? Why wasn't He spending time with the "right" people—the savvy political types who got things done?

Little wonder the mood of the people soured by midweek. "Maybe this Man's not all He's cracked up to be," they may have reasoned. "Maybe He's been pulling the wool over our eyes all this time. He's probably powerless to do any real good around here."

The rest is history. The crowds turned on Him and screamed for His crucifixion—not more than a week after they had celebrated His entry into the city.

I wonder . . . are we all that different from those people?

When expectations are running high, when we think we've got God's plan neatly figured, when we've convinced ourselves that the King's job is to make our lives easier, relieve our burdens, and take away our everyday pressures . . . don't you think our praises may sound a bit empty?

What happens when the shouts of Palm Sunday fade into Blue Monday? What happens when we hit mid-week and all our plans have splintered like a ship's hull on a reef? Can we still sing our hosannas? Or do we turn on God in bitterness or resentment because He didn't follow through on our list of expectations?

Let's be sure we give Jesus praise for who He is . . . not what we think He ought to be.

STRONGHOLD

Psalm 103 is a great psalm to use when you want to praise God for exactly who He is. Notice how the psalm begins and ends. Ask God right now to help you praise Him from your innermost being.

Next, personalize verses 2 through 5. Slowly and thoughtfully consider His benefits toward you—how He has forgiven your sins, healed you when you were sick, and lifted you when you were at your lowest.

Decide right now to keep Psalm 103 handy and ready for when Blue Monday, Wednesday, or Thursday comes along.

Let Down Your Net

It was one of those dry times.

The Bible seemed about as inspiring as the Los Angeles phone book. Prayer felt like an exercise in futility. My prayers never seemed to make it more than two or three feet into the air. I would have been happy to get them as high as the ceiling.

My Christian friends kept going on and on about all they were learning and how they were growing and what God was telling them and *wasn't the Lord wonderful?* I felt little interest in spiritual things. Faking it made me feel even more guilty.

The hardest part was that I couldn't trace the dry spell to anything specific. No besetting sins. No fights with my husband. No roots of bitterness. No great lapses in my prayer life or Bible study. No lack of fellowship.

Yet my spirit felt as arid as July in the Mojave Desert. It was like those times when your smile loses its shine, your soul becomes dim, and your countenance tells you and everyone around you that something's not quite right.

Strange as it sounds, the closest biblical analogy I can find for those dry days takes place in the middle of a lake. Let's pick up the story in Luke chapter five.

[Jesus] went aboard one of the boats, which belonged to Simon, and asked him to push out a little from the shore.

Then he sat down and continued his teaching of the crowds from the boat.

When he had finished speaking, he said to Simon, "Push out now into deep water and let down your nets for a catch."

Simon replied, "Master! We've worked all night and never caught a thing, but if you say so, I'll let the nets down."

And when they had done this, they caught an enormous shoal of fish—so big that the nets began to tear. So they signaled to their partners in the other boat to come and help them. They came and filled both the boats to the sinking point (vv. 3-8).

That's a story for dry times—when you feel a little tired of trying . . . when you're a little weary of praying prayers that don't seem to get answered . . . when the pages of the Bible might as well be written in Egyptian hieroglyphics.

Simon, too, was weary. Tired of trying. His back ached and his eyelids drooped. He'd been at it all night long without so much as a sardine to show for it. Yet at the command of Christ, he let down his nets. One more time.

Perhaps all of your nets are empty today. You've tried and tried but come up with nothing. You feel dry and dull, and wonder if God has misplaced your file somewhere on His desk.

He hasn't! God has been listening to your prayers. As a matter of fact, it's often those petitions offered in the dry times that please Him best.

Your heavy heart is no secret to the God who loves you. As David wrote: "All my longings lie open before you, O LORD; my sighing is not hidden from you" (Psalm 38:9, NIV).

He's asking you today to let down your net. One more time. Even though you haven't seen amazing results in recent weeks. Even though your emotions say, "What's the use?" Even though running an uphill marathon seems more appealing than seeking the Lord right now . . . . nevertheless, obey the word of Christ and let down your net. Keep in the Word. Return to prayer. Confess your sin. Get accountable to a Christian friend. Worship with God's people. Sooner or later, He'll surprise you just like He surprised Simon Peter. He's going to bring you out of that long night—out of that dryness. You're going to experience His joy . . . more than you can handle.

Be faithful. Trust Him. Wait.

Jesus can still fill an empty net.

STRONGHOLD

Have you ever seen a dry, barren desert suddenly spring to vibrant life after a rain shower? You wouldn't believe how drastic and miraculous the change can be. That's exactly how the Spirit of Christ can revive us out of a dry spell. Suddenly. Unexpectedly. Gloriously.

For a good word picture, read Isaiah 35:1-7. That portion of Scripture is talking about the return of the Lord Jesus, but the beautiful descriptions can also apply to you today.

For extra encouragment, underline verses 3 and 4!

High Stakes Attitudes

Let's talk about a few facts of life.

Tires have blowouts, computers pop circuits, toddlers get colds, and picnics invite rain. If that isn't enough, somebody gets a promotion ahead of us, a baby-sitting arrangement falls through, a long-planned vacation gets canceled at the last minute, we don't make the team at school, and the heartthrob we're interested in dating is "busy" on four consecutive weekends.

Some things simply can't be avoided.

Now, we aren't always responsible for the circumstances in which we find ourselves. When things happen they just happen, and many times there is little we can do about it.

But before we think we're totally absolved from any responsibility in a difficult circumstance, let's look at one additional fact of life: We *are* responsible for the way we *respond* to those everyday setbacks. We can either choose to indulge ourselves in depression, backbiting, or bitterness . . . or we can choose to look to our Sovereign God who has everything under control.

You see, we are not without choices!

I'm impressed with the way the apostle Paul assumed responsibility in his attitude toward trials. In the midst of an undeserved prison sentence and in the face of an uncertain future, he told a group of his friends, "I want you to know, brothers, that what has happened to me has really served to advance the gospel" (Philippians 1:12, NIV).

Paul must have realized that he had very little control over many of the devastating circumstances of his life. He couldn't have avoided the shipwrecks. He had no control over the phony apostles who were jealous of him and tried to slander his reputation. He never asked to be dropped unceremoniously over the city wall in a basket. Nor did he enlist the services of a demon-possessed girl to follow him around Philippi shouting obscenities. And when he answered people's direct questions, could he help it if the truth made them angry?

Yet Paul realized that his reaction to negative circumstances was serious business. How he responded could either advance Christ's gospel or set it back. In other words, *there was much more at stake than simply Paul's life*. Other lives would be influenced by his godly response to trials. The reputation of the gospel was at stake. Angels were watching. God was taking notice.

Now, I'm not in prison like Paul. No guard stands outside my bedroom door. There are no chains dangling from my wrists or manacles biting into my ankles. But I do have a wheelchair and, like Paul, I can't claim direct responsibility for this particular circumstance.

But I am responsible. I will be held accountable for my response. Like Paul, I'm learning to rejoice in suffering . . . simply because this wheelchair, much like those chains, is being used to advance God's cause.

No, you may not be responsible for that irritating phone call from your neighbor, or for the fact that your husband is going to be home late from work, or that your wife can't seem to balance the checkbook—but you are responsible for your response, and you will be held accountable by the living God for the choices you make.

If you keep a good attitude in the tough times today, it will, in effect, turn out for the advantage of the gospel. As others see, as your husband takes notice, as your children observe, as your neighbors look on, as you speak out with boldness and humility—you will advance God's cause.

There's so much more at stake here than simply your own life. Others can be influenced to make eternal decisions. The gospel has a reputation. Angels are observing.

So is God.

STRONGHOLD

Sometimes we demonstrate better responsibility for our attitude when we enlist the help of others. Ask a trusted friend to hold you accountable, to help you make the right choices. Ask your friend to nail you when he or she observes you handling a certain tough time with a complaining or grumbling spirit.

Feel uncomfortable with the idea? If so, remember this— Someone far greater than your friend is watching.

CHAPTER 92

If You Can Glorify God in This . . .

You hear mothers say it all the time.

Their kids want to stay home, complaining of cramps or a headache, but as soon as the school bus leaves the corner, they bound out of bed, pull the games off the shelf, flip on the TV, or run downstairs to raid the fridge.

And what do moms all over this country say?

"If you're well enough to do *that*, then you're well enough to go to school."

I heard a similar line while dieting a few months ago. At a friend's house, I turned down a luscious-looking piece of walnut cake topped with whipped cream icing, sprinkled with nuts.

My friend regarded me for a moment. "If you can turn down *this*," she said, "then you can turn down anything."

Maybe you've said something similar as a student . . . taking way too many units for your own good—and working nights to boot. As the pressure builds, the midnight oil burns, and finals loom, you hear yourself say, "If I can make it through *this* semester, I can make it through anything!"

You can almost hear God say the same thing to us . . .

. . . as we wade through crushing disappointments

. . . or battle a confusing family problem

*. . . or grit our teeth and learn contentment in the middle
of a painful illness*

. . . or tearfully accept the sudden loss of a loved one.

We might at first think it curious that God so often uses suffering to make our lives "to the praise of His glory," as it says in Ephesians. I mean, aren't there better ways we can glorify God—or at least easier ones?

But do you know what God says to us?

"If you can praise and glorify Me in *this* circumstance, My child, you can glorify Me in anything."

In other words, whenever a Christian is found faithful in affliction, repaying good for evil, returning love for abuse, holding steadfast through suffering, or loving in the middle of loneliness or grief . . . the Lord receives the truest, brightest, most radiant kind of glory possible.

And if we can be found glorifying Him in that manner, God will open up all kinds of new opportunities, new circumstances in which to glorify Him. He'll do so because He knows we can be trusted, we can handle it with His grace.

Maybe today you just can't see glory to God issuing forth from your response to trials. The dishes are piling up, your friend continues to misunderstand you, you haven't had a restful weekend in a month of Sundays, and your painful arthritis just won't be eased.

Let me tell you something. If you can glorify God through a patient response right now—in the middle of those things—then you can glorify God anywhere.

Kind of puts you on the victory side doesn't it?

STRONGHOLD

The Westminster Shorter Catechism says, "Man's chief end is to glorify God and to enjoy Him forever." Giving God glory no matter what our circumstances—ordinary or extraordinary—has to be top priority.

Sometimes we need a sharp reminder from Scripture to help us do that. Take a look at 1 Corinthians 10:31. Eating and drinking—very average, ordinary circumstances—remind us that all of our average, daily routines can be opportunities to give God glory. Think of five everyday responsibilities and decide how you can give God glory through each one.

Reflections in the Furnace

The only thing that caught fire were the ropes that bound their hands and feet.

Free of their restraints, Shadrach, Meshach, and Abednego seemed content to walk about in the great fiery furnace of Babylon. And no wonder. They were not alone.

Then King Nebuchadnezzar leaped to his feet in amazement and asked his advisers, "Weren't there three men that we tied up and threw into the fire? . . . Look, I see four men walking around in the fire, unbound and unharmed, and the fourth looks like a son of the gods (Daniel 3:24,25, NIV).

The king, who had ordered the servants of God thrown into the fire for refusing to worship his golden image, stood as close as he dared to the mouth of the furnace and shouted to them.

"Shadrach, Meshach and Abednego, servants of the Most High God, come out! Come here!"

So Shadrach, Meshach and Abednego came out of the fire . . . The fire had not harmed their bodies, nor was a hair of their heads singed; their robes were not scorched, and their was no smell of fire on them (3:26,27).

Not only were the three young men free from burns or injuries, they didn't even smell like smoke!

At one time or another, all of us have felt the flames of the refiner's fire. It's the one experience we all share in common. No matter how we balk at the idea, God has promised to refine His children.

> *I will bring [them] into the fire;*
> *I will refine them like silver*
> *and test them like gold.*
> *They will call on my name*
> *and I will answer them*
> (Zechariah 13:9, NIV).

To refine, says Webster, is "to make fine or pure; free from impurities, dross, alloy, or sediment . . . to free from imperfection, coarseness, crudeness, etc." A refiner's fire, of course, is supposed to improve whatever commodity goes into it. Look at your gold wedding band, or maybe that gold chain around your neck. After all these years, it still gleams. It still wears well. It has the luster and richness pressed into it long ago when it went through the refining flames.

Look at your best silver, your flatware that you got when you were married, those silver bowls and trays tucked away in your china cupboard. You pull them down once in a blue moon, yet they glow with that soft shine even after many years.

The refining process is supposed to turn out things all the more beautiful, all the more durable.

But how many of us go through the refiner's fire and come out the other end looking like . . . charcoal? Or rusty iron. Or smoking ashes. We may be like the Pharisees of old who wore long faces and rumpled clothes when they fasted. Often when we come through a period of suffering, we want to make sure that everybody knows all the sad and sordid details. The thing of beauty that God wanted to create by sending us into the flames becomes tarnished by our complaints and woebegone expressions.

Be honest. If you've had one of those days where you feel like you've been dragged through the refiner's fire, how do you show it?

By taking a casual greeting like "How are you doing?" as an excuse to list every minor and major casualty of your day?

By using your prayer group time as an excuse to gripe or gossip?

By painting a picture of your marriage that colors your spouse as the culprit and you as the hero?

By living like a martyr . . . and making sure everybody knows it?

If you do, I'm afraid people are going to smell smoke. Your testimony may end up tarnished. Even scorched.

There's a better way. Let's offer sincere, wholehearted praise to God as we walk through the refiner's fire. Perhaps those who pause to peer into our furnace will see the Son of God walking with us.

STRONGHOLD

Take a look at 1 Peter 1:6-9. According to Peter, exactly why does God permit trials to come our way? Just how precious is your faith?

It will help you to know that Peter was writing to Christians who *really* were being tested by fire. They lived under the reign of the madman Nero and refused to worship him. As a result, believers had to face lions in the coliseum, not to mention everyday abuse and maltreatment. Theirs was a genuine test of faith. Yet history records that many of these early believers remained undaunted in their testimony. Their faith was neither scorched nor tarnished by complaints. They shined for God.

How can their gleaming example encourage you today?

CHAPTER 94

The Sound of a Cry

Nobody is as in touch, in tune with our heart's longings as God.

In Psalm 5, David opens his prayer by saying, "Give ear to my words, O LORD. Consider my groaning. Heed the sound of my cry . . ."

Up to his ears in trouble, his heart pounding in fear, David wants God to hear the *sound* of his cry.

Does that ring a bell with any of you mothers? Your baby is nestled in his crib upstairs and suddenly you hear him cry. After a moment of listening, you know what that child wants by simply interpreting the *sound* of his crying. You can tell whether he's just tired and grumpy—or if he's waking up and wants you to come running. You can tell if he's afraid, lonesome, or actually in pain. Mothers learn to heed—and read— the voice of crying. They know what their child wants simply by the sound of his voice.

God is like that. When we pray, He knows just what our need is—even if we can't shape the words. He can tell if it's an urgent prayer for help, a sighing prayer of discouragement, or maybe just a deep-down groan that we only half understand ourselves. Much like a mother with a child, God heeds and pays special attention to the voice of our cry.

He also listens for our praise.

Just as that mom is deeply moved by the cry of her child, she is overjoyed with the sound of his laughter. A smile, a gurgle, and a squeal delight a mother. And as that child grows, it means even more to hear him say, "Mom, you're something special . . . you're the neatest mom on the whole block."

That mother may receive the "Mother-of-the-Year" award from the local Jaycees, or be voted Den Mother par excellence by the Cub Scouts Council, but it will all pale in comparison to the spontaneous praise of her own son.

Wouldn't you think our praise to God would delight Him all the more? If God heeds the sound of our cry, it makes sense that He also delights in the sound of our praise.

What about taking time out today to go before your Lord? Invite Him to read your heart, those secret pages no one has ever turned. Let Him hear the voice of your cry, all of those deep, inexpressible fears and longings. It doesn't have to involve a lot of words or carefully constructed phrases. Your time with the Lord can just be a quiet pause in the day, perhaps even a time of silence. God knows that voice of yours. Just like a mother, He knows exactly what you need when you cry to Him.

STRONGHOLD

Take a stroll down memory lane and pull out an old family photo album. Let your eyes linger over each snapshot of mom, dad, children, aunts, and cousins—hugging, smiling, and laughing. Reach back in your mind and recall the most meaningful times you've enjoyed with family—that picnic in the park, the family softball game, a special anniversary or memorable birthday party.

Feels nice, doesn't it?

Now—transfer some of those warm, family feelings to your relationship with your heavenly Father. Imagine for a moment His joy when He hears your praise. Think of how instant He is in responding to your cry.

While the smiles and laughter are still dancing in your mind, talk with Him now—straight from the heart.

The Groaning of the Spirit

Immediately after church, a young woman with cerebral palsy approached me in her wheelchair.

CP is usually characterized by paralysis, weakness, or loss of coordination due to brain damage. Sometimes there are uncontrolled movements and slurred speech. This woman's speaking was especially difficult to grasp. She kept groaning a certain sentence over and over again. Even though I patiently asked her to repeat each word one by one, I still couldn't understand. The expression on her face gave me no clues at all. I couldn't tell if she was in terrible trouble or was simply trying to relay some profound experience.

Finally, after many attempts, I was able to piece her sentence together. She was asking me to help her find someone who could assist her into the restroom!

It was a simple request. But I felt helpless, so inadequate that it had taken me so long to understand her. Once it dawned on me what she was requesting, I moved quickly to get her help!

Can you imagine the hardship of not even being able to make your needs known? Wouldn't it be sad if there was no one around who could even understand you?

Ah, and yet that is the very predicament you and I find ourselves in. Listen to the words of Paul:

> *In the same way, the Spirit helps us in our weakness. We do not know what we ought to pray, but the Spirit himself*

*intercedes for us with groans that words cannot express.
And he who searches our hearts knows the mind of the
Spirit, because the Spirit intercedes for the saints in ac-
cordance with God's will* (Romans 8:26-27, NIV).

There are times when we want to talk to God . . . but
somehow can't manage it. The hurt goes too deep. Fear locks
our thoughts. Confusion scatters our words. Depression
grips our emotions.

I'm so glad God can read my heart and understand
what's going on even when I am handicapped by my own
weakness for words. As it says in Hebrews 4:13, "Nothing . . .
is hidden from God's sight. Everything is uncovered and laid
bare before the eyes of him to whom we must give account."

Words are not always necessary. When we are in such
trouble that we can't even find words—when we can only
look toward heaven and groan in our spirit—isn't it good to
remember that God knows exactly what's happening? The
faintest whisper in our hearts is known to God. Even if it
should be a sigh so faint that you are not even aware of it
yourself, He has heard it. And not only heard it, but He *understands* it—right down to the slightest quiver registered in
our innermost being.

You and I may certainly be handicapped when it comes
to understanding the groans and sighs of one another. And
others— even those closest to us—may never be able to hear
or interpret our deepest sorrows and longings.

But the One who searches hearts knows and understands. The Spirit is never handicapped by our weakness for
words.

Our heavenward groans have a voice before God.

STRONGHOLD

Aren't you glad the Holy Spirit wraps words around your feelings—especially when you don't seem to have words to pray?

Sometimes it's helpful to borrow the Spirit-inspired words of someone from Scripture when you pray. I'm sure Solomon, who incidentally never seemed at a loss for words, would not mind loaning you his prayer recorded in 1 Kings 8:56-61. Personalize it and make it your prayer to God.

CHAPTER 96

What Makes Heaven "Home?"

*The city was laid out like a square, as long as it was wide
. . . The wall was made of jasper, and the city of pure
gold, as pure as glass. The foundations of the city walls
were decorated with every kind of precious stone . . . The
twelve gates were twelve pearls, each gate made of a
single pearl. The street of the city was of pure gold, like
transparent glass . . . Then the angel showed me the river
of the water of life, as clear as crystal, flowing from the
throne of God and of the Lamb down the middle of the
great street of the city . . .* (Revelation 21:16, 18, 19,
21; 22:1, 2, NIV).

Reading the descriptions of heaven and the New
Jerusalem in the Bible gives us an incredible picture. All
sorts of word pictures describe the beauty and majesty of
that place . . . streets of translucent gold, gates made of precious stone, a throne from which flows a river, walls made of
brightly colored gems.

Sounds fantastic, doesn't it? For most of us, a place like
that is hard to even imagine.

Now, I do like to think about heaven, but rarely in those
terms. Oh sure, I know Jesus says in John 14 He has gone on
ahead to prepare a place for us, and each of us is to have
some sort of mansion—no down payment or mortgage to
worry about, thankfully—on a golden avenue.

When I think of heaven as a *home*, however, I hardly
ever think about mansions or glittery streets. If heaven re-

ally is our long-awaited dwelling, what draws us to that place if it's not gates and domes, spires and gleaming gold walls? For that matter, what makes any house a home? It's not necessarily its shape or size or furniture, is it? When we think of our earthly home, we don't usually think about the four walls. *What makes home is not what a place looks like, but who lives there.*

As far as I'm concerned, that's what makes heaven so appealing. It's no longer a bunch of word pictures describing rainbow thrones and 24-karat asphalt. It's a place where *people* live—and wonderful people, at that. Friends of mine who have left this earth. Relatives who have long since gone to be with the Lord. Add to that the countless saints of the ages like Moses and David, Joshua and Daniel, Naomi and Ruth, Paul and Peter, and even saints in our own age—Amy Carmichael or Corrie Ten Boom—people who have inspired my walk in the Lord.

I can't wait to meet them.

On top of that long list of people is Jesus Christ Himself. And the Father. And the Holy Spirit.

Certainly, heaven is a prepared place. But more importantly, it's a place for prepared people. People who will not only enjoy fellowship with one another, but with our great Creator and Savior.

If you find it difficult to muster up longing for those celestial mansions and glimmering vistas, try taking your focus off heaven as a *place*. Put your focus on heaven as a home . . . a home for people like you, who love the Lord Jesus.

STRONGHOLD

Are you one of those "prepared people"?

Heartaches and hardships down here on earth have a way of preparing us to meet God when we arrive in heaven. When we meet Jesus face to face, our hardships will have given us at least a *tiny* taste of what He went through to purchase our redemption. We will appreciate Him so much more. After all, what proof could you bring of your love and faithfulness if this life left you totally unscarred? How could you appreciate at all the scarred hands with which Christ will greet you?

Get better prepared today by spending a few moments alone with Colossians 3:1-4.

Praying in His Name

Handicapped people are puzzled, and I can't say I blame them.

One pastor tells them faith healing is theirs to "claim." Another insists divine healing is theirs only if God sees fit. Cassette sermons urge "emotional healing" and Christian magazine articles describe "spiritual healing." *No wonder* they're puzzled.

A Heinz-57-variety of theological "answers" on the subject of healing appear in books, seminars, tapes, and on Christian television and radio. The mail we receive at Joni and Friends is full of questions, perplexity, and outright frustration.

I had to see for myself, so I flicked on Sunday evening television last week. Sure enough, the clergyman at the microphone was expounding that God WANTS you well, so you CAN and SHOULD be well.

I just wish that TV preacher could visit our office, sit quietly for a few hours, and read some of the letters we receive from disabled people who have viewed his program. After years of praying, these people have nearly had their faith shipwrecked by the "health-wealth" way of looking at their problems.

When I was first paralyzed, you can imagine how interested I was in what the Bible had to say about healing. I desperately wanted out of my wheelchair!

As I pored over Scripture, I was impressed with the kind of healing that Jesus performed. He never seemed to pass up anybody. He showed His concern for the suffering by opening the eyes of the blind and the ears of the deaf— and even raising up the paralyzed.

I was also struck with the number of Bible verses that seemed to indicate I could ask whatever would be in God's will— and Jesus would do it. I put two and two together and figured if Jesus healed back then, He'd want to raise me up now. Why shouldn't He? Why shouldn't healing a suffering teenaged girl be perfectly consistent with His will?

I clung to John 16:23-24 with all my might:

My Father will give you whatever you ask in my name. Until now you have not asked for anything in my name. Ask and you will receive, and your joy will be complete (NIV).

Well, I asked.

To make a long story very short, I never got healed. At least . . . not the sort of healing I was after. It was years later that I began to catch a glimpse of all that a verse like John 16:23 might mean.

What does it mean to pray in Jesus' name? I've come to understand it means to pray in a manner consistent with Christ's character, or life.

If you think about it, the life of Christ sets quite an example for the kinds of requests we might include in our prayers.

Jesus' reputation was mocked and slandered . . . but we might assume that a pure and polished reputation is obviously God's will.

Jesus never had a real home, a place to lay His head . . . but we're convinced it's God's will that we have that new house down the street.

Jesus was a man of sorrows and acquainted with grief . . . yet there was a time when I thought words like *suffering* and *disappointment* shouldn't even be in the Christian's vocabulary.

Do you see what I'm saying? When we pray in Jesus' name, we should expect to receive qualities consistent with that name—with His character. Traits such as patience and self-control and assurance. We might pray for financial prosperity, a new career, success with the opposite sex, or physical healing, but God may choose to give us something even more precious, something even closer to what His name and character are all about.

His presence. His perspective. His endurance. His deep and lingering peace in the midst of turmoil and pain and loneliness and disappointment.

Will God give us health and a clear reputation? Friends who won't turn their backs on us? A new job? A mate? Perhaps. But then again, God may give us just what John 16:23 says He will give.

Joy. Joy that we might be complete . . . whatever our circumstances.

STRONGHOLD

Do you and I really appreciate the power behind those few precious words . . . in Jesus' name? Do we understand the broad and sweeping access we have before the Father?

When the Lord invited His followers to go to the Father in His name, He was talking about a brand new relationship between the believer and God. Previously, men and women approached God with caution and great fear through the priests. But since the resurrection of Jesus, all believers can talk to God personally . . . directly . . . any time we want!

To get a clearer idea of what it means to go to God "in Jesus' name," take a close look at Hebrews 10:19-23. Then tonight, as you lay your head on your pillow after your nightly prayer, take a moment to reflect on the marvelous access you enjoy before the Father.

CHAPTER 98

Thoughts By the Spring

When I was a child on our family's farm, one of my favorite places was the pond down in the pasture by the barn. It was filled with tadpoles, crayfish, and—oh, all kinds of attractions for an adventurous little girl on a hot summer afternoon.

As a child, I always wondered where the water in the pond came from. I'd walk all the way around its edge but could never see any stream splashing into it. No waterfall. No pipes. What was flowing into the pond to make it so fresh and clear and full?

My dad patiently tried to explain that the pond was fed by a spring, a source of water from deep down in the earth. That spring, he told me, bubbled up from within and filled the little pond area.

To me it was a big mystery. But I was satisfied with the answer and went contentedly on my way, playing with the frogs and crayfish.

I don't know how many times that little spring has come to my mind through the years . . . especially when I think about the Holy Spirit.

Let me explain.

We've all heard people say we should be "filled with the Holy Spirit." Now, that's good, biblical counsel. Ephesians 5:18 says, "Do not get drunk on wine, which leads to debauchery. Instead, be filled with the Spirit" (NIV).

What kind of image does that create in your mind? How many of us picture the Spirit being poured into our lives from the *outside* . . . as if we were hollow mannequins? Just unscrew the cap on top of our heads, Lord, and fill us from the toes on up!

Do we get the idea that God's Spirit is being carried around in a massive pitcher, ready to be ladled out to us for the asking?

That thought reminds me of my old confusion about the farm pond. I kept looking for some stream pouring in. An outside source. Yet, when the Bible talks about us being filled with the Spirit, it's more accurate to picture a *spring*. When we obey God and yield our lives to Him, emptying ourselves of selfish desires, the Spirit of God is just like a spring bubbling up within us . . . from down deep in our souls. The Spirit source fills us and we are satisfied.

As Jesus said:

"He who believes in Me, as the Scripture said, 'From His innermost being shall flow rivers of living water.'" But this He spoke of the Spirit, whom those who believed in Him were to receive (John 7:38-39).

If Dad would have dug out a larger pond area in the dirt, that little spring would have continued to fill it. That might be good advice for you and me. If we would empty ourselves even further, letting go of our own rights, clearing out the debris of habitual sins, and humble ourselves further before the Lord, our *capacity* for God's Spirit would be increased.

He would fill us even more.

As our lives brim over from this ever-fresh wellspring within us, there will be plenty of refreshment for the thirsty souls of those around us.

STRONGHOLD

The word picture Jesus used in John 7:38-39 is almost startling. What does the term *river* or *stream* imply about the outflow of the Spirit's life from within us? How would you describe the outflow from your life? A stream? A trickle? Take time with your Lord today to clear out any obstructions or rubbish that might be hindering the spring from "bubbling up" within you.

CHAPTER 99

The Leaky Bucket

On the farm when we were kids, my sisters and I got involved in 4-H projects. One of those projects was raising calves. Oh boy, were they cute . . . I used to love to pet that silky, curly hair between their ears. It felt funny to get a nuzzle with a wet muzzle—and their tongues were like warm, wet sandpaper.

Feeding time was a chore—but we sure laughed a lot. My sister had a milk formula which she had to mix and pour into a bucket—a bucket with a big nipple on the bottom for the calf to suck on.

I remember one time when the only bucket I could find had a little hole in the bottom. The calf was bleating and crying for his dinner and there just wasn't another bucket around. There was no one to hop into the truck, drive to the feed store and pick up a new one. I looked into the woeful face of that little calf and decided the only thing I could use was the leaky bucket.

First, I made certain to mix a lot of extra formula. Then I poured the measured amount into the leaky feeding bucket. That little calf went for it and while he kept on drinking, I kept pouring in as much—if not more—formula as I saw dripping out from the bottom. The calf got his dinner . . . as long as I was certain to pour it in faster than it trickled out.

That memory replayed in my mind recently when I heard a pastor talking about being filled with the Spirit. He was describing the despondency of so many Christians he counsels. Believers who find themselves filled with the Spirit one day, and emptied out the next. They're frustrated, and tired of getting drained-and-filled, drained-and-filled.

Those Christians, I reasoned, are simply leaky buckets. Welcome to the club! *All of us* are like leaky buckets, simply because we're human. And this whole cycle of getting drained and then filled up can be tiring if we try and go it alone.

The answer? It's simple. Make sure you've got somebody (or perhaps a great many somebodies) pouring their love and counsel and prayers into you faster than you find it leaking out.

Fellowship. That's the solution. Brothers and sisters who will hold you accountable, study with you, sharpen you, and keep you on the straight path. Imperfect, "leaky" Christians who will pray for you as you pray for them.

Oh sure. You'll keep leaking . . . losing the zeal and fervor and excitement as you walk through life. Sorry, but this side of heaven that's inevitable. Just make sure you're part of a fellowship where you'll be filled up faster than you empty out. You might even find your "leaky" bucket overflowing into some of the empty buckets around you.

That's what being in the Body is all about.

STRONGHOLD

John Donne said, "No man is an island, entire of itself; every man is a piece of the continent, a part of the main." It's good to be linked with other believers, isn't it? Think of the many benefits you've received from your fellowship with other Christians.

But don't forget—you benefit others as well. Take time to fill up on the advice of Romans 15:1-7. Will you commit yourself anew to pouring your love and counsel and prayers into a fellow believer trapped in the drain-and-fill cycle?

A Better Joy

After this the Lord chose another seventy-two men and sent them out two by two, to go ahead of him to every town and place where he himself was about to go . . .

The seventy-two men came back in great joy. "Lord," they said, "even the demons obeyed us when we gave them a command in your name!" (Luke 10:1, 17, GNB).

Talk about a spiritual shot in the arm! They were the most exciting days any of the disciples could remember. A few months earlier they had been ordinary working guys, punching a time clock, carrying a lunch box, hassling the daily commute. But now . . . now they had been transformed into ambassadors of the Kingdom of God. Spiritual authority oozed from their pores. It was a heady experience, to say the least.

"Lord, You just wouldn't believe it!" they exulted. "Even the demons took off when we spoke in Your name! It was great!"

This discipleship business was suddenly very interesting. They saw answers to their prayers. They saw people come into the kingdom. They preached fearlessly, prayed fervently, and enjoyed a camaraderie they had never known before. It was like being away on a gigantic spiritual weekend retreat. *Everything* went right . . . even to the point of controlling the work of demons.

Now, understandably, Jesus was thrilled for them and their new-found joy. He responded with genuine enthusiasm to the success of their ministry. Luke 10:21 says that He was "filled with joy." He burst into prayer and thanked His Father, praising Him that these men had tasted life the way it should be lived.

Yet at the same time, without dampening the spirits of His men, the Lord gently brought fresh focus to their gathering.

> *Jesus answered them, "I saw Satan fall like lightning from heaven. Listen! I have given you authority, so that you can walk on snakes and scorpions and overcome all the power of the Enemy, and nothing will hurt you. But don't be glad because the evil spirits obey you; rather be glad because your names are written in heaven"* (Luke 10:18-20, GNB).

Can you identify with those seventy-two excited missionaries? Perhaps you've found yourself in a similar circumstance.

"Wow, what a great retreat that was!" you say to your friends. You've been away for a week of fellowship with a group of exuberant believers. You've sat under the instruction of a first-rate Christian communicator, and you come home a changed person. I mean, you've got joy! And that joy carries over for days, even weeks. Your prayers seem to have more energy, you pray more specifically, with more faith. You even share Christ courageously and fearlessly—you're so excited!

Have you had that happen? Can you recall that feeling of spiritual elation? You thought to yourself, "Oh, if we could only have it this way all of the time. If we could only have that speaker join our church. If we could only experience that sort of fellowship and prayer and excitement on a regular basis! Why does it have to end?"

I think the Lord would like to give us the same focus He gave to His disciples on that first, joyous day home from their journey. Don't let your joy depend on a lot of spiritual activities, highlights, and emotions. Don't let your gladness hinge on the next celestial lightning bolt or sun-splashed moment of meditation.

God wants our joy to rest on the simple fact that our names are written in heaven. There is no joy like the joy of our salvation! "Restore to me the joy of my salvation," was the first request David made of God after he got his spiritual act together.

If Jesus Christ is your Savior and Lord, there is an entry on an actual page of an actual book in the highest heaven with YOUR NAME on it!

If *that* isn't enough to make you shout for joy, then you'd better close your prayer closet door behind you and find out why.

STRONGHOLD

Take a look at your address book. There are probably big circles around the names of special people in your life. Now, take a glance at those names you've crossed out or erased. Have any idea where those people are or what they're doing?

Aren't you glad that God's Book of Life doesn't resemble your address book with all its splotched and smeared names? Want to know more about that Book of Life which includes your name? Turn to Revelation 20:11-15 and then praise God in your heart that He always uses permanent ink!

Have any doubt about that? For assurance, read Revelation 3:5.

Every Good Gift

Have you ever sat down with a pencil and pad to write out a "count your blessings" list? Maybe you've gotten as far as listing twenty items and thought you were done. After all, you had to stretch your thinking to be even *that* specific.

But there's more. So much more than we can possibly imagine. If we let the full impact of a verse like James 1:17 blow apart our old ideas about God's blessings, we'd see our list suddenly stretch past the horizon.

Listen . . .

Every good and perfect gift is from above, coming down from the Father of the heavenly lights.

Think about that! James is saying that every good time you have ever had in this world comes directly from God. (I mean *good* times—not sinful times.)

Can you think of the times you ever laughed and enjoyed yourself on an evening with friends? Can you remember the funny jokes?

Can you remember your first date? Well, maybe you'd like to *forget* the first date. How about your fifth date, when things got a bit more comfortable?

Can you recall the first time you won a game of Monopoly?

How about your first crack at water or snow skiing?

Or a special walk with a little child who loved you?

Or that evening with your family by the campfire?

Can you remember hearing some music that went right to your heart and brought goose bumps to your back or tears to your eyes?

The Bible says here that your Father is the origin of every joyful smile that has ever crossed your face.

How about God's provision of good food? Don't you just love the flavor of hot corn on the cob with lots of butter and salt and pepper? Or maybe a juicy hamburger with all the trimmings? God *could* have given us our nourishment with pills. But no, instead He chose to make food taste good.

And then there is color. The Creator didn't have to make a world in color. He could have wrapped it all in battleship gray. Think of all the beautiful sunsets—one every minute, all over the world. Picture the spongy green of spring-fresh grass or the pink of a hyacinth or crocus. In a recent news item about a middle-aged man who gained his sight after a lifetime of blindness, the awestruck man was quoted as saying, "I never imagined that yellow could be so—*yellow*."

Our God is the God of sunsets

. . . and hot buttered popcorn

. . . and red rosebuds

. . . and spring rain

. . . and Thanksgiving turkey

. . . and bear hugs from your best friend

. . . and freshly laundered towels

. . . and ice tea on a hot summer day

. . . and the laughter of a child.

Every good thing comes from the Father. Every single one. And more than that, those good things are *gifts*. Gifts to be received with heartfelt gratitude. As David wrote, "How precious to me are your thoughts, O God! How vast is the sum of them! Were I to count them, they would outnumber the grains of sand" (Psalm 139:17, 18, NIV).

All too often, though, you and I save our mental checklists for all the bad and discouraging things. We file away in our thinking all the times we've ever been disappointed, embarrassed, used, humiliated, or hurt. And soon we find ourselves irritated and complaining—clutched at the throat by an ungrateful spirit.

Even though our own pain might scream for our undivided attention, God wants us to come to Him with a heart full of thankfulness for all the good things in this life. Everything from the joy of a Christ-centered friendship to the first lick of a Baskin-Robbins pistachio ice cream cone.

Every good gift comes from the same Giver.

STRONGHOLD

"Count Your Blessings!" You've probably sung this old hymn (or heard it sung) scores of times. Whether at old-fashioned camp meetings or at Sunday evening services in a country church. Remember the tune? Maybe you haven't sung it for a while, but now is the time to sing it afresh. And remember . . . sing it with gusto. After all, you've got a lot of good gifts to thank God for!

When upon life's billows you are tempest tossed,
When you are discouraged, thinking all is lost,
Count your many blessings, name them one by one,
And it will surprise you what the Lord hath done.

Are you ever burdened with a load of care?
Does the cross seem heavy you are called to bear?
Count your many blessings, every doubt will fly,
And you will be singing as the days go by.

Count your blessings, name them one by one;
Count your blessings, see what God hath done;
Count your blessings, name them one by one;
Count your many blessings, see what God hath done.[7]

First Line Defense

By all rights it was a battle God's people should have never won.

The odds against King Jehoshaphat and his outnumbered troops were astronomical. Several neighboring military powers had banded together, determined to wipe the little nation of Judah off the map.

By the time Jehoshaphat got the bad news ("a vast army is coming against you from the other side of the Sea") there was very little he could do about it. The awesome force was less than thirty miles from Jerusalem's gates.

The frightened king took stock of what he had on hand. It wasn't much. He had no strategy, no chariots, no defense, no allies, no time, and no army worth writing home about.

But whether he knew it or not, he did have a secret weapon.

> Alarmed, Jehoshaphat resolved to inquire of the LORD, and he proclaimed a fast for all Judah. The people of Judah came together to seek help from the LORD; indeed, they came from every town in Judah to seek him . . . all the men of Judah, with their wives and children and little ones, stood there before the LORD (2 Chronicles 20:3, 4, 13, NIV).

The king poured his heart out before God and all the people. He didn't bluff or bluster. He didn't rattle his saber or make a patriotic speech. He just prayed as though his life depended on it—and it did.

> *O LORD, God of our fathers, are you not the God who is in heaven? You rule over all the kingdoms of the nations. Power and might are in your hand, and no one can withstand you . . . We have no power to face this vast army that is attacking us. We do not know what to do, but our eyes are upon you* (vv. 6, 12, NIV).

The enemy was a determined marching multitude, but Jehoshaphat's only armor was his faith in a prophet's message.

> *Do not be afraid or discouraged because of this vast army. For the battle is not yours, but God's . . . You will not have to fight this battle. Take up your positions; stand firm and see the deliverance the LORD will give you* (vv. 15, 17, NIV).

This was to be no usual battle. So the king didn't even pretend to follow accepted military procedure.

> *After consultation with the leaders of the people, [the king] determined that there should be a choir leading the march, clothed in sanctified garments and singing the song "His Lovingkindness Is Forever" as they walked along praising and thanking the LORD!* (v.21, TLB).

Talk about your out-of-the-ordinary weapon of warfare! Who ever heard of putting a choir out in front of an army? Harps and lyres leading the infantry instead of tanks and artillery? How could such a thing work? And yet work it did.

> *At the moment they began to sing and to praise, the Lord caused the armies of Ammon, Moab, and Mount Seir to begin fighting among themselves, and they destroyed each other! . . . When the army of Judah arrived at the watchtower that looks out over the wilderness, as far as*

they could look there were dead bodies lying on the ground—not a single one of the enemy had escaped (vv. 22, 24, TLB).

Now that marvelous story is more than just a historical event. It has meaning for you and me this very day. Like Jehoshaphat, we are surrounded by multitudes of enemies. Well trained and well equipped, the armies of Satan are experts at battling believers. And what one of us, in our own strength and with our meager personal resources, can withstand all those fiery darts?

How do we face such an overpowering enemy?

Ask Jehoshaphat. He would tell you that the answer is *praise to the Lord*. The demons hate it. Nominal Christians are irritated by it. But you and I need to learn to praise God in such a way that our enemy will be thrown into a complete rout. When we step out into spiritual warfare (which by the way, happens every day) we have the resources in Christ to totally confuse our foe.

We do it with our praise.

This is such a difficult lesson for me to learn. When things go haywire in my life, it's my second nature to *do* something—anything—to remedy, rectify, or resolve the problem. Make lists . . . set goals . . . get counseling . . . go shopping . . . raid the fridge . . . read a book on the subject . . . talk it out with others. Keeping busy seems like such a logical front-line defense against the devil's attacks.

But praise? What good can talking into thin air do? How is it that words pack enough power to thwart a determined adversary? Won't my enemies—discouragement and despondency—be better defeated by rolling up my sleeves, making fists, and meeting them head on?

Yet we learn from Jehoshaphat that praise must be our *first* line of defense.

Paul put it in a nutshell for the Corinthians:

For though we live in the world, we do not wage war as the world does. The weapons we fight with are not the weapons of the world (2 Corinthians 10:3-4, NIV).

All those legions lined up against us will turn on one another when they hear us lifting high the name of our mighty Lord Jesus.

You've got power over the enemy. Right now. It's praise.

STRONGHOLD

Wouldn't you like praise to be a bigger part of your daily routine? I know I would. Let me give you an idea that has helped me to praise God . . . from my heart.

Try memorizing, if you haven't already, the Doxology:
> *Praise God from whom all blessings flow;*
> *Praise Him all creatures here below;*
> *Praise Him above, ye heavenly host;*
> *Praise Father, Son, and Holy Ghost.*

Now, say it! Sing it in the shower as you start your day. Think about it while you're waiting in line . . . at the fast-food drive-in, the bank window, or the grocery store check-out. Say it at the dinner table to replace your usual blessing for the food. Finally, whisper it as you feel yourself drifting off to sleep at night.

CHAPTER 103

Thoughts on a Clear Day

The morning broke crisp and clear, electric with excitement. Several days had passed with hardly a problem . . . no inconveniences, no last-minute pressures, no disagreements with my husband. Nothing but clear sailing.

I was on my way to work, looking forward to digging into the day's duties. My painting was going well. I was in good health. I was caught up on all my correspondence. I felt great.

Right out loud in my van I exclaimed, "Oh, Lord, You're just so good! You're really a wonderful God." And I meant it. God is good—and wonderful beyond telling.

But . . . why is it that I am most *certain* of His goodness when things are going smoothly?

We get so excited about God when circumstances are delightful—when the weather invigorates us, when the bills are all paid, when the medical check-up went just fine, when no problems plague us and no hassles hound us. Praise at those times comes so easy.

But what if . . . ? What if the weather was miserable and the first call you answered in the morning was the collection agency? What if the medical check-up hadn't been positive?

Would praise swell in your heart and slide off your tongue just as easily? Probably not. But welcome to the club.

You and I are so prone to let our *circumstances*—whether good or bad—dictate our view of God. If things are great, then God is good. If we feel threatened or anxious, then God must be off somewhere—watching over the saints in Australia or answering some grandmother's prayer in Iceland.

Needless to say, it shouldn't be that way . . . and you and I know it. Time and time again the Bible tells us that God is faithful. The same good and steadfast Father yesterday, today, and forever.

Moses wanted there to be no doubt. "Know therefore that the LORD your God is God," he told his people. "*He is the faithful God*, keeping his covenant of love to a thousand generations of those who love him" (Deuteronomy 7:9, NIV).

The apostle John underlined the truth in a way we can never forget. "If we confess our sins, *he is faithful and just* and will forgive us our sins and purify us from all unrighteousness" (1 John 1:9, NIV).

The writer of Hebrews urges us to "hold unswervingly to the hope we profess, for *he who promised is faithful*" (Hebrews 10:23).

Psalm 146:6 assures us that the Lord remains *faithful forever*.

Paul signs off a letter to Thessalonica with the reminder that "*the one who calls you is faithful* and he will do it" (1 Thessalonians 5:24, NIV).

You see, Scripture, and Scripture alone, should be our frame of reference for who God really is. Circumstances, if we let them guide our thoughts, would have our faith going every which way but right. In fact, if we were to get our theology from a casual view of the world's events—what with wars, disease, earthquakes, famines, and catastrophes—God would come out looking like an ogre.

Circumstances do not a good theology make.

So let's remember the next time we're so quick to tell God how great He is on a golden morning or tranquil evening by the fireside. Let's remember to say the same thing when the day grows gloomy and the night weighs heavy with fear or disappointment.

Scripture tells us that *every* day is a great day to give praise to God.

STRONGHOLD

You think *your* circumstances are bad! Take a look at 2 Kings 25:1-12 at what God's people faced during the Babylonian invasion of Jerusalem. Now, picturing all that horror and confusion, read Jeremiah's assessment of those circumstances in Lamentations 3:21-25.

Did Jeremiah's faith rest on what he knew to be true about God, or on his own assessment of the cruel and horrible circumstances?

Can you pray Jeremiah's beautiful prayer in Lamentations 3 today as you consider your own circumstances, good or bad?

A Kingdom Unshaken

It was the middle of the night, and the first thing I heard was the windows rattling. Then everything in the room started to sway.

Usually a solid sleeper, even Ken woke.

"Ken—that was an *earthquake*, wasn't it?"

"Yeah," he replied, "and a pretty big one, too." Then he rolled over and went back to sleep! No big deal, I guess, for a California native.

But that was not the case for me. This Maryland girl lay awake for hours.

What a strange, helpless feeling it had been—not knowing how long or how hard the earth was going to shake.

What if it had been . . . "the big one"?

Would our roof collapse?

Where would we turn off the gas?

Were we ready with stored up food and water?

Shouldn't we bolt the headboard of the bed to the wall?

Oh, the questionings and imaginings that can go through my mind in the middle of the night—especially when I'm the only one awake.

It wasn't long, though, before those panicky thoughts gave way to a still, persistent voice speaking from a room inside my heart. How long had the voice been speaking—since the earthquake began? The Lord comforted me with a verse we had just studied in our women's Bible study a couple weeks before.

> *Therefore, since we are receiving a kingdom that cannot be shaken, let us be thankful, and so worship God acceptably with reverence and awe* (Hebrews 12:28, NIV).

Now there's a verse that fit the need of the moment! Believe me, when I felt the good old solid ground start quaking like crystal ready to crack, it was encouraging to be reminded that we believers are receiving a kingdom that *cannot be shaken*. Not even by "the big one."

That earthquake was God's audio-visual aid to me that the solid rock-bottom things we tend to depend on—like the earth, for instance—could be here today and gone tomorrow.

The verse in Hebrews tells us that because we're receiving this steady, immovable kingdom, our hearts are to overflow with worship and awe and thanksgiving. What a mighty God we serve! What a powerful refuge He offers His weak, vulnerable children!

I simply can't describe the amazement and wonder I felt after the last aftershock of that earthquake rumbled away into the distance. I was filled with praise for God. He and the things which He is creating for us will never shake or shatter.

What things around you keep shifting and changing?

Have you found yourself comfortable with good health, secure in a loving relationship, or fulfilled in a steady job, only to have the props unexpectedly knocked out from under you? You and I don't need an earthquake to remind us that our confidence and hope must always rest in the One who never changes.

As the psalmist wrote:

God is our refuge and strength,
an ever-present help in trouble.
Therefore we will not fear,
though the earth give way
and the mountains fall
into the heart of the sea,
though its waters roar and foam
and the mountains quake
with their surging . . .

The LORD Almighty is with us;
the God of Jacob is our fortress
(Psalm 46:1-3,7, NIV).

We live in a world that lives in terror of a sliding Dow Jones Average and a rising Richter Scale . . . of falling missiles and a climbing cancer rate.

Let's praise God for a future that can never be shaken.

No matter what.

STRONGHOLD

Here in southern California you'll hardly ever find newly-built homes made of brick. Know why? Because bricks crumble in earthquakes. That's another reason you won't find too many houses with basements. Most homes are built on concrete slab foundations so they will give more easily when the ground moves.

What kind of "home" are you building? Read Matthew 7:24-29 for a good master-building plan.

Memories

Memories,
pressed between the pages of my mind,
memories,
sweetened through the ages just like wine . . .[8]

I like that song. And even though it's a contemporary tune, it could well have been penned by a lonely apostle named Paul, passing the long hours in a dark Roman dungeon.

Paul talked about memories in a letter to his friends in Philippi, scratching the words on soiled parchment, squinting in the halflight of his damp cell.

I thank my God every time I remember you . . .

Cut off from fresh air, sunlight, and—most of all—companionship, Paul was warmed by memories of his friends, the Philippians. Closing his eyes, he could see their faces, hear their voices, feel their warm embrace.

So it is during life's longest, darkest hours. In lonely intervals away from our family . . . in an extended stay in a hospital . . . in an overseas assignment that seems to stretch on and on . . . in the vacant room once filled with the presence of a loved one. At times and places such as these, light-filled memories can help fill the emptiness and ease the ache of loneliness. Like Paul, we can find our spirits bolstered and our hearts inspired to stick with it through drawn-out days of difficulty.

Today, as I write these words, marks the seventeenth anniversary of that hot summer day when I broke my neck—and altered the whole course of my life. I was seventeen on that day when I dove into the shallow waters of the Chesapeake, so I've now spent as many years in a wheelchair as on my feet. It's been a long journey . . . yes, and a difficult one.

Yet seventeen years have given me plenty of time to adjust and cope. I've even come to the point where I can give thanks. I don't allow myself to live in the past—daydreaming or fantasizing about what might have been. But that's not to say I don't enjoy a good memory now and then. Nice memories have a way of buoying my spirits—especially when I'm feeling frustrated with limitations in general and wheelchairs in particular.

I treasure some of those memories.

Like the sensation of walking on the warm concrete apron of a swimming pool.

Or the feel of wet leather reins in my hands.

Or the chill of an ice cold bottle of Coke in my grip on a hot day.

Or the wonderful exhaustion of tired muscles after a long jog with my friends.

Or snapping flowers off their stems with my fingers.

Or scouring a sink with a sponge and cleanser.

Or creaming my own hands.

Or having my ankles rubbed.

Or the cool ivory keys of a piano beneath my fingers.

Or brushing a horse's coat.

Or sewing with a needle and thread.

Or even drumming my fingers on a desk. Kind of a funny feeling, especially if my nails were long.

Those might not sound like much to you, but to me they represent warm and sunlit moments of my past . . . part of a life that was good and sweet and worth remembering.

So on this seventeenth anniversary of my injury I say, *Thank you, God, for the wonderful things I can still remember. Thank you that these memories help me to appreciate how precious our health really is. Oh, and help me, Lord, not to take for granted those things I still can feel and do and experience. So many things. And Father . . . may the next seventeen years be as rewarding and enriching as what I've experienced so far. Let me keep making memories . . . memories to savor for years to come.*

STRONGHOLD

"I thank my God every time I remember you . . ." What kind of memories did Paul have of Philippi? Turn to Acts 16:11-15 for the beautiful story of Lydia. Read the verses and imagine the scene, picturing what went through Paul's mind. For another memory, skip down to Acts 16:25-40 and read about the amazing midnight conversion of an entire family.

Don't you think these beautiful memories—thrilling reminders of God's marvelous works—helped Paul in his loneliness? You bet!

Choosing Your Attitude toward Work

An attitude is something you wear—like skin. Like it or not, you're wearing one right now. And it's showing! If you're alive you're neck deep into an attitude, and you have no choice about that.

But you *can* choose what sort of attitude in which you're going to robe yourself on any given day.

A friend and I were talking recently about the attitudes Christians hold toward their jobs—whether inside or outside the home.

"It's Ephesians 6:6 that goes right to the heart of it, Joni," my friend told me. "Paul says that we shouldn't go about our tasks in order to please men, but 'as servants of Christ, doing the will of God from the heart.'"

I immediately thought of Joseph. If there was ever anybody who did his best at a job in order to do God's will from the heart, it was this young teenager in the book of Genesis.

Loved and trusted by his father, Joseph was probably the most conscientious shepherd in the whole family. He took those sheep seriously. In fact, he did such a good job of shepherding that his jealous brothers sold him into slavery.

So what did Joseph do then? He became the best slave he could possibly become. He was such an honest, honorable slave that he chose faithfulness to his master rather than playing games with his master's wife. He was rewarded by being thrown into prison.

So what did Joseph do then? He concentrated on becoming a model prisoner—the best in all of Egypt. So guess how he was repaid. No, not with parole. Not even with honorable mention on the warden's good behavior list. He was forgotten by the very ones who should have remembered his faithful service and remained imprisoned for two long years. (For the full story, read Genesis 40-41:1.)

Joseph's journey from shepherd to slave to prisoner is ironic. He was so sincere. So filled with heartfelt obedience. You would expect his lot to get lighter as he went along. *We* expect that . . . but should a *servant* expect that? Isn't it a servant's duty to do his master's bidding, whatever the task? Overall, God seemed less concerned with Joseph's release and relief and more concerned with seasoning his character.

The day came, however, when God decided his man was ready. In a single hour, Joseph went from a corner in the dungeon to the right hand of Pharaoh. From a lifer in the federal pen to the Secretary of the Treasury.

What's remarkable is that none of those years spent as a slave or prisoner were wasted. God had neither forgotten him nor lost track of his situation. The discipline and endurance and patience and obedience were all needed to mold Joseph for a key role in his generation.

Feel like a slave to your computer today?

Does it seem like you're manacled to that desk—with just enough slack in your chain to reach the file cabinet, the coffee pot, and the washroom?

Or maybe your chain is hooked to the kitchen sink and a vacuum cleaner . . . or the wheel of a delivery truck . . . or a study carrel in the lonely back corner of a library.

Wherever we find ourselves today, let's all take a little encouragement from Joseph. We may not end up as Secretary of the Treasury, but we are servants of the King.

And no matter how lofty or lowly the role He has given us to play in this old world, He simply asks us to do His will.

Let's do it with joy, from the depths of our hearts.

The choice is ours.

STRONGHOLD

Speaking of attitudes, the entire second chapter of Philippians reads like an attitude check-list. Verse 5 even says, "Your attitude should be the same as that of Christ Jesus."

Read verses 5 through 11 and take a check-up from the neck-up!

A Rose

This morning Ken and I went out to smell the roses . . . and took a tape measure.

Encouraged by a wet California winter and spring, the blooms on our backyard rose bushes are outdoing themselves. One rose measured eight inches across. That's something for *Ripley's Believe It Or Not*.

When I moved into our little house a number of years ago, I could tell the roses had been tenderly cultivated. All were well-rooted, with thick, thorny stems. As the years have passed, they've grown larger and more luxuriant before our wondering eyes. Ken snipped one this morning and put it in a vase on our kitchen table. When something is that beautiful, you want it close. Close enough to inhale its fragrance. Close enough to let your eyes linger on it.

Nothing is more beautiful than the gradual unfolding of a rose bud into its full glory. Each petal unfurls, layer by layer, revealing ever-increasing loveliness. At each stage you say to yourself, *How could it be more beautiful? Right now it's at its best. I've got to get my camera!*

When I consider the way God reveals His glory to us, I picture a rose. In the book of Genesis, the bud of God's plan opened just enough to show the promise of vivid beauty. Through successive chapters of history, the bloom opened more and more before the wondering eyes of His people.

One glory followed another.

. . . His glory as a Warrior, striking Egypt with plagues, bringing His people safely through the depths of the sea, while the pursuing Egyptian army floundered and drowned.

. . . His glory in the desert, moving out in front of His people in a pillar of cloud by day and a pillar of fire by night, symbols of His constant presence.

. . . His glory at Sinai, with the blast of a trumpet, quaking earth, black sky, rumbling mountain, and laws for living inscribed by the finger of God.

. . . His glory blazing between the cherubim in the wilderness tabernacle.

. . . His glory filling the mighty temple of Solomon in Jerusalem, so intense it virtually drove the priests from the building.

At each stage, as the rose unfurled petal by petal, there were probably those who reasoned, "This is the ultimate! It can't get any better than this!"

Yet the prophets promised something even more startling. The rose would unfurl yet another layer of perfect beauty. The glory of God would be fully revealed and all flesh would see it.

The Glory came . . . and His name was Jesus.

No one could have been prepared for what was to be revealed in and through the life of the One called *Immanuel*— "God with us."

The Word became flesh and lived for awhile among us. We have seen his glory, the glory of the one and only Son, who came from the Father, full of grace and truth (John 1:14, NIV).

It was certainly no mistake that Jesus was called "the Rose of Sharon." People marveled at each new turn, each new facet, each new unfolding or unfurling of His nature and character. Beholding His glory must have been something beyond description. No wonder people wanted to be near Him!

God wants to reveal His glory to you. Did you know that? As you take time to draw close to Jesus today, He'll unfold Himself to you . . . like a rose . . . showing you glory which will change your life.

At times you will think that it just can't get any better—*How can it get more beautiful than this?* But it does get better. And it will.

The Rose of Sharon wants to reveal Himself to you today. Take time to inhale the fragrance of His nearness. Let your eyes linger on His beauty.

STRONGHOLD

If the season is right, clip a rosebud from a backyard bush. Or splurge and purchase an American Beauty bud from your florist. Place it in a vase near your desk or near your kitchen sink and watch it blossom from day to day. As its glory unfolds, take a moment to glory in one of Christ's amazing and lovely attributes.

CHAPTER 108

Encores

Have you ever been so moved by the music at a concert you found yourself wishing that "last song" would never come?

When it finally came, what did you do? You probably jumped to your feet, applauding wildly, and called for an encore. What an exhilarating feeling to see that entertainer come back out on stage, pick up the mike, and launch into one more song.

Encores. They give you the illusion of squeezing one more measure of light and joy and goose bumps out of a happy circumstance. Somehow, they suspend time and allow you to savor the golden moment just a little longer.

Do you remember a special weekend retreat with a bunch of Christians? The close friendly feelings were like nothing you'd experienced before. The speaker was on target. The spiritual atmosphere seemed supercharged. Unsaved friends came to know the Lord. Christians got their lives back on track.

Didn't you feel like . . . asking God for an encore? With those memories fresh in your mind, didn't you feel like imploring God for more of the same? To reproduce that precise environment and those same feelings just "one more time?"

Well, you know what? He won't do it. God doesn't give encores. Psalm 62:11 tells us that "one thing God has spoken." The Lord states it even more forcefully in the book of Isaiah:

> *Forget the former things; do not dwell on the past. See, I am doing a new thing! Now it springs up; do you not perceive it?* (43:18-19, NIV).

God will never do the same thing exactly the same way a second time around. But He *will* do something better. He will perform something new, something different, that is just as special, just as significant as any of your most memorable moments with Him.

So how about it? Are you looking forward to an upcoming get-together with a few other Christians? A retreat perhaps? A Bible study? Are you in the middle of plans for an annual event and you're wringing your hands, hoping and praying it will turn out "like last year"?

Don't let your prayers get mediocre! Don't ask God for something He did last year. Don't simply expect Him to do an encore, the same thing exactly the same way. Don't dwell on "the former things."

But do expect Him to speak.

Do expect something new, something fresh, something appropriate for the needs of the moment.

Remember, this is the God who is "able to do immeasurably more than all we ask or imagine, according to His power that is at work within us" (Ephesians 3:20, NIV). So stretch your faith and believe Him for something far greater than a simple encore.

He's ready to do "a new thing" in your life . . . *today.*

STRONGHOLD

It's great to think that God wants to do something new in our lives. But sometimes we feel tired of the way God works. We have a ho-hum "I've-seen-it-all-before" attitude. Read Isaiah 48:3-8 to see what God said to a bunch of Israelites who felt the same way. Learn from the Israelites' mistake. Start believing in the God who always tells us new things!

Hope on Tiptoe

Getting out into nature is serious business for the Tadas.

This is one Maryland flower that begins to wilt if she can't escape the confines of Los Angeles now and then for short forays among God's handiwork.

Yes, my wheelchair limits our excursions, but it doesn't stop us! Ken and I still love to go camping and boating and fishing—or just exploring.

It could be a desert . . . we don't live too far from the Mojave and always look forward to desert camping in the early spring. You should see the blooms on the cactus and the yucca plants!

Or the mountains. If we want to catch a breath of fresh air, a short drive along the Los Angeles Crest Highway tops the San Gabriel mountains and offers vistas of craggy peaks and Ponderosa pines.

And then there's the ocean. Only twenty minutes from our house. We'll often take a bag lunch on a Saturday afternoon, park on some cliff, and watch the sea gulls swirl and swoop along the crest of the breakers. We always return home with spirits revived and refreshed.

Yes, nature is personal to me. And—did you know? Nature even has its own personal verse in Scripture. Romans 8:19 tells us that "The creation waits in eager expectation for the sons of God to be revealed."

J. B. Phillips renders it like this:

The whole creation is on tiptoe to see the wonderful sight of the sons of God coming into their own.

On tiptoe . . . In some mysterious way, the flowers and plants and animals and seascapes and landscapes wait in eager expectation for . . . a glory yet to be revealed.

Paul tells a little more about this anticipation.

The world of creation cannot as yet see reality, not because it chooses to be blind, but because in God's purpose it has been so limited—yet it has been given hope. And the hope is that in the end the whole of created life will be rescued from the tyranny of change and decay, and have its share in that magnificent liberty which can only belong to the children of God! (vv. 20-21, Phillips).

The creation is groaning and longing for the day when God will release it from its bondage and usher in a new era with Christ as King. Can you hear the sighing in the wind? Can you feel the heavy silence in the mountains? Can you sense the restless longing in the sea? Something's coming . . . something better.

But consider this: If the creation has an earnest expectation, surely we believers—the sons and daughters of God— should have nothing less! If the whole inanimate and brute creation is eagerly expecting, earnestly looking forward to the appearing of Jesus and all that means, this same kind of hope should be much more evident in you and me.

How's *your* hope today?

Do you find yourself longing and looking forward to the glorious appearing of the Lord Jesus Christ? We mustn't wait in a dull sort of way with a ho-hum attitude. We must rejoice in our hope. It's that joy that makes us eagerly expect— like a big St. Bernard when he strains at his leash. Anticipation means stretching our necks. Yearning. Fervently hoping.

If that's the sort of attitude that nature has about the coming of that great day, you and I can learn a thing or two from the creation around us. Next time when you see a ray of sunlight suddenly pierce through a heavy, dark, afternoon sky, think about Romans 8:19.

If nature waits on tiptoe for the coming of Jesus, you and I shouldn't be caught flat-footed!

STRONGHOLD

Chuck Swindoll urges believers to meditate on passages such as 1 Thessalonians 4:13-18—verses that describe the day when Jesus Christ will return to earth.

"Talk about high drama!" he writes. "Take a walk outside, weather permitting, with your New Testament in hand. Read again this startling glimpse into the future—*your* future. Let your eyes sweep the skies. Feel the thunder and joy and awe. Remind yourself that this experience could happen at any moment—even before you return from your walk . . . or draw your next breath."[9]

A Sparrow Makes the Point

I was just a little girl when my mom and dad took me to the Baltimore Zoo. But there is one part of that visit I will never forget.

For some reason, the aviary seized my attention more than the elephants, monkeys, and giraffes put together. A large bird exhibition, it was aflutter with fascinating feathered creatures . . . brightly-colored parrots, funny-looking toucans, huge, stern eagles, and know-it-all owls. But flittering around the *outside* of all the cages were common sparrows, making their homes in the rafters of the aviary.

They weren't important enough to put in a cage for everyone to admire and ogle. They didn't rate an explanatory plaque. Their pictures didn't appear in the zoo guidebook. Mostly, they weren't even noticed.

Yet of all the birds He created, God chose the sparrow to make a crucial point on the subject of fear.

Jesus hit the nail on the head when He made an issue of our fears and anxieties. He knew how vulnerable we feel at times. How weak mentally, how frail emotionally. Words like *paranoid* and *neurotic* are not just reserved for residents in mental wards. A surprising number of us let our apprehensions press us to the edge of our mental limits every once in awhile. Ah . . . how insecure we tend to be!

Just recently I was there. Walking the lonely border between anxiety and panic. So gripped by fears and dreads that I could hardly think. I did, however, have enough presence of mind to follow my own prescription—the one I'm always dispensing to others. I went back to my Bible.

That's when I came across our Lord's little lecture on sparrows.

Jesus was speaking to His men about future events. When He read the fear rising in their hearts, He paused to reassure them.

> *Are not two sparrows sold for a penny? Yet not one of them will fall to the ground apart from the will of your Father. And even the very hairs of your head are all numbered. So don't be afraid; you are worth more than many sparrows* (Matthew 10:29-31, NIV).

How wise of our Lord to use the example of a sparrow! He could have used eagles. Or hawks, or falcons, or wide-winged storks. Yet out of the world's nine thousand bird species, the Lord chose one of the most insignificant, least-noticed birds flying around.

A scruffy little sparrow.

Jesus obviously wanted to make His point clear. Those who believe and follow Him mean more to the Father than anything else. If God takes note of each humble sparrow, where they are and what they're doing, you'd better believe He keeps tabs on you.

"Even the very hairs of your head are all numbered" He tells us! That's rather incredible, especially when you take a look at your brush after you've combed through your hair a few times. God takes such an interest in each of our lives that even our individual lost hairs matter to Him.

"Do not be afraid, little flock," Jesus tells us, "for your Father has been pleased to give you the kingdom" (Luke 12:32, NIV).

So why be anxious? Why be assaulted by fears? Why be pressed with worry and doubt? Why get the heebie-jeebies? If the great God of Heaven concerns Himself with the little sparrow clinging to a twig outside your window, He cares about what concerns you.

STRONGHOLD

Read Psalm 55:22, and then 1 Peter 5:7. Pour out your anxieties before Him today. He invites you to! You've nothing to lose but your fear.

Frame of Reference

There are no hard and fast rules about jigsaw puzzles. All of us have our own system. But when Ken and I clear off one end of the kitchen table on a lazy Sunday afternoon and go to work on one of those 600-piece beauties, experience has taught us to begin with the edge of the picture.

It only makes sense. You start with the puzzle pieces that have the straight sides. Fitting them together completes the frame of the picture and after that—well, it usually comes together without a lot of hair-pulling or guesswork.

Once Ken and I get the frame nicely laid out on the table, then the hard stuff starts. Filling in the middle. But like I said, once the frame is in place, you're encouraged to tackle the harder pieces. Before you cement the edges together, it's an impossible jumble of colors, curves, and irreconcilable fragments. Just a pile of stuff. No one piece seems to make any sense. But after you get the boundaries staked out, everything seems to have context. You know in your heart that it's all going to come together.

"Oh boy, only 549 little jigsaw guys to go."

The work is slow and hard, but as you fill in the picture, you begin to see the complete scene take shape—a meadow, a lake, Garfield the cat, a pepperoni pizza, a busy street scene in Paris. The key is to keep going back to the completed edge of the picture. That always seems to give Ken and me a frame of reference as to what the whole scene should look like. Sometimes when I get stuck with an unfamiliar puzzle piece, I'll go back to that frame to match the colors and objects.

Before long—taa-daaa!—the puzzle is finished.

It struck me recently that working on a jigsaw puzzle isn't all that different from working on our Christian walk. I like to think of God's truth in Scripture as pieces of some grand puzzle. And the frame . . . the most important part . . . is Jesus. *Start there*. Begin with the Gospels. Learn what He thinks about your sin. Observe His love. Study His conversations. Memorize His words. Learn how He went to the cross and died for you. Rejoice in the resurrection. All these things are like a gigantic frame. The Lord Jesus is like the completed edge around the picture of your life.

And with that frame completed? Well, you have a reference point. Not that filling in the rest is going to be easy!

There are many portions of Scripture that are difficult to understand and simply don't make sense.

There are many events in our lives that are difficult to understand and simply don't make sense.

Sometimes our world seems like a big box of puzzle pieces turned upside down and jumbled around. Nothing seems to fit together. Nothing seems to take any recognizable shape. Confusion reigns and broken pieces resist reassembly.

That's when you need a Frame. That's when you need to keep going back to the Lord Jesus Christ. Listen to what Paul tells us in Colossians:

For by Him all things were created, both in the heavens and on earth, visible and invisible . . . all things have been created by Him and for Him. And He is before all things, and in Him all things hold together (1:16-17).

In Him all the universe holds together. How much

more so the details of our lives. He's the glue that binds the stars and planets in their orbits and bonds the very atoms and molecules. How much more the fragmented pieces of my life.

In Him all of Scripture holds together. On the Emmaus road, the resurrected Jesus Christ walked and talked with two grieving disciples. At that point, they didn't recognize their Lord. So they spilled their frustration and sorrow into the ears of the Stranger who walked in their midst. Now that Jesus of Nazareth had been crucified, what was going to come of the promises in Scripture that Messiah would redeem His people? It was a puzzle to them. A hopeless jumble. The pieces didn't begin to come together.

Yet the Lord replied to them:

"O foolish men and slow of heart to believe in all that the prophets have spoken! Was it not necessary for the Christ to suffer these things and to enter into His glory?"

And beginning with Moses and with all the prophets, He explained to them the things concerning Himself in all the Scriptures (Luke 24:25-27).

What did Jesus do? He took them to the Frame. He traced His fingers over the straight edges of Scripture and gave them context. And then . . . "their eyes were opened and they recognized Him" (24:31).

Flip ahead to the book of Acts and you'll find a similar situation. An official of Ethiopia was riding along in his chariot puzzling over a scroll of Isaiah. Who in the world was the prophet talking about? Who was this "Lamb" being led to slaughter? Who was this "Sheep," silent before the shearer? The official was bewildered. He wanted to understand, but couldn't put it together.

That's when the Holy Spirit brought Philip onto the scene.

"Do you understand what you are reading?" Philip asked.

"How can I," he said, "unless someone explains it to me? . . . Tell me, please, who is the prophet talking about, himself or someone else?"

Then Philip began with that very passage of Scripture and told him the good news about Jesus (Acts 8:30-31, 34- 35, NIV).

There it is again. Jesus is the Frame of Reference that draws all of Scripture together into one grand design, one complete picture. All that we learn in Scripture relates to Him.

Puzzling today over the odd-shaped, varicolored fragments of your life? Need a frame of reference?

Take a peek at the picture on the puzzle box. It's a portrait of Jesus.

STRONGHOLD

Every puzzle piece of Scripture has a purpose. Some pieces are to make us "wise for salvation through faith in Christ Jesus." Other pieces are "useful for teaching, rebuking, correcting, and training in righteousness" (2 Timothy 3:15, 16).

In John 5:16-47, Jesus had a talk with some religious leaders who got hung up on a few of the puzzle pieces of Scripture. They were ignoring the frame. Take time to read those verses, zeroing in on verses 39-40, and see what Jesus has to say about the completed picture of the puzzle.

Job's Wife

Which of us hasn't read, or at least heard, of the story of Job? Countless books and Bible commentaries have been penned about this man and his avalanche of adversity. His life has inspired untold sermons. Great reservoirs of ink have emptied over the centuries as writers have praised and puzzled over his life.

Oh sure, he voiced his share of complaints, and wrestled with more than a few doubts. But not once did he curse God. In fact, not long after he learned of the terrible destruction which ripped through his family, his possessions, and his servants, the heartbroken man replied:

> *"Naked I came from my mother's womb,*
> *and naked I will depart.*
> *The LORD gave and the LORD has taken away;*
> *may the name of the LORD be praised"*
> (Job 1:21, NIV).

The Bible goes on to say that in all this Job did not sin by charging God with wrongdoing.

Yes, Job went through a lot, but . . . have you ever stopped to think about Job's *wife*? When it comes right down to it, his wife went through just as much as he did. She, just like him, felt the crushing loss of her sons and daughters. She, just like him, lost her possessions and cherished household servants. And what's more, she had to stand by and watch as her husband—the only one left of her family—suffered indescribable pain and sorrow. Only someone who has spent a long night in the waiting room of an intensive care unit or experienced the helpless anxiety of watching a loved one suffer can identify with that hurt. I know that there were times in my own suffering when my mom or dad would have given anything to trade places with me.

We hear so often about the "trials of Job," but what do we ever hear about the trials of Mrs. Job?

There may be some good reasons why this woman doesn't hold an honored place in history. One glance at Scripture tells us that she had anything but the patience of her husband. She sees her life falling to pieces around her, all her secure props knocked out from underneath her. She sees her husband driven to the point of despair. And what does she do? Her first piece of advice is recorded in Job 2:9:

"Are you still trying to be godly when God has done all this to you? Curse him and die" (TLB).

From her words, you get the impression that she's as angry with her husband as she is with God! Whatever her wedding vows may have been, she evidently ignored the portions that said, "For better or for worse, for richer or for poorer, in sickness and in health . . ." Blinded by her own misery and despair, she could only lash out in anger and bitterness.

My heart goes out to her. Few of us will ever be touched by that kind of grief and loss. And what one of us can really be sure of how *we* would respond if all of those things happened to us?

It would be a good idea to think about a response *before* a major trial or testing descends upon our life. How, by God's grace, would we respond . . . to Him . . . to our loved ones?

And what about those upsetting "small" difficulties that intrude daily? Those things that are less like a boulder crashing down a hill and more like a sharp pebble in our shoe. Do those sorts of troubles cause us to nag and complain at our spouse or those close to us—to even lash out in anger?

Patience, the apostle Paul tells us, is a gift from God. A gift that the Holy Spirit supernaturally produces as we daily yield our lives (even the little things) to His control.

Who knows? If our response can reflect Job's patience, we may go down in God's history as one of the select number who can say, "I'm going to obey God—no matter what. The Lord gives and the Lord takes away . . . blessed be the name of the Lord."

STRONGHOLD

Mrs. Job may not have known how to handle her bad times because she didn't learn how to successfully deal with the good times. We take so much for granted—good health, full stomach, family safety, job security, sturdy roof over our heads.

How do we learn to respond well when life is good? It would help to remember that we must urgently seek God in the happy times as well as in the bad.

Read Habakkuk 3:17-18. Are you enjoying an abundant time of safety, good health, and happiness? You may not have sheep in a pen or cattle in the stalls, but list your favorite people and possessions and commit them to God right now.

Conclusion

To whom are God's secrets told?

Perhaps in reading—looking up Scriptures or contemplating a new thought—you have felt the Spirit of Christ beckoning you, pointing the way. Sometimes you've sensed Him in front, leading. At other times He's been beside or even behind you. Occasionally, you've been aware of His nudge. You've heard Him calling you into a deeper intimacy with Himself, directing your steps toward the higher, hidden roads.

You feel very much like one of those who sat at His feet, listening, hanging on every word, hoping to understand more. Do you see yourself, let's say, among the "crowd that gathered around Him" in Mark 4:1? Picture it now. Can you imagine elbowing your way to the front of the masses? You find a spot and look around. The crowd is so large that He gets into a boat and sits in it a short distance out in the lake. People line the shore, crowding up to the water's edge. He begins to teach—many things. Men and women strain to see and hear this marvelous man who speaks in such mysterious parables.

And you, along with the rest, listen.

But the story He tells weaves itself through ideas and images that don't quite make sense—something about a farmer scattering seeds among rocky places, thorns, shallow and good soil. The story ends, and looking around at the crowds the Teacher says, "He who has ears to hear, let him hear."

You feel the crowd dispersing behind you. You hear the murmured comments. Some of the people are perplexed. Many are frustrated by things they can't seem to understand.

You, too, feel puzzled. Yet something about what He said— or didn't say—summons you to stay. As the crowd dissolves, you find a closer spot, move forward, and look around again. Like you, a few others have also drawn near to hear more. You wait, quietly, listening to the lap of the water on the sand.

As He steps back onto the shore, the Twelve and a few others such as yourself, crowd around Him, asking Him the meaning of the parables. "The secret of the kingdom of God has been given to you," the Teacher says (Mark 4:10-11, NIV).

And there, away from the scattered crowd, together with fellow seekers, the Lord takes you into His confidence. To you He reveals the secrets—unraveling His innermost thoughts, dreams, and heartfelt hopes. Voicing His desires for you and for the rest of those who search.

Sitting at His feet, you are full of awe and wonder. That Jesus would share Himself so warmly, so intimately with you—it's astounding! His words make the future, the distant, the almost unreachable appear as if it were the present, the near and very real. You feel as though you are already "seated with Christ in heavenly places" (Ephesians 2:6).

This is your secret strength.

A strength that throws back into the far distance the things of earth.

A strength that seems to bring you into contact with the unseen world.

A strength that enables you to realize your true position as a pilgrim.

All things are yours, whether . . . the world or life or death or the present or the future—all are yours, and you are of Christ, and Christ is of God (1 Corinthians 3:22-23, NIV).

With a sigh of satisfaction, or maybe exhilaration, you realize what this special strength is . . . your life now hid with Christ in God.

He will never let you be shaken or moved from your place near His heart.

Like many authors, Joni Eareckson Tada receives letters in response to her books. In 1979, as a result of her books and a film about her life, thousands of letters were received from people—both able-bodied and those with disabilities—who identified with her struggle to accept her circumstances.

Responding to the needs identified in these letters, *Joni and Friends* was formed that same year as a Christian organization to bring together the church and disabled people through evangelism, encouragement, inspiration, and practical service. Although the ministry is focused toward addressing the needs of the disabled, many different people—hurting and confused by difficult circumstances—have benefited. In addition to counseling correspondence, resource materials, radio programs, seminars and other resources, *Joni and Friends* also helps provide financial assistance to disabled people through the *Christian Fund for the Disabled.*

If you or someone you know might benefit from the ministry of *Joni and Friends,* or if you would like more information, please write to:

> *Joni and Friends*
> P.O. Box 3333
> Agoura Hills, CA 91301
> 818-707-5664

Notes

1. Elisabeth Elliott, *A Slow and Certain Light* (Nashville, Tenn.: Abingdon Press, 1982).

2. Samuel Rutherford (1600-1661), *The Letters of Samuel Rutherford*, (Banner of Truth, 1985 reprint).

3. Joni Eareckson Tada, *One Step Further* (New York: Bantam Books, 1978), pp. 54-55.

4. Margaret Donaldson, "His Hands," copyright 1972. Used by permission.

5. Thomas O. Chisholm, "Great Is Thy Faithfulness." Used by permission.

6. William Hiley Bathurst (1769-1877), "In Pain," quoted by Margaret Clarkson in *Grace Grows Best in Winter* (Wm. B. Eerdmans, 1984), p. 54.

7. Johnson Oatman, Jr., "Count Your Blessings."

8. "Memories," © Hal Leonard Publishers. All rights reserved.

9. Charles R. Swindoll, *Growing Deep in the Christian Life* (Portland, Ore.: Multnomah Press, 1986), p. 280.

Scripture Index